D1547975

HUMAN RIGHTS IN CRISIS

Human Rights in Crisis

Edited by

ALICE BULLARD
Georgia Institute of Technology, USA

ASHGATE

Published by
Ashgate Publishing Limited
Gower House
Croft Road
Aldershot
Hampshire GU11 3HR
England

Ashgate Publishing Company
Suite 420
101 Cherry Street
Burlington, VT 05401-4405
USA

Ashgate website: http://www.ashgate.com

British Library Cataloguing in Publication Data
Human rights in crisis
  1. Human rights 2. Human rights advocacy 3. Torture
  (International law) 4. Women's rights 5. War on Terrorism,
  2001-
  I. Bullard, Alice
  323

Library of Congress Cataloging-in-Publication Data
Human rights in crisis / edited by Alice Bullard.
    p. cm.
  Includes bibliographical references and index.
  ISBN 978-0-7546-7028-5
  1. Human rights. 2. Human rights advocacy. 3. Torture (International law). 4. Women's rights. 5. War on Terrorism, 2001- I. Bullard, Alice.

JC571.H8664 2008
323--dc22

2007041400

ISBN: 978 0 7546 7028 5

Printed and bound in Great Britain by TJ International Ltd, Padstow, Cornwall.

Contents

List of Illustrations

List of Contributors

Ashley Barr, J.D., Carter Center for Human Rights, Atlanta, Georgia

Alice Bullard earned her Doctorate in History at the University of California at Berkeley in 1994. She was a Professor of History at Georgia Institute of Technology, Atlanta, Georgia from 1994 to 2007. Bullard is now pursuing a law degree at Georgetown University Law Center, Washington, DC (J.D. expected 2010). She may be reached at ab654@law.georgetown.edu

Richard Burchill, Ph.D., Director, McCoubrey Centre for International Law, Law School, University of Hull, UK

Lisa Hajjar, Ph.D., Professor and Chair, Law and Society Studies, University of California, Santa Barbara

Dina Francesca Haynes, J.D., Associate Professor, New England College of Law, Boston, Massachusetts

Matt Eisenbrandt, J.D., Consultant and former Legal Director, Center for Justice & Accountability

Marsha A. Freeman, Ph.D., J.D., Senior Fellow, University of Minnesota Human Rights Center, and Director of the International Women's Rights Action Watch, an international resource center on gender and human rights

Peter Redfield, Ph.D., Associate Professor of Anthropology, University of North Carolina, Charlotte, NC

Amy Ross, Ph.D., Associate Professor of Geography, University of Georgia, Athens, Georgia

Acknowledgments

I would like to thank B Wardlaw and the Wardlaw Human Rights Fund for so generously supporting the Human Rights Initiative. Their support made writing this volume possible. My colleagues in the Human Rights Initiative, especially Gregory Nobles, deserve special thanks. All who participated in the Human Rights in Crisis conference in the spring of 2005 contributed to this volume, even if no chapter bears their name as author. Bert Lockwood's kind advice and support has its effect throughout these pages. Richard Burchill's assistance in bringing this collection to print was invaluable. To all the contributors and participants, I give heartfelt thanks. I hope this volume creates a record of the dedication of the scholars and professionals who contributed their work. This dedication marks a path for those who come after us.

Introduction

Alice Bullard

This volume began to take shape during a conference organized by the Human Rights Initiative at the Georgia Institute of Technology in the spring of 2005. At that time, the reports of human rights abuses by American soldiers and interrogators in Abu-Ghraib prison and the Guantanomo detention facility sparked deep concern among human rights advocates. We conceived of "human rights in crisis" in relationship to the defense and advancement of human rights in the context of the US-led War on Terror. The crisis, in its original conception, recognized the possible loss of human rights both in the United States and among detainees in US-governed detention facilities. It also contained an element of hope derived from a conviction that the pursuit of human rights happens on many fronts and in many ways around the globe; that a retreat from human rights in the United States did not necessarily signal a global retreat. The need to defend human rights and the possibility of advances in human rights and emerging means of pursuing human rights inspired this project from its inception.

Hence, this volume is dedicated to expanding our understanding of the pursuit of human rights in the era of the Global War on Terror, but in identifying robust defense of human rights in this era it looks beyond the boundaries of this war. This is a necessary step not only to obtain a more comprehensive outlook, but also to allow a more nuanced understanding of the multiple means by which human rights are pursued. Law and legal studies are often recognized as the discipline most closely associated with the study and advancement of Human Rights, but here we broaden our methodologies to include anthropology, sociology, and history as well as legal studies. If law enshrines human rights and structures a means of pursuing them, nonetheless broader forces create the possibility of sustaining a culture of human rights.

The innate dignity of human life and the imperative to preserve and sustain this dignity is the broadest philosophical foundation for human rights. Compassion couples with the abstract concept of dignity, providing the emotional impetus to engagement in the struggle for human rights. Rooted in the loving care of oneself, compassion extends such love to all humanity, recognizing fellowship in life's struggles and triumphs. We can look to philosophers – for example, Immanuel Kant, philosopher of human dignity, and Jean-Jacques Rousseau, philosopher of compassion – to provide depth to this formulation, but building and sustaining a culture of human rights goes far beyond paying homage to long deceased philosophers and erecting legal scaffolding as monuments to their ideas. Compassion, moreover, can entail paternalistic relationships – those who have much deigning to dispense small kindnesses to those in need. The assertive demand for human rights by the marginalized or disenfranchised easily disrupts such pious sentimentalism, thereby exposing those seeking their rights to counter-attacks and criticism. Compassion as well is a fickle emotion, not always reliable or sustainable, susceptible to wax or wane in the wake of personal circumstances, cultural trends, and media campaigns. Paradoxically, the "crisis" that threatens human rights can also be the "crisis" that floods hearts with compassion; in this way, the culture of crisis is bound up with the culture of human rights. "Human rights in crisis" can mean both human rights threatened and human rights defended.

The terrain is fertile for human rights when individuals are impassioned by the power of human dignity and by assaults upon this dignity. Compassion is the emotion that drives individuals to reach out and defend the human rights of themselves and of others, but these processes are caught in broader networks that enable, constrain, direct, and sometimes impede efforts. Political goals and allegiances, media campaigns, donor preferences and perceptions, volunteer organizations and the politics of their organizers, the culture of victimhood in contemporary America, the limited political tolerance for compassion – these are just some of the forces that form and limit human rights culture.

In times of crisis the rule of law is often challenged, with preference given to concerns of sovereignty and security. Crisis thus can precipitate an assault on human rights. Wars and times of trouble create vulnerable individuals; in flight from armed conflict or economic ruin, those seeking to preserve their dignity run the risk of entering the enclosures – encampments, detention centers, or prisons – of refugees and asylum seekers (Arendt 1976, 277–280). These enclosures, counterparts to the prisons and detention facilities for enemy combatants, are liminal spaces from which it is difficult to emerge via the successful claim to legal protection, the guarantee of which is grounded in human rights law. Crisis can provoke broad waves of compassion in the citizenry, but the lability of emotion is such that fear and loathing are also likely responses. Individuals caught up in the crisis risk running afoul of public sentiment; they can be portrayed in the media and in the courts as opportunistic or threatening rather than dignified, as too eager for profit and self-enrichment. The mobilization of fear and hatred can extend as well to scapegoating – the modern enactment of the ancient ritual of sacrifice to cleanse the social body (Freud 1918, 171–189). Callous indifference (sometimes called compassion fatigue) is the banal reality in a world pulled by a seemingly endless variety of demands. Envisioning new means of committing to human rights and bringing them to more and more of the globe's peoples is the provenance of social visionaries. Reconfiguring the boundaries of the acceptable, raising the standard of human dignity for women, the poor, the socially marginalized and politically exploited, is deep cultural work dependent on multiple reinforcing transformations.

This present exploration of human rights in crisis begins with an examination of United States policies in the Global War on Terror, moves to further considerations of the historical and legal underpinnings of human rights culture, and finally turns to the pursuit of human rights in three detailed case studies.

Part I

The hallmarks of the current era in human rights – the era of crisis – are the controversial policies of torture, rendition, and of holding so-called enemy combatants without recourse to legal representation and without guarantee of just treatment as outlined by the Geneva Conventions. Lisa Hajjar assesses the policies and practices of the Bush administration as it attempts to refute allegations of torture and simultaneously seeks to secure legal standing for its unprecedented methods and immunity for its agents in the field. Hajjar weighs the evidence and allegations that torture has been routinely employed against so-called enemy combatants at the Guantanomo military base on the island of Cuba, and discusses how such abuses spread from "Gitmo" to the Abu-Ghraib prison in Iraq.

These are troubling assaults on human rights by the United States, but the crisis of human rights is deeper and more complicated than these examples might lead us to believe. Human rights activist Ashley Barr argues that the radical departure of George W. Bush's administration from the culture of human rights carries with it global consequences; from standard-bearer and chief defender of human rights, the United States has changed into a seemingly cynical actor that denies torture, kidnapping, and arbitrary imprisonment, are assaults on human dignity, and advocates Executive privilege unbounded by legal constraint. Barr describes with sensitivity and a wealth of detail how the war on terror has become a pretext around the globe for states to prosecute human rights defenders. Allegations of terrorism leveled against those seeking to defend and further human rights is the cynical outcome of a policy climate that values military might and perceived state interests above the rights of the individual.

Part II

The uneasy juxtaposition of the ideals of human rights, the realities of state sovereignty, and the cultural contingency of politics, are explored in Part II. The ideals of human rights flow from the conviction that human life is sacred and that compassion for living humanity should guide and inform our actions. It is perhaps too easy to claim adherence to this creed, to claim to be a defender of human rights. In truth, a more limited scope of loyalties and compassion usually prevails over an encompassing universalism. Sovereigns exercise prerogatives that infringe on rights. Sentiments localized in communities and the nation short-circuit the dedication to universal rights. Promises of rights in treaties, constitutions, and statutes are neglected or left unrealized. Some individuals remain vested with more significance than others. Women, in particular, persistently seek elusive equality within the so-called universal rubric of human rights. The chapters in this section impress upon us that human rights law and culture occupies a variegated terrain, unevenly hospitable and productive, yet nonetheless subject to the demands of those seeking tangible human rights.

Amy Ross takes us into the world of "collateral damage" and the morally murky terrain in which questionable calculations lead us to classify deaths as legitimate wartime occurrences, or as homicides, or even war crimes. Drawing on skillful historical analysis and intimate knowledge of contemporary war crimes tribunals, Ross guides us through the world of aerial bombing and mass killings that accompany contemporary warfare. What body counts as a legitimate wartime death? What counts merely as "collateral damage"? And how is that reconcilable with destroyed relations in a community, in a family, torn apart by senseless wartime losses? The status of any individual and the meaning of that individual's death appears deeply conditioned by one's relation to the state and to the military power exercised. In Ross' account we see how the individual lives lost are not each counted in the same manner; the naked individual is shrouded in various layers of identity that give valance to death. Murder, execution, accident, vanquished foe: accounting for the transmutation of human life lost into culturally coded indices of warfare emerges as central to the pursuit of human rights. As demonstrated by the political controversy subsequent to the findings of Gilbert Burnham and his research team, that 654,965 civilians have perished since the US invasion of Iraq, bodies do count and must be counted (Burnham, Lafta, Doucy, and Roberts 2006).

Richard Burchill explores the political grounding of human rights institutions in a way that makes clear that the divide between state's rights and individual rights is written into the history of human rights. The very institutions charged with defending human rights enshrine the rights of states, and engender difficulties for the pursuit of individual rights *vis-à-vis* these states. Burchill weighs the power of rhetoric, however, combined with the existence of international human rights laws, and demonstrates that the interests of the sovereign states can be overcome via a concerted effort to assert human rights claims. If, as he finds, states' actions in the fight against international terror have overridden international human rights law, nonetheless, he claims the established language of human rights offers a powerful recourse for on-going redress.

The jockeying for position and power that pits states against each other in the international arena, and that sometimes pits states against their own citizens: these are the conditions that drag the ideals of human rights into the real world of politics. When the individuals in question are women, however, the normal equations often cease to be relevant. In her chapter, Marsha Freeman is eloquent on the history of women's human rights as she shows us the hard fought gains of the 1980s and 1990s. Her analysis of interest groups, political trends and philanthropic fashions, moreover, leads us to realize that the gains of an earlier generation are far from guaranteed to prevail in the current era of retrenchment. Personal beliefs and cultural trends among big donors prove crucial to creating and sustaining momentum in the pursuit of women's human rights.

Part III

We conclude this investigation into human rights in crisis with three investigations into the contemporary pursuit of human rights. These case-studies demonstrate the complicated terrain of human rights, terrain that demands far more than legal argumentation for adequate understanding, advocacy, or enforcement.

Matt Eisenbrandt explores the world of torture and international accountability as victims confront their persecutors in American courts of law. Eisenbrandt addresses the advances made by the Center for Justice & Accountability (CJA) in establishing important legal precedents in its cases against death squad leaders and top military officers from Chile, Honduras, El Salvador and Haiti who have settled in the United States. CJA has won key decisions in the areas of statute of limitations, command responsibility, conspiracy, and crimes against humanity. Each of these issues is critical to the success of lawsuits in US courts under the Alien Tort Claims Act and Torture Victim Protection Act. Eisenbrandt concludes his chapter with reflections on how these cases have reinvigorated the search for justice for past abuses in the defendants' home countries. The apparent contradiction between the successful claims against torturers in American courts and the US Executive branch insistence that extreme interrogation tactics are not in fact torture reminds us that successfully claiming or upholding human rights can be a fundamentally political process; the clash of law and sovereignty sometimes produce irrational inconsistencies.

Dina Haynes provides a vivid analysis of a gendered struggle for human rights, and in so doing provides flesh and blood examples for Freeman's earlier chapter. Haynes portrays the indignities suffered by trafficked persons – largely women – as they petition for immigration relief in order to avoid deportation to the country of abuse. The US government ostensibly recognized the gravity of trafficking in enacting a special law in 2000 to protect victims and to provide them with a special visa status. This legislation, however, has not led to sizable numbers of women acquiring protection or legal status; focusing on trafficking as a crime has had the perverse result of impeding the assertion of the human rights of those trafficked. The life stories of those trafficked are seldom simple stories of victimization; rather individuals seeking to better their lives, to escape societies torn by war or economic devastation, fall victim to traffickers precisely because they are looking for a way to escape dire situations. Haynes' chapter seems to be haunted by Hannah Arendt's famous lament that human rights are most impossible to assert precisely when they are most needed (Arendt 1973, 298–301).

Those caught beyond the boundaries of state sovereignty, those with no recourse to a state-based legal identity, are most vulnerable and thus need their "human rights" the most. Yet those in flight, in transit, or in forced migration, are simultaneously easy prey for traffickers and without recourse to legal protections. Haynes, however, gives no ground to the human rights skepticism that flavors Arendt, arguing instead that states must respond with respect to those who aggressively pursue their human rights, including their economic rights. Strong recommendations for approaching those trafficked in terms of human rights rather than in terms of the crime of trafficking, accompany a lament by Haynes that those served by trafficked women are rarely if ever prosecuted.

Peter Redfield explores the effort on the part of Doctors without Borders/ Médecins Sans Frontières (MSF) to reorient humanitarian intervention from acute to chronic situations and the problems entailed in such an endeavor. His ethnography of recent MSF work in Uganda addresses human rights in crisis, exploring the fact that human rights are both deeply threatened and highly defended in moments of crisis, and that much human rights work depends on a culture of crisis to maintain interest and funding. Founded three decades ago as an alternative to the International Red Cross, MSF has since grown into a complex and transnational fixture of global crises. Along the way it has also expanded its operation to include a wider range of medical problems, addressing "neglected diseases" as well as emergencies in an effort to confront human suffering. Redfield examines how MSF's efforts to distance itself from recent military actions conducted in the name of humanitarianism and the establishment of any international "right to intervention" parallel its increased engagement in struggles to advance the right to medical treatment – including the right to pharmaceuticals – on a global scale. Redfield's investigation reveals how MSF's work has revised the human rights equation, shifting away from state-sponsored interventions and toward a "right to health" conceived at the level of medical reach and development. Undermining the media sustained culture of crisis is part of MSF's attempt to change the moral economy of suffering and humanitarian values. If the humanitarian sensibilities driving MSF have only limited impact in effecting systematic change, nonetheless their actions render visible the global economy of health care, suffering, and human life.

Works Cited

Agamben, G. (1998), *Homo sacer; sovereign power and bare life*, Palo Alto, CA: Stanford University Press.

Arendt, H. (1976), *The Origins of Totalitarianism*, New York: Harvest Harcourt.

Burnham, G.H., Lafta, R., Doucy, S. and Roberts, L.F. (2006), "Mortality after the 2003 invasion of Iraq: a cross-sectional cluster sample survey," *The Lancet* 368: 1421–1428.

Freud, Sigmund (1918), *Totem and Taboo*, New York, Vintage.

Sunder Rajan, Rajeswari (2003), *The scandal of the state: women, law, citizenship in postcolonial India*, Durham, Duke University Press.

Universal Declaration of Human Rights adopted by the General Assembly of the United Nations Resolution 217A (III) December 10, 1948. Available at http://www.un.org/Overview/rights.html.

PART I
The Post-9/11 Climate

Chapter 1

Human Rights Law, Executive Powers, and Torture in the Post-9/11 Era

Lisa Hajjar

Declaiming that "we do not torture" has become routine for President George W. Bush. Every time the torture and abuse of foreign prisoners in US custody makes the headlines, as it has with regularity since photos from an interrogation wing of the Abu Ghraib prison were first published in April 2004 (CBS's *60 Minutes II* 2004; Hersh 2004), he expounds some version of this denial (see Lederman 2005A). In November 2005 President Bush repeated this no-torture claim several times in response to an article in the *Washington Post* (Priest 2005, A01) that some CIA "black sites" – secret places where so-called "high value targets" had been disappeared for interrogation – were located in Eastern Europe (subsequently confirmed by Human Rights Watch to be Poland and Rumania; see HRW 2007).

The CIA black sites-in-Europe scandal was intensified by official acknowledgment that CIA tactics include "waterboarding," a form of mock execution through simulated drowning (see Priest 2004, A1). However, waterboarding, American advocates and apologists have claimed, does not constitute "torture" (as interpreted by Bush administration lawyers) because the pain that results is not "protracted" (Smith and Eggen 2004, A1). Former CIA head Porter Goss went so far as to characterize this tactic, a favorite of medieval inquisitors' "professional interrogation practice" (Diamond 2005).

On December 6, 2005, Secretary of State Condoleeza Rice went to Germany to issue her own version of the "we do not torture" routine in response to revelations about the CIA's abduction (from Macedonia) and detention (in Afghanistan) of German citizen Khaled el-Masri, who they wrongly suspected of complicity in terrorism, and who they subsequently dropped off in a remote spot in Albania after the error was realized (see Democracy Now! 2005). Rice was dispatched to reassure European allies that whatever was done to prisoners in US custody was not "torture," but, as ABC News reported on December 5, in advance of Rice's visit the CIA "scrambled" to move 11 detainees from European locations to a new black site somewhere in North Africa (later revealed to be Morocco).

These official denials are typical of torturing regimes and come in several forms (see Cohen 2001). "Literal denial" is when a state accused of torture (or some other gross crime) responds by saying that nothing happened and that those who claim otherwise are liars or "enemies of the state." This was the official American pattern of response to allegations of torture until December 2002, when the *Washington Post* reported that unnamed officials confirmed the use of "stress and duress" (position abuse, sleep deprivation, exposures to extremes in temperature, sound and light, and other tactics), as well as the transfer of prisoners who could not be "broken" by these means to countries whose intelligence services are known to use torture (Priest and Gellman 2002, A1). This ground-breaking article shifted the American pattern to "interpretative denial," namely refutation through euphemism. This entails acknowledging the practices but saying that they do not constitute "torture" but "something else" – "stress and duress" and "coercive interrogations" are two American euphemisms of choice (Bowden 2003). This interpretative denial was aided by prodigious work of some government lawyers to interpret laws to exclude tactics used by American interrogators from their interpretation of the definition of torture. The third variation is "implicatory denial" – that is, denial by implicating others – which occurs when a state acknowledges torture but blames it on "aberrant agents," claiming that rogue elements have breached official norms and policies. Official responses to the Abu Ghraib prison photos exemplify implicatory denial, as officials initially blamed the problem on "bad apples" (see Carter 2004).

The reason American officials – or officials from any country – are inclined to deny *torture* is, above all, because it is illegal and those who engage in or abet it are liable to prosecution. Since 2002, the plausibility of such American denials has eroded apace with continuing allegations and mounting evidence about the routine and pervasive use of torture against people in US custody in Afghanistan, Guantanamo and Iraq (see Human Rights Watch 2005; 2006A; 2006B). Photos, first-person accounts and even official investigations into interrogation and detention policies have confirmed that prisoners have been held naked in chilled cells, tied in stress positions and sleep deprived for protracted periods, subjected to deafening music and snarling dogs, sexually humiliated, and beaten. The *coup de grâce* is the plethora of declassified and leaked documents that these practices were sanctioned as policy by American authorities at the highest levels (see Greenberg and Dratel 2005).

In this chapter, I elaborate on the prohibition against torture and various efforts in the twentieth and twenty-first century to carve out exceptions, including America's post-9/11 development into a torturing regime. I also provide some discussion about the efforts to expose and prevent torture, including roles played by some military lawyers and others working to close the gap between "we don't torture" rhetoric and the reality of interrogation and detention practices.

Law and (International) Order

During the Enlightenment, the common and quite pervasive practice of torture began to be criticized as illegitimate and ineffective (see Dubois 1991; Peters 1996). Consequently, the renunciation of torture spread as country after country enshrined prohibitions in the processes of modernizing their legal systems. The prohibition constituted a limit to what state agents could do to people in custody who had not been found guilty of a crime. In US law, forbidding torture traces back to the founding of the nation and was enshrined in the Eighth Amendment of the Constitution barring cruel treatment, an enlightened repudiation of the tyrannical excesses of kings. Along with *habeas corpus* and the separation of powers, the ban on extralegal cruel treatment served as a foundation of the modern rule of law, because it was understood as essential to curbing tyranny and enabling conditions of human dignity, liberty, security and due process to thrive.

In the twentieth century, torture garnered universal prohibition and criminalization through developments in international law. The unprecedented horrors and violence of World War II provided the negative inspiration for a revolution in international law to forge the principle that people should have rights as humans, and not merely as protected classes of subjects, such as citizens, civilians or prisoners of war. The right not to be tortured became a human right when international law prohibited the practice, and established legal liabilities and penalties (see Foley 2003).

As a matter of law, torture is a crime with rather unique strength and scope (see Hajjar 2000). It is absolutely non-derogable, meaning that it is prohibited under all circumstances. In the words of the UN Convention Against Torture and Other Cruel, Inhuman or Degrading Treatment or Punishment (1984), "No exceptional circumstances whatsoever, whether a state of war or a threat of war, internal political instability or any other public emergency, may be invoked as a justification for torture." The prohibition of torture is also "universal" because it has status as a *jus cogens* norm and constitutes a part of customary international law, which means that it applies everywhere (i.e., territorially universal) and can be prosecuted anywhere. This means that anyone suspected or accused of torture is "an enemy of all mankind" because the crime of torture attaches universal jurisdiction; any perpetrator who is not prosecuted in his or her own country can be prosecuted in any competent legal system anywhere in the world (see Macedo 2003).

The right not to be tortured is dialectically related to the prohibition, which is absolute and universal. This means that the right applies to all people everywhere, regardless of their social status, their political identity or affiliations, or any aspect of their activities. In contrast, even the right to life is not nearly as strong as the right not to be tortured since there are many ways in which people can be killed "legally." Even the right of persons not to be exterminated through genocide, as prohibited by the Genocide Convention (1948), depends on the intent of the killing, which hinges on a collective identity as members of a national, religious or ethnic group. The right not to be deliberately targeted in war hinges not on one's humanity but rather on one's status as a civilian or non-combatant, or a surrendered or captured soldier.

Why is the Prohibition of Torture So Strong?

Torture occurs when someone who is *in custody* – unfree to fight back or protect himself or herself and imperiled by that incapacitation – is purposefully harmed (physically and/or mentally). Historically, the purposes have included punishment (penal torture) and extraction of a confession (judicial torture; see Foucault 1977). In the modern era, an additional purpose is extraction of security-related intelligence (interrogational torture) which may or may not also be a basis for prosecution (i.e., confessional; see Peters 1996). Other violent practices, like domestic violence and battery, also involve purposefully causing pain, but they lack the public dimension of custodianship and therefore do not constitute "torture," despite that pain and suffering, humiliation and injury are common to all. Legally, severe pain, suffering, humiliation and injury constitute torture only if they serve some public purpose and if the status and role of the torturer emanates from a public authority and if the person being harmed is in custody.

Notwithstanding these qualifications, there is no bright line empirically distinguishing torture from "everything else." Rather, torture is like a core within layers of violence. For example, being beaten while being arrested changes from "cruel treatment" to "torture" only when "custody" has been achieved, obviously a very blurry and contestable line. The combination of "torture" and "cruel, inhumane and degrading treatment" in the same international laws contributes to this confusion, which is further compounded by the exclusion of painful – but lawful – punishments such as floggings, amputations or the death penalty. Many forms of violence may lead to torture and many forms of violence may result from torture, but the core violence that is torture – and what makes torture a "core international crime" – is violence (physical or psychological) against a person already in the custody of an authority.

An "authority" obviously would include states and their agents, but it would not exclude non-state groups and their agents, or civilians. Torture is not contingent on legitimacy, jurisdiction or international recognition of the custodian; it is contingent on an organized rather than individualized capacity to take people into custody and then harm them for a purpose that is public rather than personal.

Torture and Terror

One of the great paradoxes of torture is that although it is so strongly prohibited and so widely construed as fundamentally illegitimate, it is shockingly common. According to Amnesty International, about two-thirds of the world's governments utilize tactics that could be deemed to constitute torture. While states torture people for numerous reasons, one common reason invoked by many states is that they claim to be engaged in conflicts with "terrorists." Consequently there is a tendency to proclaim that "coercion" (i.e., euphemized torture) is crucial for the protection of national security and/or to assert that terrorist enemies lack the right not to be abused in custody (see Ignatieff 2002).

Terrorism is a broad and flexible concept, and there is no clear, internationally accepted definition. It is used, variously, to describe certain kinds of actions, including attacks on civilians, hijackings, organized resistance or repression, and to identify certain types of actors. In national security discourse, the term terrorism typically is used to refer to non-state actors or organizations engaged in attacks or struggles against the state, emphasizing but not necessarily limited to violence, to which the state responds with "counter-terrorism."

Terrorism is not a figment of the politically paranoid imagination. Any and every instance of deliberately targeting civilians or civilian infrastructures as a tactic in the furtherance of some cause, whatever the political or ideological motivation and whomever the targeting agents, is terroristic. If the deliberate targeting of civilians constitutes terrorism, then states can be as culpable as non-state groups. However, as Richard Falk (2002, xix) explains:

With the help of the influential media, the state over time has waged and largely won the battle of definitions by exempting its own violence against civilians from being treated and perceived as "terrorism." Instead, such violence was generally discussed as "uses of force," "retaliation," "self-defense" and "security measures."

National security is a legitimate interest of any state, and states have responsibility to provide for the security of their citizens. But the tendency to characterize all "enemies" as "terrorists" or "terrorist sympathizers" contributes to the delineation between "legitimate" and "illegitimate" communities, leaving the latter vulnerable to state violence, including torture and other violations of human rights (see Palti 2004).

A Distinction is Born

Israel was the first state in the world to break the "torture taboo" by *publicly* authorizing interrogation practices for Palestinians that constitute torture, albeit under the euphemistic term "moderate physical pressure." In the 1967 Arab-Israeli war, Israel captured and occupied the West Bank and Gaza and established a military administration to rule the Palestinians residing in these areas. A military court system was established to prosecute Palestinians suspected of violating Israel's military and emergency laws, which criminalized not only violence, sabotage and militancy, but also a vast array of political and non-violent activities. Israel used prosecution as one of its key strategies to rule Palestinians and to thwart and punish resistance to the occupation (Hajjar 2005A). Since 1967, over half a million Palestinians have been prosecuted in the military court system, out of a population that now numbers 3.2 million. There have been periods when incarceration rates in the West Bank and Gaza were among the highest in the world.

For two decades (1967–87), allegations that Israeli soldiers and interrogators were routinely torturing Palestinian detainees were consistently refuted by Israeli officials as lies and fabrications of "enemies of the state." Then for reasons unconnected to the interrogation of Palestinians, the Israeli government established an official commission of inquiry to investigate the General Security Services (GSS). The report produced by the Landau Commission (Landau 1987) was path-breaking in a number of ways: It confirmed that, in fact, GSS agents had used violent interrogation methods routinely on Palestinian detainees since at least 1971, and that they had routinely lied about such practices when confessions were challenged in court on the grounds that they had been coerced. The Landau Commission was harsh in its criticism of GSS perjury, but adopted the GSS's own position that coercive interrogation tactics were necessary in the struggle against "hostile terrorist activity." The Landau Commission accepted the broad definition of terrorism utilized by the GSS, which encompassed not only acts or threats of violence, but virtually all activities related to Palestinian nationalism.

The most radical aspects of the Landau report were its conclusions and recommendations. The report's authors argued that national security requires physical and psychological coercion in the interrogation of Palestinians, and that the state should sanction such tactics in order to rectify the problem of perjury. The Landau Commission's justification for this recommendation was based on a three-part contention: that Palestinians have no right to legal protections given their predisposition for terrorism, that the GSS operates morally and responsibly in discharging its duties to preserve Israeli national security, and that GSS interrogation methods do not constitute torture. Thus, the Landau Commission proposed a way for the state to engage in torture while simultaneously denying it by terming it "moderate physical pressure."

This Israeli euphemism traces back to British torture of Irish prisoners in Northern Ireland. A legal challenge was mounted against Britain's "five techniques" in the interrogation of suspected Irish Republican Army members on the grounds that they violate the European Convention on Human Rights. In *Ireland v. United Kingdom* (decision available at: http://www.worldlii.org/eu/cases/ECHR/1978/1. html), the majority decision by the European Court of Human Rights ruled that the five techniques (wall standing, hooding, subjection to noise, sleep deprivation, and deprivation of food and drink) do not amount to "torture" but to the lesser – and also prohibited – category of "inhumane and degrading treatment." But the British government accepted the minority opinion of the Court that the techniques constitute (or come close to) torture (especially when used in combination), and decided to forego their use. The Landau Commission, noting that Israeli interrogation tactics resembled the five techniques, embraced the Court's majority decision that they do not constitute "torture." Thus was born the euphemization of "moderate physical pressure" as "not torture."

The Israeli government adopted the Landau Commission's recommendations to "legalize" torture in November 1987. This prompted a concerted campaign and protracted litigation by Israeli lawyers and human rights organizations to end Israeli interrogation practices that constitute torture (see Pacheco 1999). In 1999, the Israeli High Court of Justice finally issued a ruling prohibiting the routine use of "pressure" tactics (though not calling these tactics "torture") while preserving the option to use such tactics in "exceptional circumstances" (reprinted in Levinson 2004).

The Pinochet Precedent

Perhaps the most vivid illustration of the strength of the prohibition on torture and the universal jurisdiction that attaches to it is the case of former Chilean dictator Augusto Pinochet. Pinochet was arrested in 1998 in London when the British government conceded to act on an indictment by Spanish judge Balthazar Garzon. The Spanish indictment charged Pinochet with genocide and other forms of murder (see Kornbluh 2004), but the only charge that held up as the case made its way through the British legal system was torture. Although Pinochet ultimately was released from British custody because of "ill health," the "Pinochet precedent" – holding that he was indictable – was a landmark (see Woodhouse 2000). No *raison d'état* could be invoked to justify torture, and no one, not even a former head of state, could claim legal immunity from prosecution on charges of torture (see Feitlowitz 2000).

Of course, the Pinochet case did not solve or even alter the problem of torture. But the Pinochet precedent did illustrate that the right not to be tortured is stronger than the rights of a state, regardless of the circumstances or suspicions against those in custody. It also illustrated that there is no sovereign immunity, even for a former head of state, for the crime of torture, and also that accountability can go to the top of the chain of command. Pinochet probably never tortured anyone personally, but he was deemed responsible for torture by his soldiers and secret service agents.

The "New Paradigm"

In the US, prior to the 9/11 terror attacks, the prohibition of torture was rarely debated in public. It was recognized as a customary international legal norm when Congress passed the Torture Victims Protection Act in 1992 which allows a torture victim to sue his/her torturer in US courts, regardless where the torture occurred. The 1949 Geneva Conventions, which prohibit torture and cruel, inhuman and degrading treatment of prisoners captured in war, are incorporated into the US Uniform Code of Military Justice (UCMJ), and federal anti-torture and war crimes statutes passed in the 1990s establish criminal liability for violations in times of war or peace.

This black-letter law would seem to settle that torture and inhumane treatment were not legitimate options for US interrogators. But in the wake of 9/11, dominant voices in the Bush administration's inner circles subscribed to the idea that if "coercively interrogating" prisoners could provide intelligence to save American lives and win the "war on terror," then "quaint" laws should be no obstacle. The administration's embrace of torture was a direct result of the policy preference for reinterpreting the law to assert that all those taken into custody were "terrorists" who have no legal rights whatsoever, including, if deemed to be of "military necessity," no right not to be tortured. This lawless approach was termed a "new paradigm" (see Barry, Hirsch, and Isikoff 2005).

The top advocates for torture and other extra-legal policies were Vice President Dick Cheney and his counsel (later appointed chief of staff), David Addington (see Mayer 2006A). The license to torture was varnished with legal opinions from the Justice Department's Office of Legal Counsel (OLC), most prominently by Berkeley law professor John Yoo, who served as deputy assistant attorney general from 2001–2003. The new paradigm had several components and goals. One, termed the "unitary executive thesis," was to expand executive power at the expense of the courts and Congress. To these ends, Yoo and his OLC colleagues produced a series of secret memos opining that the president, as commander-in-chief, has unfettered powers to wage war, that any efforts to subject executive discretion over interrogation and detention policies to federal, military or treaty laws would be "unconstitutional," that the legal restriction on cruel, inhuman and degrading treatment is unenforceable outside the United States, and, for good measure, that prisoners designated as terrorists by presidential fiat (rather than status review by a tribunal) should have no *habeas corpus* right to contest their detention and no right not to be maltreated (see Yoo 2006; Margulies 2006). These OLC opinions were treated as "controlling legal authority" and utilized by the CIA and Pentagon civilians to authorize practices that the International Committee of the Red Cross (with unique access to prisoners) characterized in 2003 in a rare public critique as "tantamount to torture" (Lewis 2004). The clandestine drive to evade the laws of the land prohibiting torture and ill treatment started in earnest in January 2002, when then-White House counsel

(Attorney General 2006–2007) Alberto Gonzales asked the Defense Department to instruct intelligence officers at Guantánamo Bay, Cuba to fill out a one-page form on every detainee certifying the president's "reason to believe" that the detainee was involved in terrorism (Golden 2004A and 2004B). Those whom the president so suspected were to be tried by the special military commissions created by Bush's November 2001 executive order. Within weeks, the officers began reporting back that interrogations were not producing the information needed to fulfill Gonzales' request. At a time when these prisoners were touted as the "worst of the worst," the presumption was that legal restraints on interrogation were the problem.

The first legal obstacle was cleared on February 7, 2002, when President Bush embraced the OLC opinion that suspected al-Qaeda detainees were not protected by the Geneva Conventions, and that suspected Taliban detainees are categorically not entitled to prisoner-of-war status under the conventions. This laid the ground for a "no crime without law" approach to the handling of prisoners. In the preceding weeks, the State Department had sharply criticized the legal flaws and political dangers of this position, for which it was rewarded by exclusion from discussions of interrogation and detention policies thereafter (see Hajjar 2005).

By the summer of 2002, official agitation was mounting over the lack of intelligence that could lead to the capture of Osama bin Laden and other top al-Qaeda and Taliban leaders, whose continuing evasion of the US-led military campaign in Afghanistan was a political embarrassment. The most infamous torture memo, dated August 1, 2002 and signed by then-Assistant Attorney General Jay Bybee but authored by Yoo, was written in response to the question of how far CIA agents, anxious about the risk of future prosecution under federal anti-torture laws, could go in interrogating high-value al-Qaeda suspects. It was prompted by the March 28, 2002, capture of Abu Zubaydah, believed to be a top al-Qaeda strategist. Yoo opined in the August 1 memo that a tactic is not "torture" unless it causes pain comparable to "organ failure or death." His reasoning was that torture (i.e., physical) entails "severe pain" and in searching the US statutory record the only American law that uses this phrase pertains to emergency medical care, hence the reference to organ failure or death. (The analysis in this memo was so shoddy and embarrassing that it was repudiated by the administration as soon as it became public in June 2004 and replaced that December with a new OLC memo.)

At the time this August 1 memo was produced, American interrogation practices were shrouded in secrecy. This changed with the publication of the above-mentioned *Washington Post* article in December 2002 (Priest and Gellman 2002, A1). The tactics unnamed officials described to the journalists were identical to Israeli "moderate physical pressure," including keeping prisoners "standing or kneeling for hours, in black hoods or spray-painted goggles … [and holding them] in awkward, painful positions and deprived of sleep with a 24-hour bombardment of lights – subject to what are known as 'stress and duress' techniques."

Priest and Gellman also reported that detainees who could not be broken by the "restrained" stress and duress tactics might be given mind-altering drugs or "turned over – 'rendered,' in official parlance – to foreign intelligence services whose practice of torture has been documented by the US government and human rights organizations." They continued, "While the US government publicly denounces the use of torture, each of the current national security officials interviewed for this article defended the use of violence against captives as just and necessary. They expressed confidence that the American public would back their view." Priest and Gellman also quoted Cofer Black, former head of the CIA Counterterrorist Center, who testified before Congress on September 26, 2002. According to Black, the CIA and other security agencies need "operational flexibility," and therefore cannot be held to the "old" standards. "There was before 9/11, and there was an after 9/11. After 9/11 the gloves come off."

Like the Landau Commission report when it was published in Israel in 1987, this *Washington Post* story dramatically altered both what is known about American interrogation and how torture was talked about in the US. Human rights advocates assailed official admissions of "stress and duress" as defenses of torture. And defenders of the administration responded in kind. For example, on January 11, 2003, in a letter to the *Washington Post*, two former Justice Department officials who served under Presidents Ronald Reagan and George Bush cited the European Court ruling (i.e., *Ireland v. U.K.*) as evidence that "stress and duress" is not torture. "Indeed," they retorted to the human rights advocates, "to say these practices do [constitute torture] ultimately trivializes the torture that does take place in so many areas of the world."

Even before the publication of the Abu Ghraib photos in 2004, there was a growing debate about torture spurred by revelations about interrogation tactics and detention conditions that arguably constitute torture, and the rendering of prisoners to states with well-established records of torture – including Jordan, Egypt, Syria, Morocco, Pakistan and the Philippines (see Mayer 2005). The question is why officials at the highest levels would authorize such policies.

Yooification and Gitmoization

Although the August 1 torture memo was written specifically for the CIA, the White House forwarded it to the Pentagon, where it was seized upon as a solution to military interrogators' frustration that Guantánamo detainees were tenaciously resisting lawful interrogation methods. It should be noted that in August 2002, a senior Arabic-speaking CIA analyst dispatched to assess Guantánamo detainees' intelligence value concluded that few had any meaningful ties to or information about al-Qaeda. One exception was Muhammad al-Qahtani, alleged to be the twentieth hijacker. The desire to "break" him was the reason for authorization to use dogs, protracted sleep deprivation and stress positions, forced nudity and other forms of degrading treatment (see Zagorin and Duffy 2005). A memo by Army Lt. Col. Diane Beaver, dated October 11, 2002, noted that coercive tactics are "per se" illegal under the UCMJ, but that this might be circumvented on the basis of the commander-in-chief's authority (one of the key arguments in the August 1 memo).

A December 2, 2002 Defense Department memo authorizing a three-category menu of interrogation tactics was rescinded on January 15, 2003, apparently because of concerns among the uniformed military about the ramifications of abandoning the UCMJ. The Pentagon then convened a working group to produce new military interrogation guidelines for Guantánamo. The working group was instructed by the Pentagon's General Counsel William Haynes to accept the OLC's August 1 analysis, and forbidden from developing analysis that would conform to military law or 50 years of military practice (see Lederman 2005B).

Top lawyers in the Judge Advocate General's Corps from all four branches of the military wrote memos to the Pentagon leadership in February and March 2003 conveying uniform dismay at the authorization of "torture lite" tactics. They protested that this contravenes the UCMJ, which enshrines Geneva Convention rules and governs the military, regardless of the status of prisoners, that it would expose soldiers to the risk of court martial, and that it would undermine military doctrine and discipline, as well as public support for the war (see Mayer 2006B).

On March 14, 2003, Yoo sent a memo to Haynes responding to the JAGs' concerns, which was used by Pentagon civilians to silence the dissent. (The contents of this memo, which has not yet become public, are apparently so sensitive or embarrassing that even a 2005 official investigation into prisoner abuse, headed by Vice Adm. Albert Church, was barred from making a copy and had to read it in a secure location.) The working group issued its final report on interrogation policy for Guantánamo on April 4 (Pentagon 2003). (This document was also declassified in June 2004, and in March 2005 was officially rescinded and declared to be "a historical document with no standing in policy, practice or law to guide any activity of the Department of Defense.")

The coercive tactics authorized for military interrogators at Guantánamo, where the Bush administration claimed that the Geneva Conventions do not apply to prisoners, "migrated" in late August 2003 to Iraq, where there was no dispute that the Geneva Conventions did apply (since this was, at least originally, a "conventional" war between states). Lt. Gen. Ricardo Sanchez, commander of the Iraqi theater of operations, signed off on tactics that would "Gitmoize" Iraqi prisons, including use of dogs, sexual humiliation, stress positions and other forms of prisoner abuse that were conveyed to the world in the Abu Ghraib photos (Hersch 2004B).

The Bottom Line

While the Abu Ghraib photos proved immensely embarrassing to the Bush administration, they did not lead to any immediate change in policy. Although the declassification or leakage of numerous official documents illuminated dots running up the chain of command, the twelve official commissions of inquiry tasked to investigate interrogation and detention policies were unanimous in their refusal to connect those dots. In July 2005, Lt. Gen. Mark Schmidt issued his report on FBI allegations of detainee abuse at Guantánamo to Congress. The report remains classified, but according to the executive summary that has been published, Schmidt and his fellow investigators certified that some detainees were subjected to tactics that were clearly "abusive" (20-hour interrogations for 48 days in a row, short-shackling to the floor for extended periods) and "degrading" (being smeared with fake menstrual blood, being forced to bark like a dog and perform dog tricks). In an Orwellian twist, the report concluded that these tactics were not unlawful. In Schmidt's view, echoing

Yoo's logic, the "abusive" tactics were not "inhumane," and nothing in US law prohibited degrading and humiliating treatment of "unlawful combatants."

Defining "humane treatment" became a key focus in the subsequent battle over interrogation and detention policies. The universally recognized baseline standard for the treatment of prisoners in wartime is Geneva Convention Common Article 3, which extends to all detained persons. It states that they "shall in all circumstances be treated humanely," and that "[t]o this end," certain specified acts "are and shall remain prohibited at any time and in any place whatsoever" including "cruel treatment and torture," and "outrages upon personal dignity, in particular humiliating and degrading treatment."

The universal applicability and standards of Common Article 3 were resolutely rejected by the Bush administration. This official resistance flew in the face of the 9/11 Commission, lawyers in the JAG corps and numerous others who declared that, even where Common Article 3 might not apply as a matter of treaty obligation, the standards must be the point of reference for the treatment of prisoners. The Bush administration's only concession on this matter was to state that prisoners would be treated "humanely" as a matter of policy, implying that some people still have no legal right to their humanity. Cheney and other pro-torture advocates continued to insist that there is no baseline in a war on terror because no law can bridle executive discretion and that the president is under no obligation to abide by customary international law.

But the scandals and revelations had some significant political effects. In July 2005, Sen. Lindsey Graham (R-SC) finally succeeded in his year-long quest to obtain the release of the JAG memos written in the spring of 2003 (available at: http://balkin.blogspot.com/2005/07/jag-memos-on-military-interrogation.html). Upon their release he said, "The JAGs were telling the policymakers: if you go down this road, you are going to get your own people in trouble...and they were absolutely right." The memos spurred Graham, an Air Force reserve lawyer himself, and fellow Republicans John McCain and John Warner to draft legislation that would bring all interrogations conducted anywhere in the world by any US agents (including the CIA) back within the rubric of the law. Cheney led the White House campaign to thwart their initiative, thus earning himself the nickname "vice president for torture." The language of the 2005 McCain amendment was endorsed by dozens of retired military officers, including former Secretary of State Colin Powell, as well as otherwise stalwart Bush administration backers from the American Enterprise Institute and the *Weekly Standard*.

On October 5, 2005, the Senate voted 90-9 to attach McCain's initiative as an amendment to the 2006 defense appropriations bill, prompting the threat of a presidential veto and a lobbying campaign directed at Republicans in the House of Representatives. Rather than veto the overwhelmingly popular legislation, Bush signed a secret "signing statement" stating, essentially, that he was not bound to abide by it, a variation on the "unitary executive thesis" (Savage 2006).

The Dénouement

Throughout 2006, battles over interrogation and the law grew more pitched, and the question about what was gained by allowing torture more pointed. As was increasingly clear to anyone paying attention, one of the many adverse effects of utilizing "enhanced interrogation techniques," conducting "extraordinary renditions" to countries that torture and "disappearing" people in CIA custody was to undermine the prospect of ever bringing to justice any of the captured authors of the September 11 attacks, or other suspects. As David Cole points out in a December 3, 2005, *Los Angeles Times* op-ed, "One probable reason for the military's reluctance [to charge and prosecute most detainees in US custody] is the real risk that any trial will turn into a trial of the United States' own interrogation practices. Although the military tribunal rules do not exclude the use of testimony extracted by torture, no trial will ever be viewed as legitimate if it allows such testimony, and defense lawyers are certain to make this a central issue in any proceeding."

The military defense lawyers assigned to represent the first Guantanamo detainees slated for prosecution before the military commissions were among the most visible critics of US interrogation practices. These JAGs mounted a vigorous defense of their clients by speaking out against the government's authorization of violent and degrading interrogation tactics, as well as the military commission rules that permitted the use of information from others that might have been extracted through torture. In November 2005, the Supreme Court agreed to hear the case of *Hamdan v. Rumsfeld*, which was brought by Navy Lt. Cmdr. Charles Swift on behalf of his client Salim Ahmad Hamdan, challenging the constitutionality of the military commissions themselves.

In June 2006, the majority of the US Supreme Court in *Hamdan v. Rumsfeld* ruled that prisoners captured in the "war on terror" have rights under the Geneva Conventions (at minimum those designated in Common Article 3 that unequivocally prohibits torture and degradation), thus rebuking the administration's claim that they are rightless. The *Hamdan* ruling also declared the statute for the military commissions in Guantanamo unconstitutional. Finally, the ruling raised the specter that those who had violated – or ordered the violation of – the Geneva Conventions could be prosecuted under the federal War Crimes Act (1996). For the first time since the 9/11 attacks, euphemistic denials would no longer suffice.

In response to *Hamdan*, President Bush criticized the Supreme Court and sought to push through Congress legislation that would essentially negate the ruling and restore all that it had taken away (White and Smith 2005), including a statute for military commissions that would permit the use of evidence and confessions extracted through "coercive interrogations"; and an amended version of the War Crimes Act to provide immunity (i.e., impunity) for past violations of Common Article 3. This legislative campaign was pursued using strong partisan pressure (easily heightened by the fact that 2006 was an election year) to rally Republican legislators who composed a majority in both houses, and a media campaign casting opponents of proposed legislation as "terrorist sympathizers."

McCain, Warner and Graham drafted legislation that would have comported with the *Hamdan* ruling in most ways, and it was endorsed by dozens of retired military officers, including former Secretary of State and head of the Joint Chiefs of Staff Colin Powell, and numerous legal experts and human rights organizations. However, Bush and Cheney prevailed to crush the Republican dissenters' resistance to the legalization of torture. In October 2006, less than a month before the election (that would ultimately sweep both houses of their Republican majorities), Congress passed the Military Commissions Act. This act essentially gave Bush everything he desired and signaled the caving of the Republican dissenters (McCain has presidential ambitions for 2008) to the pro-torture policies of the administration. Whether the Democratic-led Congress will undo the appalling MCA remains to be seen, but either way, lawyers are poised to litigate all the way to the Supreme Court in order to store what that notorious piece of legislation has taken away.

Meanwhile, it was because Congress passed the MCA that Germany was finally willing to entertain a case against Donald Rumsfeld and other top officials, on the grounds that domestic accountability was, for the present, off the table in the US.

Conclusion

Since September 11, the Bush administration has articulated positions and pursued policies that blatantly contravene the law (federal and international), on the grounds that terrorists do not deserve legal rights and protections. The administration has adopted policies that were repudiated during the Enlightenment, including incommunicado and indefinite detention, denial of *habeas corpus*, violent and abusive interrogation, and for some, trial in courts with Star Chamber secrecy and partiality. Although the US government continues to claim that torture has never been authorized, these clandestine and extralegal conditions are evidence to the contrary. The Abu Ghraib images and the thousands of pages of documentation, not to mention the numerous first-person accounts by former prisoners and members of the military, are hard evidence that the US has joined the list of countries – Egypt, Israel, Uzbekistan – that are fighting "wars on terrorism" partly through the use of torture.

The US government has a right to pursue justice for the September 11 attacks and for other acts of terrorism that target civilians. But justice is a matter of law, not policy, and it requires lawful treatment of prisoners and witnesses, and legal venues that are able and willing to function independently to interpret and enforce the laws of the land. At this juncture, it is vital that many more citizens school themselves in the legal issues at stake, and speak out loudly to demand lawful policies. Torture is inimical to law and justice.

Works Cited

Barry, John, Michael Hirsch, and Michael Isikoff (2005), "The Roots of Torture," *Newsweek*, May 24.

Bowden, Mark (2003), "The Dark Art of Interrogation," *The Atlantic Monthly*, October.

Carter, Philip (2004), "The Road to Abu Ghraib," *Washington Monthly*, November.

CBS's *60 Minutes II* (2004), April 29.

Cohen, Stan (2001), *States of Denial: Knowing about Atrocities and Suffering*, Polity Press.

Democracy Now! (2005), "Extraordinary Rendition Under Fire: Lawsuit Charges CIA with Kidnapping and Torture of German Citizen," December 7.

Diamond, John (2005), "CIA Chief: Interrogation methods 'unique' but legal," *USA Today*, November 20.

Dubois, Page (1991), *Torture and Truth*, Routledge.

Feitlowitz, Margaret (interviewer) (2000), "The Pinochet Precedent: Who Could Be Arrested Next?" Crimes of War Project, available at: http://www.crimesofwar. org/expert/pinochet.html.

Foley, Conor (2003), *Combating Torture: A Manual for Judges and Prosecutors*, Human Rights Centre, University of Essex: United Kingdom.

Foucault, Michel (1977), *Discipline and Punish: The Birth of the Prison*, Pantheon.

Golden, Tim (2004A), "After Terror, A Secret Rewriting of Military Law," *New York Times*, October 24.

– (2004B), "Slow Pace of Pentagon's Courts Set off Friction at White House," *New York Times*, October 25.

Greenberg, Karen and Josh Dratel (2005), *The Torture Papers: The Road to Abu Ghraib*, Cambridge University Press.

Falk, Richard (2002), *The Great Terror War*, Olive Branch Press.

Hajjar, Lisa (2000), "Sovereign Bodies, Sovereign States and the Problem of Torture," *Studies in Law, Politics and Society*, vol. 21.

– (2005A), *Courting Conflict: The Israeli Military Court System in the West Bank and Gaza*, University of California Press.

– (2005B), "In the Penal Colony," *The Nation*, February 7.

Hersch, Seymour (2004A), "Torture at Abu Ghraib," *New Yorker*, April 30.

– (2004B), *Chain of Command: The Road to Abu Ghraib*' HarperCollins.

Human Rights Watch (2005), *US Operated Secret "Dark Prison" in Kabul*, New York, December.

– (2006A), *By the Numbers: Findings of the Detainee Abuse and Accountability Project*, New York, April.

– (2006B), *No Blood, No Foul: Soldiers' Accounts of Detainee Abuse in Iraq*, New York, July.

– (2006C), *US: Vice President Endorses Torture: Cheney Expresses Approval of CIA's Use of Waterboarding*, New York, October 26.

– (2007), *Ghost Prisoner: Two Years in Secret CIA Detention*, Vol. 19, no. 1(G), February.

Ignatieff, Michael (2002), "Human Rights, Laws of War, and Terrorism," *Social Research* vol. 69, no. 4 (Winter).

Kornbluh, Peter (2004), *The Pinochet File: A Declassified Dossier on Atrocity and Accountability*, The New Press.

Landau, Moshe et al. (1987), *Commission of Inquiry into the Methods of Investigation of the General Security Services regarding Hostile Terrorist Activity*, Government Press Office, Israel.

Lederman, Marty (2005A), "'We Do Not Torture.' 'We Abide By Our Treaty Obligations.' 'We Treat Detainees Humanely.' (Repeat as needed)" Balkinization. com, September 21.

– (2005B), "Gitmo: Where Was the Law? Whither the UCMJ?" Balkinization.com, June 14.

Levinson, Sanford (ed.) (2004), *Torture: A Collection*, Oxford University Press.

Lewis, Neil A. (2004), "Red Cross Finds Detainee Abuse in Guantanamo," *New York Times*, November 30.

Macedo, Stephen (ed.) (2003), *Universal Jurisdiction: National Courts and the Prosecution of Serious Crimes under International Law*, University of Pennsylvania Press.

Margulies, Joseph (2006), *Guantanamo and the Abuse of Presidential Power*, Simon & Schuster.

Mayer, Jane (2006A), "The Hidden Power: The Legal Mind behind the US's War on Terror," *New Yorker*, July 3.

– (2006B), "The Memo: How an Internal Effort to Ban the Abuse and Torture of Detainees Was Thwarted," *New Yorker*, February 27.

– (2005), "Outsourcing Torture: The Secret History of America's 'Extraordinary Rendition' Program," *New Yorker*, February 14.

Pacheco, Allegra (ed.) (1999), *The Case against Torture in Israel: A Compilation of Petitions, Briefs, and Other Documents Submitted to the Israeli High Court of Justice*, Public Committee against Torture in Israel.

Palti, Leslie (2004), "Combating Terrorism While Protecting Human Rights," *UN Chronicle Online*, available at: http://www.un.org/Pubs/chronicle/2004/issue4/ 0404p27.html.

Pentagon (2003), *Working Group Report on Detainee Interrogations in the Global War on Terrorism: Assessment of Legal, Historical, Policy and Operational Considerations*, available at: http://www.washingtonpost.com/wp-srv/nation/ documents/040403dod.pdf.

Peters, Edward (1996), *Torture*, University of Pennsylvania Press.

Priest, Dana (2004), "CIA Puts Harsh Tactics on Hold; Memo on Methods of Interrogation Had Wide Review," *Washington Post*, June 27: A1.

– (2005), "CIA Holds Terror Suspects in Secret Prisons," *Washington Post*, November 2.

Priest, Dana and Barton Gellman (2002), "US Decries Abuse but Defends Interrogations: 'Stress and Duress' Tactics Used on Terrorism Suspects in Secret Overseas Facilities," *Washington Post*, December 26: A1.

Savage, Charlie (2006), "Bush Could Bypass New Torture Ban," *Boston Globe*, January 4.

Smith, R. Jeffrey and Dan Eggen (2004), "Gonzales Helped Set the Course for Detainees," *Washington Post*, January 5: A1.

White, Josh and R. Jeffrey Smith (2005), "White House Aims to Block Legislation on Detainees," *Washington Post*, July 23.

Woodhouse, Diane (2000), *The Pinochet Case: A Legal and Constitutional Analysis*, Hart Publishing.

Yoo, John (2006), *War by Other Means: An Insider's Account of the War on Terror*, Atlantic Monthly Press.

Zagorin, Adam and Michael Duffy (2005), "Inside the Interrogation of Detainee 063," *Time Magazine*, June 12.

Chapter 2

Human Rights Advocates in the Post-9/11 Era

Ashley Barr

It would be a mistake to treat human rights as though there were a trade-off to be made between human rights and such goals as security or development. We only weaken our hand in fighting the horrors of extreme poverty or terrorism if, in our efforts to do so, we deny the very human rights that these scourges take away from citizens. Strategies based on the protection of human rights are vital for both our moral standing and the practical effectiveness of our actions – United Nations Secretary-General Kofi Annan (2005).

On February 17, 2005, the US government released thousands of pages of documents detailing internal investigations into abuse of prisoners in Afghanistan and Iraq, bringing the total number of pages of army documents released to over 24,000 (Inskeep 2005). The American Civil Liberties Union (ACLU) and other human rights groups won access to many of these documents after filing a successful Freedom of Information Act (FOIA) request. The February 17 batch of documents detailed allegations of prisoner abuse at American-run detention centers in Bagram and Kandahar, Afghanistan, and in Iraq. One document referred to a compact disk found in an office in Afghanistan. The disk contained pictures of prisoners subjected to many forms of abuse, including mock executions (Inskeep 2005). Another document described results of an army investigation which concluded that many pictures of detainee abuse were destroyed following the international outrage of prisoner abuse at Abu Ghraib (Inskeep 2005). In one case, a squad leader ordered that photographs be deleted from a digital camera (Inskeep 2005). At the time of writing this chapter the ACLU is still waiting for thousands of pages to be released.

As disturbing as these revelations are, they are not surprising. Almost every day over the past months news agencies have published fresh allegations of abuse, leaked memos, and other documents that further reveal the extent of detainee abuse in Iraq and Afghanistan. The picture we now have of detainee abuse, buttressed by the FOIA documents, contradicts the Bush Administration's depiction of that abuse being the result of "a few bad apples" (*Economist* 2005). It is also revealing to juxtapose what we now know with President Bush's 2005 Inaugural speech rhetoric. At that time, President Bush magnanimously declared that, "fortunately for the oppressed, America's influence is considerable, and we will use it confidently in freedom's cause" (*CNN* 2005). He proudly put his Administration at the service of those fighting oppressive governments, promising that, "America will not pretend that jailed dissidents prefer their chains" (*CNN* 2005). He even emphasized dissent as a necessary component of a rights-based society, arguing that, "rights must be more than the grudging concessions of dictators; they are secured by free dissent and the participation of the governed" (*CNN* 2005).

Despite this heady rhetoric, the information being gathered through FOIA requests provides clear evidence of Administration policies in the Global War on Terror (GWOT) of a contrary nature. Indeed, three fundamental issues emerge clearly from a close reading of these documents:

1. The US-led War on Terrorism is leading to human rights opportunism – or copycat behavior – around the world. That should make us more concerned for our collective security than ever before, regardless of the Bush Administration's rhetoric about freedom and liberty.
2. Human rights defenders – like the ACLU and their counterparts all over the world – are essential to real freedom and security for us all.
3. Our challenge is to make Bush's language real by creating enabling environments for dissidents, civil society groups, human rights defenders, minority populations, and other vulnerable groups.

Again, it is useful to imagine the actual implementation of Bush's declared allegiances. He promised that:

> All who live in tyranny and hopelessness can know: the United States will not ignore your oppression, or excuse your oppressors. When you stand for your liberty, we will stand with you. Democratic reformers facing repression, prison, or exile can know: America sees you for who you are: the future leaders of your country (*CNN* 2005).

In a partial acknowledgement of insistent criticism of his policies, President Bush also pledged to "restore the rule of law," and in particular to restore "adherence to the Geneva Conventions and international human rights standards to which the nations of the world have pledged themselves during the last half-century" (*CNN* 2005).

President Bush's pledges at his 2005 inauguration came after a chorus of criticism leveled at his policies. To choose one example from the many possibilities, consider the remarks by Nicholas Howen, Secretary-General of the International Commission of Jurists. To an international audience of eminent jurists, Howen characterized the GWOT as, "more than a set of specific laws" (Howen 2004). Rather, he claimed, "it is a way of thinking" (Howen 2004). Howen spoke darkly of "a disturbing rhetoric … a security-dominated discourse" (Howen 2004). This GWOT rhetoric, according to him,

> says that rights and freedoms interfere with security of state. It pushes aside the usual laws and norms because they seem to constrain the unfettered discretion of the executive to take any action it thinks necessary. In this rhetoric there are only patriots and terrorists; good and evil (Howen 2004).

Howen continued his denunciation of Bush policies, reminding his audience that, "the rule of law must be the first defense against arbitrary power" (Howen 2004).

The crisis precipitated by the attacks on the US on September 11, 2001, according to him, precipitated as well a test of our political and legal systems:

> The strength of our rule of law and human rights norms will be judged by whether they hold up in times of crisis, when governments are most tempted to ignore them, yet when they are most needed (Howen 2004).

This chapter evaluates the impact of this crisis not just on the American social and legal systems, but with an eye to the global arena of human rights defenders. If President Bush softened his rhetoric in 2005, the damage done by the GWOT across the globe to human rights defenders was not thereby erased or ameliorated. In this period of crisis, when human rights defenders have vital work to accomplish, their mission has in many instances been impaired or made impossible by states aggressively pursuing sovereign interests.

That the US-led War on Terrorism is leading to human rights opportunism can be easily illustrated. Indeed, one could be forgiven for assuming, after examining government policies in a large sample of countries, that governments around the world have collectively declared a global state of emergency. By now, the tactics used by the Bush Administration and copied in countries from Colombia to India are well known.

"Assessing the New Normal," a publication by Human Rights First (formerly Lawyers Committee for Human Rights), provides an excellent compilation of post-9/11 policies and practices that US citizens now accept as a necessary component of a terrorism offensive. These policies include increased unaccountable surveillance and intelligence gathering, incommunicado indefinite detention without charges (as of March 2005 there were over 500 detainees at the US Naval Base at Guantanamo Bay, Cuba), torture and cruel, inhuman, and degrading treatment during interrogations, an abandonment of the Geneva Conventions and international human rights standards generally, and tightened administrative controls on civil society groups and political opponents. Many people, including well-meaning American voters, justify these actions as necessary in the new world order of unprecedented threats (Lawyers Committee for Human Rights 2003).

But terrorism is not new; countries around the world, from Sri Lanka to Egypt to Northern Ireland to Palestine, have dealt with these issues for decades. In November 2003 The Carter Center in Atlanta, Georgia, and the United Nations Office of the High Commissioner for Human Rights brought human rights defenders from around the world to Atlanta to discuss the protection of human rights in the context of the GWOT. Many defenders came from countries that have been battling with their own rebel or insurgent groups for years. These activists gave voice to a common understanding of human rights as integral to, rather than inimical to, a successful battle against terrorism.

Martin O'Brien, a human rights activist from Northern Ireland, presented the commonly held wisdom from a personal perspective:

> I come from a place where there has been a war on terrorism for very many years, and many of the repressive approaches spreading across the world are ones which originated or at least have been practiced for many years in the place where I live. But there is

conclusive evidence from the Northern Ireland experience and from other situations that sacrificing human rights in the name of security does not work – if anything, it leads to an escalation in violence (Carter Center 2004).

Hina Jilani, the United Nations Special Representative of the Secretary-General on Human Rights Defenders spoke to a similar point when she said that "[b]oth counterterrorism measures and respect for human rights have the same objective" (Carter Center 2004, p. 26). State security, Jilani contended, is achieved through respecting human rights, not violating them.

Certain counter-terrorism measures have both obvious and subtle effects on the work of human rights defenders. A seemingly benign but not inconsequential effect of counter-terrorism measures is a heightened public sense of fear. When people are afraid they will be more reluctant to demand respect for the rule of law, and accountability and transparency in government agencies. People will be more likely to accept infringements on fundamental freedoms because they believe the infringements will make them safer. Consequently, in climates of heightened fear human rights defenders find their target audience less receptive to their messages. Governments are conscious of this phenomenon and in this type of environment are more likely to violate human rights conspicuously. Indonesia, for example, has been fighting a rebel group in the province of Aceh. Neil Hicks of Human Rights First notes that the "long running counterinsurgency campaign … has been recast as part of the global war against terrorism" (Hicks 2004). Former Indonesian President Megawati Sukarnoputri reportedly told soldiers that they "should not be afraid of abusing human rights in Aceh" (Hicks 2004).[1] These policies are more palatable to the public and less politically damaging in climates of heightened fear.

The war against terror has propelled a burgeoning trend of states using rhetoric to stigmatize human rights organizations, with certain governments going so far as to equate human rights movements with terrorists. Just as a state of heightened public fear has the effect of making people less receptive to the message of human rights groups, this tactic benefits governments by reducing public support for organizations critical of state leaders. While the United States is certainly not the most blatant example of utilizing this tactic, government officials have floated the comparison. In December 2001 Attorney General John Ashcroft gave warning, "to those who scare peace-loving people with phantoms of lost liberty, my message is this: Your tactics only aid terrorists, for they erode our national unity and diminish our resolve … They give ammunition to America's enemies" (Hicks 2004). In September of 2003 Colombian President Uribe described human rights organizations as, "writers and politicians … serving terrorism and cowardly hiding behind the human rights flag" (Human Rights First 2004). Ana Maria Diaz of the Colombian Commission of Jurists, another participant at the Human Rights Defenders Forum criticized Uribe's outlook saying, "the government's policy known as the 'democratic security policy,' has only made the situation worse. Among the most serious aspects of the policy is, for example, the increased involvement of civilians in the armed conflict. The

---

1   Hicks quoted from the NGO Coalition for Human Rights in Aceh, *Aceh: Perjuangan Sipil versus Representative Negara*, 2002.

president of Colombia refutes the principle of distinguishing between combatants and noncombatants" (Carter Center 2004). Similarly, the Zimbabwean government claims the real goal of human rights organizations is regime change and that they label their operations as human rights work in an effort to conceal their actual purposes. State officials maintain these NGOs are a threat to national security (Pyati 2004). Former Indian Deputy Prime Minister L.K. Advani made a less radical comparison that was closer to Ashcroft's words. Speaking about a piece of legislation called the Prevention of Terrorism Act, he said, "[i]f the opposition opposes the ordinance they will be wittingly or unwittingly helping terrorists" (Tully 2001).

Putting administrative restrictions on non-governmental organizations (NGOs), on political opponents, and on journalists is a slightly more overt tactic that governments have used to impede the work of human rights and democracy advocates. Administrative obstacles are often attempts to divert NGOs' resources and staff energy from the substantive work they want to do. However, there are more severe examples of restrictions such as denying NGOs registration or forbidding them from accepting foreign funding. Omar Mestiri of the National Council for Liberties in Tunisia attended the Carter Center's Human Rights Defenders' Forum in 2003. The Tunisian government rejected Mestiri's organization's request for legal recognition, so the Council currently operates "in a legal limbo" (Human Rights Watch 2005b). Political surveillance, interrupted phone service, and travel bans are among the many tools Tunisia uses to disrupt and frustrate the work of human rights defenders (Human Rights Watch 2005b). Russia used a draconian piece of legislation from 2002 called the Law on Extremist Activities to temporarily shut down the Krasnodar Human Rights Center, an organization that monitors human rights abuses in Chechnya and the North Caucasus. Hicks said that "[p]rior to the passage of the new law, the organization would have been able to contest the closure order in court while continuing with its work, but the new law left it with no legal redress" (Hicks 2004). A 2002 Egyptian law gives President Hosni Mubarak unwarranted control over the operation of NGOs, along with the power to issue excessive penalties, including prison terms, to unauthorized organizations that accept donations (Human Rights Watch 2005a).

If there were a prize for the most discreet use of administrative obstacles to harass NGOs, the United State's Internal Revenue Service (IRS) would be a sure winner. In July 2004 Julian Bond, the chairman of the National Association for the Advancement of Colored People (NAACP) gave a speech that disparaged Democrats and Republicans, but focused its criticism on President Bush for not accepting an invitation to the organization's national convention. In October, months following Bond's speech and one month before the national elections, the IRS began an investigation into the NAACP for violating its tax-exempt status (Montagne and Inskeep 2005). Nonprofit organizations categorized as 501c3 such as the NAACP, are prohibited from endorsing political candidates. The NAACP suspects the IRS initiated its investigation in October in an attempt to disrupt the NAACP's voter registration drives by forcing the organization to divert energy and resources to the IRS' demands (Associated Press 2005).

Moving much closer to the top of the ladder of overt state interference in the work of human rights defenders, we reach Liberia. Liberian journalist Hassan Bility had written articles that piercingly criticized then-President Charles Taylor. Taylor was fond of saying that those critical of his administration were an extension of the global threat of terror (Lawyers Committee for Human Rights 2003). Bility was arrested and reportedly tortured in prison. In June 2002 he was rearrested on the unfounded accusation that he was operating a terrorist cell. The government asserted that Bility did not have the right to a trial in front of a civilian jury because of his "illegal combatant" status. A Liberian information minister freely acknowledged the term had been borrowed from US terminology. After being held incommunicado for almost six months, Bility was released (Amnesty International 2002). Arbitrary detention, long prison sentences, and the use of torture are all tools the Bush Administration has used for the war on terror and that other governments around the world have copied.

Howen and the International Commissions of Jurists are on the right track with their creative and holistic project to define acceptable limits of counter-terrorism measures. To accomplish this, the Commission has convened a panel of eminent jurists. Howen described how the jurists, "will spend at least one year listening to lawyers, human rights defenders, and victims. They will bring together the lessons of history and of many different peoples and nations" (Howen 2004). Following the panel's conclusion, "The [International Commission of Jurists] will hold a series of Roundtable Policy Dialogues to begin to change both attitudes and policies" (Howen 2004; see this volume's conclusions for further comments).

The Human Rights Defenders' Forum mentioned earlier proved an affective way to change counter-terrorism policies that infringed on human rights. Following the 2003 forum, Carter Center staff traveled with some of the defenders to Washington D.C. to meet with policy makers and bring attention to the effects that US counter-terrorism policies are having on the work of human rights activists in other countries. For example, in February 2004, following the forum and aggressive criticism from local human rights organizations, Kenya decided to rewrite a controversial piece of anti-terror legislation. In its original form, the law would have allowed indefinite detention and restricted the freedom of assembly, expression, and association.

Human rights organizations have taken a variety of vocal approaches to combat the concept that some human rights violations must be accepted to ensure security. Amnesty International, Human Rights Watch, Human Rights First and others advocated against the nomination of Attorney General Alberto Gonzales, who as White House Counsel provided a legal justification for torture. Similarly, John Negroponte's nomination to be Director of National Intelligence elicited scorn from human rights groups during confirmation hearings. Critics accuse Negroponte of ignoring human rights abuses committed by the Honduran military and arming Nicaraguan contra rebels during his stint as ambassador to Honduras (*BBC* News 2005). Human Rights First and other groups repeatedly call for a 9/11-style commission to thoroughly investigate abuse at US-run detention centers in the US and abroad.

Finally, all citizens must affirm the rule of law and encourage adherence to international standards. People of all nationalities must communicate their desire to their governments and legislators that the rights of all citizens and non-citizens are protected. Unless governments are constantly reminded that their populations are not willing to accept undue infringements on their rights in the name of national security, leaders will continue to retreat from the decades of progress that has been made toward increasing the global respect for human rights.

Works Cited

Amnesty International (2002), "Liberia: Hassan Bility Released but Other Human Rights Activists Remain Held," Press Release, December 9, 2002, available at: http://web.amnesty.org/library/Index/ENGAFR340322002?open&of=ENG-LBR.

Annan, Kofi (2005), "In Larger Freedom: toward development, security and human rights for all," Report of the United Nations Secretary-General, March 21.

Associated Press (2005), "NAACP Calls IRS Probe Timing Political, Refuses to Cooperate," *Boston Globe,* February 1.

BBC News (2005), "Profile: John Negroponte," BBCnews.com, February 17, *available at* http://news.bbc.co.uk/1/hi/world/americas/3640787.stm.

Block, Melissa (2005), "New Details About the Military's Investigations of Prisoner Abuse at the Hands of US Troops in Iraq and Afghanistan," *All Things Considered*, National Public Radio, February 18. Carter Center (2004), *Human Rights Defenders on the Frontlines of Freedom: Protecting Human Rights in the Context of the War on Terror*, Atlanta, May p. 74.

CNN (2005), "Bush: 'No Justice Without Freedom,'" CNN.com, January 20, 2005, transcript available at: http://www.cnn.com/2005/ALLPOLITICS/01/20/bush. transcript/.

Economist (2005), "Just a Few Bad Apples?" *Economist*, January 22, 2005.

Hicks, Neil (2004), Remarks by the Director of International Programs of Human Rights First at "The Impact of Counter Terror on the Promotion and Protection of Human Rights: A Global Perspective," University of Connecticut, September 2004.

Howen, Nicholas (2004), Remarks by the Secretary-General of the International Commission of Jurists, at the International Commission of Jurists Biennial Conference, "Counter-Terrorism and Human Rights: Challenges and Responses," Berlin, August 27, 2004.

Human Rights First (2004), "Protect Colombian Priest Defending Human Rights," December 22, 2004, available at http://www.humanrightsfirst.org/defenders/hrd_columbia/alert010405_mayorga.htm.

Human Rights Watch (2005a), "Egypt: Human Rights Overview," World Report 2005, available at http://hrw.org/english/docs/2005/01/13/egypt9802.htm.

Human Rights Watch (2005b), "Tunisia: Human Rights Overview," World Report 2005, available at http://hrw.org/english/docs/2005/01/13/tunisi9801.htm.

Inskeep, Steve (2004), "Federal Court, Following Freedom of Information Act, Forces Pentagon to Release More Documents Concerning Potential Prisoner Abuse at Guantanamo Bay," *Morning Edition*, National Public Radio, February 18, 2004.

Lawyers Committee for Human Rights (now Human Rights First) (2003), *Assessing the New Normal, Liberty and Security for the Post-September 11 United States*, New York.

Lewis, Neil A. and Jehl, Douglas (2005), "Files Show New Abuse Cases in Afghan and Iraqi Prisons," *New York Times*, February 18, 2005.

Montagne, Renee and Inskeep, Steve (2005), "NAACP vs. IRS," *Morning Edition*, National Public Radio, February 9, 2005.

Pyati, Archi (2004), Remarks by a senior associate of the Human Rights Defenders Program of Human Rights First, Archi Pyati, to the Center for Human Rights and Conflict Resolution at the Fletcher School of International Affairs, "Ending Zimbabwe's Conflict: Finding Synergy in Human Rights and Conflict Resolution Approaches," Medford, MA, November 19, 2004, available at http://www. humanrightsfirst.org/defenders/hrd_zimbabwe/Zim_talk_111904.pdf.

Smith, R. Jeffrey (2005), "Army Files Cite Abuse of Afghans," *Washington Post*, February 18, 2005.

Tully, Mark (2001), "Politics Key to India's Anti-Terror Moves," CNN.com, November 5, 2001.

PART II
Defining Human Rights in an Era of Controversy

Chapter 3

The Body Counts: Civilian Casualties and the Crisis of Human Rights

Amy Ross[1]

Introduction

This chapter explores the role of bodies within the complex historical development of the laws of war, and the contemporary crisis of human rights. Establishing the identities of the killed, and the killers, is crucial to the distinction between violence that is determined to be criminal and/or prohibited, and violence that is sanctioned and/or celebrated as heroic. Counting certain bodies as the victims of human rights abuses (and the associated failure to count other bodies), is an integral aspect of the politics of violence and human rights. By examining which "bodies count" and how, this chapter addresses the ways in which violence is understood as either acts of war, or crimes of war. Bodies are sites of struggle within the human rights universe.

The crisis of human rights, as discussed in this volume, is multidimensional. While discourse surrounding the protection of human rights has expanded steadily since the end of World War II, the widespread and systematic violation of human rights has also increased – despite the growth of laws, institutions and movements organized around the protection of human rights. It is a paradox: alongside the twentieth-century developments associated with the protection of human rights, violence against innocents is also on the rise. Whereas "In World War I only 5 percent of all casualties were civilian; in World War II that number was 50 percent; and in the conflicts through the 1990s civilians constituted up to 90 percent or more of those killed" (Chesterman 2001, 2). Central to this paradox is a debate concerning what qualifies as "human," what rights (if any) are inherent to all humans, and when an act of violence constitutes a human rights abuse. Counting (and accounting for) the bodies in violence is essential for determining the nature of the violence. When too many dead bodies turn up in war, and these bodies are determined to be "innocents," that action can be seen as the antithesis of "noble warfare," and therefore, rather, a violation of human rights.

For example, the image of the dead bodies uncovered in mass graves near Srebrenica (see Figure 3.1) depicts a horrible event. The twisted and intertwined remains invoke an image of the individual bodies that once existed; the tangle

1 Associate Professor, Department of Geography, University of Georgia, Athens, GA 30602. Comments encouraged and appreciated. The author would like to thank Wendy Wolford, Laura Briggs, and Alice Bullard for challenging and useful critiques of these ideas.

**Figure 3.1   Grave at Pilice collective farm near Srebrenica, Bosnia, 1996.
Photo by Gilles Peress, courtesy of Magnum Photos**

of multiple bones provoke the horror of the de-humanization of the body as it
becomes a part of the pit. That something incredibly dreadful happened in this place
is indisputable. But was it a crime of war, or an act of war? Is it the inevitable
consequence of battle (as the defense argued at the genocide trial for General Radislav
Krstic before the International Criminal Tribunal for the former Yugoslavia), or is it
genocide, as the prosecutors argued? (The prosecution won – see ICTY 2006).

Whether the violence is understood to be an act of war, or crimes of war, is of
critical importance in the prevention of such violence. As the contributors of the
Crimes of War project write:

> … even as they watched the Towers fall, and in the pivotal days that followed, leaders
> disagreed about how, exactly, to define what they were seeing. Was it war? Terrorism? A
> crime against humanity? An unprecedented combination of atrocities? Definitions matter,
> for they determine what sort of response is permissible and what body of international law
> applies. (Crimes of War 2001)

The chapter is organized in two parts. The first is a genealogy of the historical
evolution of the laws of war, international humanitarian law and human rights, with
an emphasis on the socially-constructed divide between violence that is sanctioned,
and that which is considered illegal. The second part analyzes how the body counts,
that is, how attempts to determine or obfuscate the identity of the victims of violence
influence the legality/legitimacy of such violence, and the consequential options
available for the prevention of abuses and protection of human rights.

Part I: A History of Innocence

Centuries of ethical and political debates have focused on the appropriate means of waging war. Over time, the idea took hold that some people should be spared the violence of war, and that if too many of these innocents were harmed the war itself could be considered "unjust." Violence directed against the weak grew to be considered criminal.

Codes of conduct for soldiers, and prescriptions concerning who could be the legitimate target of warfare, date back to early civilizations (Neier 1998). Ancient societies in Egypt and India banned certain types of warfare, and the English courts codified "rules of chivalry" to regulate warfare between knights (Beigbeder 1999; Ignatieff 1997). Such norms and practices cross time and space, indicating their centrality to the practice of warfare, rather than restricted to a particular culture or historical moment.

Michael Ignatieff (1997) calls these norms "the warrior's honor." In an essay of that title, Ignatieff explains that these codes of conduct were centered on the premise that a just, honorable war should be a competition between strong, honorable men fighting other, strong, honorable men. War had to be differentiated from mere barbarism. These rules of chivalry (allegedly) elevated the battlefield into a realm of legitimacy, where laws governed the conduct of warriors. These codes of conduct made the violence of battle legitimate, instead of simply slaughter.

Hugo Grotius, a Dutch scholar and the "father" of international law, codified many of these ancient norms into laws in 1625. In doing so, Grotius drew upon religious and philosophical traditions that sought to determine the appropriateness of battle and organized killing (McKeogh 2002). Grotius rejected the notion of collective guilt: that all members of the community of the enemy deserved to be killed in war; "Nor is it enough that by a kind of fiction the enemy may be regarded as forming a single body."[2] In the eighteenth century, a Swiss diplomat, E. de Vattel, developed Grotius' doctrine further into an argument concerning "just war." De Vattel asserted that only defensive wars are just, whereas aggressive wars are unjust (ibid).

By the nineteenth century, public awareness concerning the treatment of the sick and wounded bodies of soldiers contributed to a demand for a response. Most scholars attribute this new development to the advent of the war correspondent in the American Civil War. War became simultaneously more visible, and more savage. With the invention of Morse Code and technological advances in photography, war correspondents generated war reports. Previously, reports from the battlefields were submitted by the general, who tended to report on heroism and glory. The dead rarely had the opportunity to share their stories.

The war correspondent shifted this equation slightly, and the public reacted. In response to this new public exposure to the horrors of the battlefield, President Abraham Lincoln passed legislation (the Lieber Code for Armies in the Field 1863) governing the conduct of soldiers (Neier 1998, 14).

In Europe, similar sentiments worked their way into law. The Crimean War served as the seminal moment. Jean-Henri Dunant, a wealthy Swiss national, witnessed the

---

2   Translated from Grotius' *De Jure Belli ac Pacis* (McKeogh 2002, 104).

Battle of Solferino in 1859 and became obsessed with the images he had seen of the war dead and wounded. In A Memory of Solferino, he described the horrors of the battlefield, the ground dark with blood, severed body parts, splintered bone fragments, wounded men desperately flailing about, and local peasants harvesting the corpses for boots and other booty. Dunant's work did more than describe the horrors of battle; he went on to offer specific proposals to how the wounded should be treated; "Would it not be possible, in time of peace and quiet, to form relief societies for the purpose of having care given to the wounded in wartime by zealous, devoted and thoroughly qualified volunteers?" (see ICRC 1986). Dunant began to lobby for an international convention that would allow for first-aid societies to care for the wounded (from both sides) in battle. Dunant established the Red Cross (so named due to the association with the Swiss flag) in Geneva.

The birth of international humanitarian law is generally credited to 1868 and the Declaration of St. Petersburg, a treaty signed by the majority of the powers in Europe. These governments agreed to "the technical limits at which the necessities of war ought to yield to the requirements of humanity," i.e., to prohibit weapons that result in unnecessary suffering beyond the legitimate goal of war. The Declaration of St. Petersburg declared that "the only legitimate object which States should endeavor to accomplish during war is to weaken the military forces of the enemy" (Rosenbaum 1993; Weschler 1999; Ignatieff 1997).

The international humanitarian law of the nineteenth century led the foundations for contemporary human rights law. International humanitarian law is expressly concerned with the laws of war, the correct conduct of states and armies during war, and the treatment of civilians – specifically the sick, the wounded, prisoners, ship-wrecked persons, women, and children: i.e. those other than the "strong men" considered the appropriate target of violence during legitimate battle (Weschler 1999). International humanitarian law therefore, departs from the early norms and ideologies concerning warfare in two critical ways. First, international humanitarian law attempts to limit the damage a state can inflict during war – even if that war is considered a just war. As such, international humanitarian law impinges on sovereignty in precisely the way that earlier aspects of international law reinforced the autonomy of states. Secondly, international humanitarian law recognized and codified distinct human identities, with violence against certain bodies considered abhorrent – again, even within the practice of a just war.

Geneva, and later The Hague in the Netherlands, became the centers of a series of initiatives that greatly amplified international humanitarian law. The first "Geneva Convention" (1864) was the product of a meeting of representatives from sixteen countries, including the United States, to discuss ways to improve medical services on the battlefield. A series of agreements followed ("The Geneva Conventions"). In its early stages, this body of law was restricted to the bodies of soldiers. The Geneva Conventions, the Hague Conventions (1899, 1907) and other elements of international humanitarian law sought to impose constraints on warfare without outlawing war itself.

Despite these initiatives of international humanitarian law, the new scale of destruction of World War I was a grim reminder as to the limits of law and the brutality of battle (Winter 1995; Winter and Sivan 1999). For some, the very extent of the death and destruction was a compelling case that war would be, from that point on, out of the question. For others, World War I proved the failure of international law to prevent war, to restrict armaments, or to prevent human death and destruction.

World War II is recognized as a critical moment in global consciousness and consensus regarding the human costs of warfare. The conclusion of the war stimulated the growth of human rights law, and the emergence of a global human rights regime. Jack Donnelly (1993) argues that the human rights regime arises from the "demand" generated from the Holocaust, with the Nuremberg Trials and international laws and norms (specifically, the Universal Declaration of Human Rights and the Genocide Convention), created to "supply" a response to these demands. The international instruments and local social movements organized around human rights have become powerful and extensive, launching a "revolution" in international law (Manasian 1998). A critical feature of this transformation was the development of the concept of the innocent civilian.

The Nuremberg trials were innovative on two counts. Firstly, individuals were to be held accountable for actions taken as officials of the state. Secondly, individuals were judged guilty for "crimes against humanity" for actions against citizens of their own state. Whereas "war crimes" addressed actions between combatants, "crimes against humanity" concerned the actions of civilians (including leaders of state) against citizen/civilians.

"Victors' justice" refers to the notion that the trials were an example of justice as an execution of authority (Foucault 1979). Critics contend that the post-World War II trials represent "victors' justice" rather than justice due to 1) the lack of trials for Allied officials for war crimes, and 2) the fact that the Nazis were tried for *ex post facto* crimes, that is crimes that were established in law, after the activities of these particular individuals. In this context, the Nuremberg and the Tokyo trials are merely the result of a victorious alliance of armies imposing its will on a defeated people, in order to demonstrate its victory/authority/power to the world community. The central problem associated with victor's justice is that it takes a "victory"; increasingly, since the end of the Cold War, conflicts are being resolved through negotiated settlements, without one clear victor. Hence Nuremberg fails as a contemporary model, as "victors" and "victories" are increasingly rare. A further problem ascribed to victor's justice is that it is imposed from an outside authority (from "above") and hence fails to resonate with the local community associated with the crimes.

Despite the caveats and complaints regarding this form of "victor's justice," what is clear is that these trials represented a shift: the security of "humanity" (existing everywhere) was the domain and concern of "international" law (again, existing everywhere).

The Universal Declaration of Human Rights originated during this moment of international consensus concerning the purported need to protect populations from mass violence. The approval (1948) and entry into force (1951) of the Convention on the Prevention and Punishment of Genocide further asserted the supremacy of international law over domestic law and state sovereignty. The Genocide Convention established that perpetrators of such a crime could be held accountable under international law, even in the absence of applicable domestic law. The Genocide Convention further detailed that an individual acting in his/her role as head of state would be accountable under international law.

A series of treaties and conventions followed in the next several decades. The Geneva Conventions were upgraded and extended, and the Universal Declaration of Human Rights was divided into two parts (1952), reflecting the growing ideological divide between the United States and the Soviet Union. The United Nations served as the place where such initiatives were developed.

These initiatives were a departure from international law that had previously avoided addressing such concerns out of principles of sovereignty; "Human-rights law … touches governments at their most sensitive point: how they exercise power over their own citizens. Never before have states agreed to accept so many restrictions on their domestic behavior, or to submit to international scrutiny" (Manasian 1998, 5).

The existence of the United Nations established a communicative and normative framework, where the human rights regime found a home. The post World War II period witnessed the growth of a web of NGOs. According to the World Bank, while statistics about global numbers of NGOs are notoriously incomplete, it is currently estimated that there is somewhere between 6,000 and 30,000 national NGOs in developing countries. Individually, such organizations may cover as few as two national societies, but in their operations together they create what scholars have termed a "global network" (Keck and Sikkink 1998). NGOs can be "particularly unruly" (see Waters 1995) as their capacity to link diverse people in relation to common causes and interests can potentially challenge the state.

Despite the reluctance of the superpowers, in 1977 the Geneva Conventions were extended, partially in response to atrocities in Vietnam. Article 85 of the First Additional Protocol of 1977 specifies that grave breaches in international armed conflict include:

3a) … making the civilian population or individual civilians the object of attack; b) launching an indiscriminant attack affecting the civilian population or civilian objects in the knowledge that such attack will cause excessive loss of life, injury to civilians or damage to civilian objects (UNHCR 2007).

In sum, laws governing the appropriate reasons to go to war, and the appropriate conduct during war, have expanded the notion of protected persons, or "innocents," and therefore inappropriate targets of war. An expanding human rights movement has increased the visibility of the victims of violence. Yet despite this expansion in law, politics and social network, civilian casualties have increased. Those conducting war increasingly sought to explain away these casualties as a fact of war; the inevitable consequences of war, or "The Fog of War."

Part Two: Knowledge, Ignorance and Which Bodies Count

Katherine Verdery argues that dead bodies are particularly important symbols in the struggles that take place over what constitutes the "truth" of a particular conflict. Bodies can mean a great many different things to a great many different people, Verdery observes, hence it is the "complexity" of dead bodies that make them particularly good material for political agendas. She writes: "Dead bodies … don't talk much (although once they did). Words can be put in their mouths – often quite ambiguous words … it is thus easier to re-write history with dead people than other kinds of symbols …" (Verdery 1999, 29).

Dead bodies may influence the telling of the historical narrative. Dead bodies may also tell a particular version of events. The bodies of the dead contribute to the body of evidence (Stover and Peress 1998). Some of this evidence can reach a court of law, which may evaluate whether a crime of war or an act of war occurred.

But without knowledge of the victims of violence, it is difficult to determine what happened, and in particular to secure accountability. Struggles over the type of "evidence" provided by the bodies of those killed during conflict represent attempts to influence the aftermath of the violence. Such evidence can be powerful material in cases against perpetrators. For that reason, human rights activists have seen knowledge and accountability as essential features in curbing impunity and securing human rights.

For example, in Latin America, the principle of "the right to the truth" was a response to practices of repression such as "disappearances", extra-judicial assassinations, and other forms of violence that have been called "deniable forms of repression."[3] Ignacio Martín-Baró, a prominent social psychologist who lived and worked in El Salvador, wrote shortly before his assassination that the power of this particular form of terror was the state's ability to deny responsibility for these crimes, while simultaneously making the entire society aware that it could kill with impunity. Martín-Baró was one of six Jesuits assassinated by the Salvadoran military in November 1989.

Establishing the truth became important, therefore, precisely because the regime was able to carry out its terror by lying, presenting distortions of the truth or covering up important information. Since secrecy was an essential feature in the operation of the violence, exposure and accountability was a necessary element of the prevention of future violations. In the face of violence conducted under the cover of state secrecy, the demands for "the right to the truth" rested on the logic that if the truth could be made a matter of open and public record, accountability would replace impunity and future violations would be deterred. Demands for an accurate accounting of the violence pursued knowledge of the atrocities as a weapon against impunity.

The pursuit of "the right to the truth" in Latin America spawned social movements organized around demands of *habeas corpus*, literally "you have the body." In its specific legal usage, *habeas corpus* refers to a writ requiring that a detained person be brought before a court at a stated time and place to decide the legality of his/her detention or imprisonment. These social movements, such as the Madres de la Plaza de Mayo in Argentina, provided a vehicle for protest, and importantly, drew international attention to the occurrence and extent of the atrocities.

Although the overt demands were for information regarding the bodies of missing loved ones, the implicit political objectives were for political and judicial accountability, and in some cases, a complete regime change from the military rule associated with the violent practices, to a (theoretically) more accountable

---

3   Ayreh Neier used this term to highlight the distinctive nature of the violence ascribed to the state: "Human Rights and Accountability" lecture, Center for Human Rights, University of California, Berkeley, April 1994.

democratically elected civilian government. The "right to the truth," then, was taken as both an attack against the structures of power considered to be responsible for the repression, as well as an important therapeutic response to recover from the pattern of "deniable repression" practised (to various degrees) in Latin America.

In many sites in Latin America plagued by the phenomenon of "disappearances" and massacres conducted under the cover of state secrecy, exhumation projects have persisted. In Guatemala, public and private initiatives sought to exhume the graves of massacre victims, even at great risk (see Figure 3.2). Although commonly called "clandestine cemeteries," survivors in communities often knew exactly where the bodies were buried. In some cases, those that had managed to escape the massacre had returned home to bury their dead; in other cases the military forced villagers to bury the dead. Often the so-called "clandestine cemetery" was located in the town center.

While the body and the story it tells has inspired social movements around demands for knowledge and accountability, other sectors are driven by the need to ignore, deny or cover-up these same bodies. The construction of ignorance associated with the victims of violence often involves the deliberate failure to account for the dead body. It is difficult to determine how many Iraqis have died as a result of the US invasion (March 2003) and occupation. There are estimates – only estimates. Perhaps the best-known estimate of civilian deaths from the fighting is that of the Iraq Body Count project. This British-based group of researchers has systematically examined the western press and collated all accounts of civilian casualties. They tabulate all deaths that are independently reported by two sources. Based on this

Figure 3.2   Exhumation site in Comalapa, Guatemala, 2003. An organization of widows has struggled to gain access to the land, so as to retrieve the bodies of massacre victims. Photo by Peter Frey, University of Georgia

methodology, they estimate civilian casualties from the invasion until September 2006 at around 45,000.

As is acknowledged by Iraq Body Count, such accounts likely underestimate deaths. Certainly some battles and other military actions, and resultant Iraqi deaths, fail to be reported unless the United States and/or other foreign forces suffered casualties. Additionally, for much of the invasion and occupation western reporters have been prevented from moving about Iraq independently, meaning that even such high-profile claims of mass civilian deaths as the killing by US bombing of upwards of 45 Iraqis at a wedding party in the town of Mogr el-Deeb in May 2004, failed to be independently verified. All estimates of Iraq civilian deaths since the invasion are probably on the low side.

In order to address the question of how many Iraqi deaths have occurred, a team of public health researchers from the Johns Hopkins Bloomberg School of Public Health, the Columbia University School of Nursing, and the College of Medicine at Al-Mustansiriya University in Baghdad undertook two epidemiologic surveys of "excess Iraqi" deaths since the March, 2003 invasion. This research team combined epidemiologic expertise with a background in studying people in disaster and emergency situations and an in-depth knowledge of Iraq.[4]

The results of the research, published in the British medical journal *The Lancet*, are shocking. The researchers estimated that 650,000 "excessive deaths" have occurred in Iraq since the US invasion in March 2003 (Roberts et al 2004, 2006). Professor Juan Cole observed on his indispensible blog, Informed Comment (in response to an even earlier 2004 study), that "The troubling thing about these results is that they suggest that the US may soon catch up with Saddam Hussein in the number of civilians killed. How many deaths to blame on Saddam is controversial … (but) it is often alleged that Saddam killed 300,000 civilians" (Cole 2004). Cole pointed out that if the trends in civilian casualties were correct, than the US was outpacing Saddam Hussein in its violence.

The *Lancet* study was seconded by other experts in demography and mass atrocity, and dismissed as speculative by US President George Bush. Others, closer to the violence, remarked that the figures were totally plausible, and resonated with life on the ground in Iraq. An anonymous Iraqi female blogger, "Riverbend," wrote (in response to the failure to accept *The Lancet* report: "We literally do not know a single Iraqi family that has not seen the violent death of a first or second-degree relative these last three years. Abductions, militias, sectarian violence, revenge killings, assassinations, car-bombs, suicide bombers, American military strikes, Iraqi military raids, death squads, extremists, armed robberies, executions, detentions, secret prisons, torture, mysterious weapons – with so many different ways to die, is the number so far fetched (Riverbend 2006)?"

Why do we have only estimates? The Iraq Body Count quotes General Tommy Franks as insisting, "We Don't Do Body Counts." The same source quotes US

---

4   Members of the team have carried out research and consulting in many parts of the world, including Iraq, sub-Saharan Africa, and Eastern Europe and have worked with such organizations as the World Health Organization and the US Centers for Disease Control.

military spokesman Col Guy Shields at a press briefing in Baghdad on August 4th, 2003 saying that there was no accurate way to keep a record of civilian deaths:

> Well, we do not keep records for the simple reason that there is no really accurate way. There's times when we have conducted operations, and we're pretty certain that there are casualties, and we'll go back and check. And there's nobody there … In terms of statistics we have no definite estimates of civilian casualties for the whole campaign. It would be irresponsible to give firm estimates given the wide range of variables. For example we've had cases where during a conflict, we believed civilians had been wounded and perhaps killed, but by the time our forces have a chance to fully assess the outcomes of a contact, the wounded or the dead civilians have been removed from the scene. Factors such as this make it impossible for us to maintain an accurate account (Iraq Body Count 2006).

This "unknowability" is troubling, and it is at odds with another stated US policy of providing reparations for Iraqi civilians killed or injured in the course of the occupation. How can the military provide financial compensation to the innocent civilians, if it lacks records of who was killed or injured? Indeed the unknown – the construction of ignorance – is an essential part of the conduct of the military assault on Iraq. Without knowledge of the numbers and means in which the casualties occurred, it is impossible to determine the criminality of the events. It is this constructed ignorance that provides the Bush Administration with its alibi: Without full awareness of the extent of civilian casualties, it is difficult to make important determinations concerning the "justness," and legality, of US military actions. Determining the numbers, identities and circumstances of the civilian deaths in Iraq is a necessary step. And then the knowledge must be converted into action. Every body must be counted and then, case by case, evaluated to determine whether the lives were lost due to acts of war, or crimes of war – or a crime against humanity, masquerading as a war.

Conclusion

Killing happens everywhere. Killing has been a regular feature of human activity, thoughout time and space. Some forms of killing claim to be justifiable and moral; consider euthanasia, capital punishment, or violence conducted in self-defense. Some forms of killing claim to be legal, whereas others are considered criminal – murder. The line between what is "killing" and what is "murder" is often highly contested. In war, some forms of killing can earn a medal, and other forms of killing can lead to a court martial. For those involved at the top of power structures, sometimes one can earn power and punishment – the presidency, and then a jail cell, or a jail cell and then the presidency – consider the careers of Slobodan Milosevic or Nelson Mandela. This distinction between appropriate "killing" and that which is considered criminal (i.e. murder) – is at the heart of the distinction between violence understood as a "human rights abuse" and violence understood as legitimate warfare. The bodies involved in this violence become a site of struggle in which the meaning of the violence is contested.

The laws of war and human rights are located at a socially-constructed divide between violence that is permitted, and that which is considered illegal and subject to sanction. Attempts to conduct war (and justify its legitimacy and legality) rely upon the assertion that the war is "just" (Falah, Flint, and Mamadouh 2006). A central element to the "justness" of war is that the lives sacrificed are only those of combatants, and that if innocents are killed, these bodies are "collateral damage." Such a conversion of identities is necessary if violence is to be accepted as war, or legitimate aggression. In turn, the assertion of civilian identities (non-combatant status) is therefore a critical element in the struggle to expose acts of war as crimes of violence: when conducted in a widespread and systematic manner, crimes against humanity.

The "human rights story" is often told as one of evolutionary linear progress. But the story is hardly one of uninterrupted forward progress, rather advances alongside mounting casualties. This is consistent with the nature of the laws of war, which were developed in a complex compromise that rather than outlawing war, served to regulate and permit war. The significant violence inflicted on bodies, and the struggles over the fate of bodies are a part of a tangled dialectic of violations and the attempts to end such violations. But it is therefore necessary to have knowledge about the circumstances of the casualties. The assertion of civilian identities (non-combatant status) is a critical element in the struggle to expose acts of war as crimes of violence.

Works Cited

Bourke, Joanna (1999), *An Intimate History of Killing: Face to Face Killing in 20th Century Warfare*, Basic Books UK.

Center for the Study of Human Rights (1994), *Twenty-five Human Rights Documents*, Columbia University: New York.

Chesterman, Simon, ed. (2001), *Civilians in War*, Lynne Rienner Publishers, Colorado.

Clausewitz, Carl von (1968), *On War*, Penguin Books: England.

Cole. Juan (2004), "US Has Killed 100,000 in Iraq: The Lancet," *Informed Comment: Thoughts on the Middle East, History and Religion* (website) < http://www.juancole.com/2004/10/us-has-killed-100000-in-iraq-lancet.html>.

Crimes of War Project (website) http://www.crimesofwar.org/expert/attack-main.html.

Donnelly, Jack (1993), *International Human Rights*, Westview Press: Boulder.

Dorsey, Alan (1999), "Note on the Law and Legal Terms," in *Crimes of War*, Gutman and Reiff, eds, W.W. Norton & Company: New York.

Eagleton, Terry (1999), "Local and Global," in *The Politics of Human Rights*, Obrad Savic, ed., Verso: New York.

Falah, Ghazi-Walid, Colin Flint, and Virginie Mamadouh (2006), "Just War and Extraterritoriality: the Popular Geopolitics of the United States' War on Iraq as Reflected in Newspapers of the Arab World," in *Annals of the Association of American Geographers*, Volume 96, No. 1.

Flood, Patrick James (1998), *The Effectiveness of UN Human Rights Institutions*, Praeger: Connecticut.

Foucault, Michel (1979), *Discipline and Punish; the Birth of the Prison*, Vintage Books: New York.

Grimsley, Mark and Clifford J. Rogers, eds (2002), *Civilians in the Path of War*, University of Nebraska Press.

Gutman, Roy and David Reiff, eds (1999), *Crimes of War: What the Public Should Know*, W.W. Norton & Company: New York.

Henkin, Louis (1989), *International Law: Politics, Values and Functions*, Excerpt reprinted in Steiner and Alston, eds (1996), *International Human Rights in Context; Law, Politics, Morals*, Clarendon Press: Oxford.

Hitchens, Christopher (2001), *The Trial of Henry Kissinger*, Verso: New York.

Ignatieff, Michael (1997), *The Warrior's Honor; Ethnic War and the Modern Consciousness*, Henry Holt and Co.: New York.

Ignatieff, Michael. 1999. "Human Rights: The Midlife Crisis," in *The New York Review of Books*. Vol. XLVI, No. 9, pp. 58–62.

"A Memory of Solferino" International Committee of the Red Cross (ICRC) (website) http://www.icrc.org/WEB/ENG/siteeng0.nsf/htmlall/p0361?OpenDocument&style =Custo_Final.4&View=defaultBody2.

International Criminal Tribunal for the ex-Yugoslavia (ICTY) (website) http://www. un.org/icty/glance/krstic.htm.

Iraq Body Count (website) http://www.iraqbodycount.org/.

Joyce, Christopher and Eric Stover (1991), *Witnesses from the Grave: the Stories Bones Tell*, Little, Brown, Inc.: Boston.

Keck, Margaret and Kathryn Sikkink (1998), *Activists beyond Borders. Transnational Advocacy Networks in International Politics*, Cornell University Press: Ithaca.

Lauren, Paul Gordon (1998), *The Evolution of International Human Rights*, University of Pennsylvania Press: Philadelphia.

McKeogh, Colm (2002), *Innocent Civilians: The Morality of Killing in War*, Palgrave: New York.

Murray, Williamson (2002), "Not Enough Collateral Damage: Moral Ambiguities in the Gulf War," in Grimsley, Mark and Clifford J. Rogers, eds, *Civilians in the Path of War*, University of Nebraska Press.

Neier, Aryeh (1998), *War Crimes: Brutality, Genocide, Terror, and the Struggle for Justice*, Times Books: New York.

Nordstrom, Carolyn (2004), *Shadows of War; Violence, Power and International Profiteering in the Twenty-First Century*, University of California Press.

Ratner, Steven R. (1998), "The Schizophrenias of International Criminal Law," 33 *Texas International Law Journal*, 237 Spring 1998.

Reiff, David (1999), "The Precarious Triumph of Human Rights," in *The New York Times*, August 8, 1999.

Risse, Thomas, Stephen C. Ropp, and Kathryn Sikkink, eds (1999), *The Power of Human Rights: International Norms and Domestic Change*, Cambridge University Press: Cambridge.

"Riverbend" (2006), "Baghdad Burning" http://riverbendblog.blogspot.com/ October 18.

Roberts L., Lafta R., Garfield R., Khudahairi, J., Burnham, G. (2004), "Morality before and after the 2003 invasion of Iraq: cluster sample survey," in *The Lancet*, Vol. 364, Issue 9448, pp. 1857–64.

Roberts L., Lafta R., Burnham, G., Doocy S. (2006), "Morality after the 2003 invasion of Iraq: a cross-sectional cluster sample survey," published online 11 October 2006, www.lancet.com.

Robertson, A.H. and J.G. Merrills (1996), *Human Rights in the World: An introduction to the study of the international protection of human rights*, Manchester University Press: UK.

Ross, Amy (1999), *The Body of the Truth: Truth Commissions in Guatemala and South Africa*, Ph.D thesis, University of California: Berkeley.

Savic, Obrad, ed. (1999), *The Politics of Human Rights*, Verso: New York.

Steiner, Henry J. and Philip Alston, eds (1996), *International Human Rights in Context: Law, Politics, Morals*. Clarendon Press: Oxford.

Stover, Eric (photos by Gilles Peress) (1998), *The Graves: Srebrenica and Vukovar*, Scalo: Berlin.

Turpin, Jennifer and Lester R. Kurtz, eds (1997), "Introduction: Violence – The Micro/Macro Link," in *The Web of Violence; From Interpersonal to Global*, University of Illinois Press: Chicago.

UNHCR. Office of the High Commissioner for Refugees (1949), "Protocol Additional to the Geneva Conventions of 12 August 1949, and relating to the Protection of Victims of International Armed Conflicts (Protocol 1)", http://www.unhchr.ch/html/menu3/b/93.htm.

Verdery, Katherine (1999), *The Political Lives of Dead Bodies; Reburial and Postsocialist Change*, Columbia University Press: New York.

Waters, Malcolm (1995), *Globalization*, Routledge: New York.

Weschler, Lawrence (1999), "International Humanitarian Law: An Overview," in *Crimes of War*, Gutman and Reiff, eds, W.W. Norton & Company; New York.

Winter, Jay (1995), *Sites of Memory, Sites of Mourning; the Great War in European Cultural History*, Cambridge University Press.

Winter, Jay and Emmanuel Sivan, eds (1999), *War and Remembrance in the Twentieth Century*, Cambridge University Press.

Chapter 4

International Human Rights Law: Struggling between Apology and Utopia

Richard Burchill

Introduction

The current system of international human rights law (IHRL) has developed from the creation of the United Nations and over the past fifty years has made great strides in developing a significant body of law through treaties, declarations, resolutions, and decisions. This body of law has not resulted in the elimination of all human rights violations but it has proven to be significant in the promotion and protection of human rights throughout the world. During the early 1990s there existed an almost euphoric belief that international human rights law had turned the corner in terms of its shortcomings and had become a major factor in the ordering of the international system. This belief was based on the assessment that concern for human rights had become a significant priority in the international system as demonstrated by the actions of states and international institutions. Unfortunately, recent events in the international system have made this assessment appear a bit premature. Amongst other things, the current "war on international terrorism" has brought to the fore the tensions that exist between the promotion and protection of human rights as a primary concern for the international system and the dominance of state security as a primacy concern. It appears that despite the advances made by IHRL in promoting and protecting human interests in the international system, the interests of states remain paramount, even when the pursuit of state interests conflicts directly with the human rights. From this, it is possible to say that IHRL is facing a crisis. Joan Fitzpatrick, who wrote extensively on the protection of human rights in crisis situations, has commented that in the current war on terrorism it is necessary for IHRL to assert itself fully and constrain the actions of states so that security does not come at the price of the effective protection of human rights (Fitzpatrick 2003). However, the inability of IHRL to be effective when faced with opposing priorities of state security is not a temporary crisis but instead highlights a serious shortcoming in the overall structure of IHRL.

Despite the advances made in IHRL in support of human interests the system is far from perfect or, in many cases, even effective. It appears that despite the existence of IHRL, states do not feel overly concerned about overstepping the boundaries created in the pursuit of self-interest. Bruno Simma, a leading human rights scholar and currently a judge at the International Court of Justice, has made the following observation concerning the condition of IHRL:

> Perusing the list of parties to the major human rights treaties, any alert observer must wonder how many of these States have decided to join this great enterprise more for symbolic reasons than motivated by the desire to conform their domestic laws and practices to internationally agreed upon human rights standards and to subject themselves to international scrutiny (Simma 1998, 659).

A similar assessment has come from those directly involved with the application of IHRL. Judge Piza, a former president of the Inter-American Court of Human Rights commented in an early advisory opinion given by the Court:

> I have come to the conclusion that unfortunately the system of the Convention appears to make it [the protection of human rights] impossible because the American states in drafting it [the Convention] did not wish to accept the establishment of a swift and effective juridical system but rather they hobbled it ... by establishing a veritable obstacle course that is almost insurmountable, on the long and arduous road that the basic rights of the individual are forced to travel (*In the matter of Viviana Gallardo*, 13 November 1981, Advisory Opinion No. G 101/81, statement of Judge Piza, paragraph 11).

Both observations identify the state as being the major obstacle in attempts to further the effective promotion and protection of human rights. In many respects this comes as no surprise as international law enshrines state sovereignty as the basic foundation of the international system which results in IHRL being based upon a significant paradox: those who create the international legal rules concerning human rights are, at the same time, the greatest violators of those rules. IHRL possesses a strong rhetoric expressing the importance of human rights protection and the necessity of ensuring appropriate measures are in place to constrain the exercise of power. At the same time, the realization of the goals and objectives of IHRL remain constrained by the priority given to the actions and interests of the state in international law and relations.

This chapter examines how the structure of the international legal argument contributes to the preservation of the primacy of the state to the detriment of the effective promotion and protection of IHRL. Use will be made of Martti Koskenniemi's work that has characterized the structure of the international legal argument as existing between Apology – a system based purely on the interests of states and Utopia – a system based on some sort of higher order normative constraints not dependant upon the behavior of states (Koskenniemi 1989). This characterization will be utilized to identify the tensions that exist between the interests of states and the desire to have a system for the protection of rights based on normative values beyond the state. Engaging in this critique will demonstrate the inordinate amount of influence and control the state has over the promotion and protection of human rights through legitimate legal techniques that maintain the superiority of the interests of states (Apology). It will also be submitted that the strong rhetoric that exists in support of human rights (Utopia) is not insignificant in advancing the promotion and protection of human rights through legal and non-legal means. The focus of the chapter is on international human rights treaties and human rights obligations through customary international law will not be discussed. Customary international law has brought significant advances in the promotion and protection of human rights as demonstrated by its use before courts in the USA through the Alien Tort Claim Act, discussed in the chapter by Matt Eisenstadt. However, it is submitted, the use of customary international law in the protection and promotion of human rights also suffers from an imbalance created by the position of primacy the state holds in the development of customary rules. The main thrust of the argument presented here is equally applicable to the use of treaty law or customary international law for the promotion and protection of human rights.

The Structure of the International Legal Argument

International law, being the law of the international system, takes state values/ interests as its primary concern. While this primary concern has varied in its intensity, international law's main purpose remains as a system for regulating the international relations of states that in turn allows states to retain an exclusive position in law making and implementation (Henkin 1995, 99). The creation and development of IHRL marked a new stage in understanding the nature of international law as the concern was no longer upon inter-state relations but on the conduct of states towards individuals and groups within their territory. This shift was significant as it brought into question the position of state sovereignty with international law moving to a more prescriptive mode. However, it did not lead to a reformation of the foundations of the international legal structure where sovereignty was removed. IHRL remains a process dominated by states where state values have proven to be more important than actual concerns for human welfare (Henkin 1995, 168).

An analysis of IHRL demonstrates the existence of a "double gesture" where there is evidence of rhetorical support for human rights protection but the continuation of legal techniques that hinder the effectiveness of the law in practice. Even though it is claimed that the concept and protection of human rights has moved from being confined to the exclusive jurisdiction of individual states to a concern for the international community (Reisman 1990, 869), this has not resulted in IHRL shedding its schizophrenic tendencies inherent in the double gesture. The structure of the international legal argument allows for the maintenance of this duality as IHRL is based on two opposing, but equally valid positions; the primacy of the sovereign state on one side and the need to protect humanity from the excesses of state power on the other. As one commentator has described it, there is a constant struggle between a "nightmare" and a "noble dream." The nightmare is that "the law and institutions which are supposed to protect human rights are powerless to constrain the excesses of governments and their lackeys," and the noble dream lies in the belief that human rights can transform the lives of individuals by providing protection and empowerment (Marks 1994, 54).

To help understand the position IHRL finds itself in, Koskenniemi's work on the international legal argument is enlightening. He has shown how the structure of the international legal argument allows two seemingly opposable positions to be simultaneously maintained. He identifies the nature of international law as based upon the continual movement between extreme poles of possibility, which he terms apology and utopia. By maintaining continual motion in the formulation and application of legal arguments, international law is able to maintain an illusion of effectiveness through its own indeterminate nature. This continual movement is necessary as international law strives to be both normative and concrete at the same time, unable to reside in either pole. This combination of normativity and concreteness create what Koskenniemi calls the "objectivity of international law" (Koskenniemi 1989, 2–8). International law is seen as being objective, that is, able to provide solutions to problems, because the law is verifiable in its existence through an examination of state behavior, but the basis for the law is not exclusively dependant upon the behavior of states. Normativity and concreteness are in direct opposition to one another and the integration of the two into a single coherent concept proves impossible. By being concrete, international law is able to provide a factually strong but uncritical doctrine, and by being normative it provides a desirable basis for obligation, but one often distant from the realities of the international system.

The international legal argument attempts to deal with this conflict between concreteness and normativity through ascending and descending patterns of justification in the formulation of rules and principles (Koskenniemi 1989, 40–42). The descending patterns of justification deal with the normative aspects of international law, moving towards ideas such as human rights, justice and the common interests of the worldwide human community. This pattern of justification believes in the possibility of state behavior being guided by normative ideas that exist outside of state self-interest. This position is susceptible to criticisms for being utopian and not based on the realities of state behavior. The ascending pattern is associated with the apologist's view of international law whereby the foundations of international law are based upon what states actually do. In the apologist's pattern, actual state behavior determines what the law is and the concept of state sovereignty is paramount preventing any reliance on normative constraints that exist outside the behavior of states. This position is susceptible to criticism for not engaging with normative ideas that should guide action in the international system. Both patterns are equally open to criticisms as being overly subjective and not indicative of how the law truly works, as Koskenniemi explains:

> From the ascending perspective, the descending model falls into subjectivism as it cannot demonstrate the content of its aprioristic norms in a reliable manner (i.e. it is vulnerable to the objection of utopianism). From the descending perspective, the ascending model seems subjective as it privileges State will or interest over objectively binding norms (i.e. it is vulnerable to the charge of apologism) (Koskenniemi 1989, 41–2).

International law, in its quest to accommodate these conflicting patterns, proves to be structurally indeterminate by not being able to base itself exclusively in either extreme; it must rely on constant movement between the two to create an illusion of effectiveness.

In IHRL, this movement occurs between the utopian ideas of the nature and purpose of human rights and the apologist position based on protecting the interests of states and the preservation of state sovereignty. An obvious dilemma emerges as IHRL cannot be based solely on what states do but it also cannot be wholly dependant on some source of normative authority detached from the state as international law requires that obligations emanate from state practice and consent. A firm position in either pole is not tenable over the long run and some appeal must be made to the opposing position in order to maintain credibility. To triumph human values over state values as the primary concern for the international system is easily criticized as being too utopian. A position where human values have no role and only state values and interests are determining factors for the international system is equally susceptible to criticism for being too apologist. There is substantial evidence to support the validity of both positions but when it comes to actual utilization of IHRL it is clear that the apologist position based on state values has the upper hand. IHRL calls upon states to adhere to certain forms of behavior but it also allows for the manipulation of the legal process to minimize any unwanted impact upon the primacy of the state. States are able to utilize the international legal argument to demonstrate a concern for human values without placing any substantive limitations upon their own values or interests.

In the movement between apology and utopia IHRL remains confined by the imbalance created by the primacy of state interests. This primacy is enshrined in international law through the concept of state sovereignty that stands as the basis of the international system. Even though it is recognized that a system based solely on state sovereignty is too apologist, movement toward a more utopian world based on human values has been constrained. The basic tenets of state sovereignty ensure it is left to states to decide whether or not to create a human rights instrument, the form and content of the final instrument, whether or not to sign and ratify an instrument thereby actually creating legal obligations, and how those obligations will be applied in actual practice within the domestic jurisdiction of the state. Through sovereignty states are able to construct a body of law that is more in tune with their interests, needs and desires, rather than those of human beings, whom the law supposedly benefits. The imbalance that results creates a situation whereby "state sovereignty emerges victorious; individuals disappear from the international scene, and the violations they have suffered remain unexposed" (Cassese 1990, 57).

International Human Rights Law: Constrained by Apology

Concern for the promotion and protection of human rights at the international level has a long history. However, it was the widespread cruelty and utter disregard for human life demonstrated during World War II that shocked the conscience of humanity and spurred a range of efforts to bring a concern for human values to the fore of international relations. The current international legal system for the promotion and protection of human rights has its foundations in the creation of the United Nations in 1945 and was a direct consequence of the horrors experienced during the war. Even though the promotion and protection of human rights was not originally a major item on the agenda in the creation of the UN (Ishay 2004, 214), the organization quickly became a leading light in promoting respect for human values in the international system, but at the same time contributing to the maintenance of the primacy of the sovereign state.

Looking at the UN Charter it is possible to identify a strong concern with human values from the outset. The Charter begins with the line "We the Peoples" which is now being interpreted as an indication that the promotion and protection of humanity is the goal of the UN, even though earlier commentaries on the Charter make clear that the opening statement does not represent any sort of overriding concern for humanity (Kelsen 1964, 5–9; Jhabvala 1997, 7–8). In the preamble of the Charter, the first and second stated aims of the organization are firmly based on human values with an expressed determination "to save succeeding generations form the scourge of war" and "to reaffirm faith in fundamental human rights, in the dignity and worth of the human person." The international legal argument allows for two possible interpretations as to the significance of these statements. It is generally understood that the preamble of an international instrument is considered part of the text and may be used in the interpretation of the instrument, especially in defining the object and purpose of the instrument (Vienna Convention on the Law of Treaties 1969, Article 31). However in the case of the UN Charter, the preamble does not create any definitive legal obligations upon the member states and there is little evidence of it being utilized in interpreting the Charter. The Preamble may be seen as expressing values that should guide the actions of member states but it is not possible to ground any binding obligations upon states from preambular statements concerning human rights. To do so would easily be subject to criticism as utopian aspirations detached from the practical realities of the world.

In the substantive articles of the Charter, Articles 1 and 2, on the purposes and principles of the UN, contain a mix of concerns with both human and state values. Human rights receive mention in a variety of places in the Charter with Articles 55 and 56 being the most prominent. Article 55(c) says the UN will promote respect for human rights and in Article 56 the member states pledge to take action in this regard. The legal impact of these provisions has been disputed. Commentators have claimed that the Charter itself does not impose an obligation upon members to ensure the various rights and freedoms that are mentioned in the Preamble and text (Kelsen 1964, 29; Daes 1992, 5). An opposing position has explained that Articles 55 and 56 of the Charter combine to form clear legal obligations concerning human rights (Humphrey 1967, 46). Given that an individual could not rely upon mentions of human rights in the Charter in making a claim about an abuse of rights, the former view appears to be the most accurate in actual practice with the latter position being the more desirable. Henkin succinctly explains that the desire to appeal to the utopian vision of human rights results in an exaggeration of the actual impact of the Charter, where in practice it is state values that prevail (Henkin 1995, 174–175).

The tension between the utopian promise inherent in human rights and the reality of the primary position of the state is demonstrated by the inclusion of Article 2(7) in the Charter that prevents intervention by the UN into "matters which are essentially within the domestic jurisdiction of any state." States can rely upon this well developed and widely accepted legal rule to avoid what may be considered onerous or undesired international obligations concerning human rights by claiming a situation is within the self-defined domestic jurisdiction. The UN Charter demonstrates the struggle in the international legal argument between Apology and Utopia as it simultaneously allows for human values and state values to be given a prominent place in the declared purposes and principles of the organization. However, despite the rhetoric in support of human rights, the UN Charter maintains "the centrality of the sovereign state as the final authority in human rights" (Ishay 2004, 215; Daes 1992, 3).

The early years of the UN saw human rights enter the international agenda with the adoption in 1948 of the Convention on the Prevention and Punishment of the Crime of Genocide and the Universal Declaration of Human Rights (UDHR). The UDHR has subsequently become the cornerstone for IHRL and is of great symbolic and rhetorical value for the promotion and protection of human rights. As a legal document that may be directly relied upon for ensuring the protection of human rights, it is much less successful (Cassese 1986, 299).

The nature of the UDHR, as a declaration, demonstrates that states were not wholly willing to adopt legal measures that more clearly defined obligations and responsibilities toward humanity. Further, even though the UDHR does set out "a common standard of achievement" it maintains respect for the sovereign state by leaving it up to the individual state to determine how the UDHR affects the domestic sphere (Falk 2000, 38). Writing prior to the UDHR Lauterpacht observed "it is clear that governments will show less hesitation about the recognition of human rights which are not ultimately subject to international supervision and enforcement" (Lauterpacht 1945, 79). This observation was proven correct as the adoption of explicit legal instruments for the protection of human rights has been a much more arduous task. Even though it was decided during the drafting of the UDHR that further legal instruments would be developed, final agreement on what would become the two International Covenants was not achieved until 1966, and then it took another ten years for these treaties to enter into force even though they only required ratification from thirty-five states.

The considerable delay in translating the principles of the UDHR into legal obligations may be due to a number of factors. One aspect that stands out is the obstinacy of states to agree to legal treaties that limit the exercise of sovereign power (Pechota 1981, 65). A similar reluctance can be seen with other international human rights treaties that have experienced significant delays from the initial declaration on principles to the agreement on a final legal document. The Declaration on the Rights of the Child (General Assembly Resolution 1386) was adopted in 1959 with the belief that children need "special safeguards and care, including appropriate legal protection." However, it took over forty years before a legal treaty, the Convention on the Rights of the Child entered into force. In 1981, the UN General Assembly issued the Declaration on the Elimination of All Forms of Intolerance and of Discrimination Based on Religion or Belief (General Assembly Resolution 36/55) expressing that "religion or belief, for anyone who professes either, is one of the fundamental elements in his conception of life and that freedom of religion or belief should be fully respected and guaranteed" along with the observation that denial of these rights has "brought, directly or indirectly, wars and great suffering to mankind." To date no international treaty has been agreed upon ensuring further legal protection of these rights as issues of religious practice are often seen by states to pose a direct threat to the interests and security of the state. The same pattern holds in the area of minority rights where the General Assembly adopted in 1993 the Declaration on the Rights of Persons Belonging to National or Ethnic, Religious and Linguistic Minorities (GA

Resolution 47/135) reaffirming the importance of protecting the rights of minorities, but little progress has been made on developing a legal treaty.

Eventual adoption of a legal instrument is only part of the struggle for the effectiveness of IHRL as the final treaties did not necessarily ensure states could be held to the obligations agreed to. Following World War II states could not maintain the position whereby it is held that state sovereignty trumps all other considerations and international law had no role in determining how a state treated its population. Since states remained the primary actor in the international system, any advance in producing limitations upon behavior was limited. Within international law generally, and with IHRL more particularly, the sovereign state is extremely reluctant to agree to any sort of compulsory enforcement mechanism. This has meant that enforcement has been primarily left to the domestic sphere, but relying upon states to actively and effectively enforce standards that place limitations upon the sovereign prerogative is problematic (Donnelly 1989, 266–8). Dinstein points out the extreme paradox of this situation in that no matter how impartial a domestic judicial system of a particular state may be, it is still an instrument of the state and its absolute impartiality may not always be relied upon (Dinstein 1995, 234). Even if the judiciary can be relied upon, there is no guarantee the executive and legislative branches of government will ensure IHRL is given an appropriate place in the domestic sphere, as discussed below.

The majority of international human rights treaties do possess some form of enforcement, or at the very least, a method for supervising obligations under a treaty. It is not possible to identify any major overcoming of the primacy of the state in determining how the system will operate as the mechanisms in place still focus on the interests of states and not on individuals. Treaties such as the International Covenant on Civil and Political Rights (ICCPR), the African Charter on Human and Peoples Rights and the European Convention on Human Rights (ECHR) all contain inter-state complaint mechanisms that are included in the treaty itself. However, these procedures have never been used under the ICCPR and have rarely been used in the African and European systems. It is difficult to see how effectiveness in the protection of human rights may be achieved in this way when states will be reluctant to complain about the behavior of others for fear of being a target themselves.

These state-based procedures are to be contrasted with individual complaint procedures that are not always included in a treaty, making it necessary to adopt a completely separate treaty. Even when a system for individual complaints is included in a treaty it will often require an explicit statement of recognition from the state. In all of these cases it is the prerogative of the state to decide whether individual complaint procedures will be adopted, or put another way, whether or not individuals will be allowed access to an impartial body for the protection of human rights. For individuals to have access to the supervisory bodies of the ICCPR, and the Convention for the Elimination of Discrimination against Women (CEDAW), a state must first decide to sign and ratify a separate treaty, a true sign of the primacy of states as no state is required to adopt the separate treaty allowing for individual complaints. With the ICCPR of the 152 states parties, 104 have accepted the Optional Protocol for individual petitions, but under the CEDAW, of the 177 states parties, only 60 have accepted the optional protocol.

Even where individual petition procedures are included in the original human rights instrument it is not a straightforward process as individuals once again have to negotiate an obstacle course where state interests have primacy. For example, Articles 11 and 12 of the International Convention on the Elimination of All Forms of Racial Discrimination (ICERD) establish an inter-state complaint mechanism that states automatically accept through ratification of the treaty. Article 14 allows states to make a separate declaration allowing individuals to petition the Committee on Racial Discrimination in relation concerning alleged violations of the Convention, which may be withdrawn by the state at any time. Of the 169 states parties to ICERD, 42 have made the declaration allowing individuals to lodge complaints to the Committee on the Elimination of Racial Discrimination. With the Convention against Torture there are 136 states parties, with 53 accepting the right of individual petition under Article 22.

Overall the dominance of states in the creation of an effective system for the protection of human rights is clear. An international legal instrument for the protection and promotion of human rights cannot come into existence unless states agree to create one, something they have proven reluctant, in many cases, to do expeditiously. The language and provisions contained in the final treaties that will determine the extent to which an individual is able to access and utilize the instrument must receive final approval by states even though a number of non-state bodies may work to influence the final text. Once a legal treaty is created, states are left with the option of whether or not to sign the instrument, whether or not to ratify it and then to dictate the terms of incorporation into the domestic legal system. Ratification, reservations, and derogations are all legitimate legal techniques that allow states to appear to be supporting the development of international human rights law but at the same time allow for minimizing the actual impact. The ability of states to utilize these legal maneuvers demonstrates that IHRL does not always mean the negation or weakening of state sovereignty, rather it clearly demonstrates the assertion of the primacy of state sovereignty over the promotion and protection of human interests (Kirby 1995, 42–3).

Ratification

The adoption of a treaty at the international level is only the first step in ensuring the effective legal protection of human rights. Before a state is legally bound in international law by the obligations contained in an international treaty the treaty must be ratified according to domestic constitutional procedures. However, ratification does not automatically ensure the domestic implementation or application of human rights obligations as the nature of the ratification process depends upon the rules and practices of the domestic system. The process of ratification differs among individual states and no full comprehensive study can be undertaken here, except to say international law does not prescribe any procedures or standards to be followed, it is wholly up to the state to determine the nature of the ratification process. While ratification is a statement to the international system that a state is willing to be bound in international law by the obligations of a particular instrument, this will not ensure individuals are able to rely upon the international instrument in trying to ensure the state lives up to its obligations.

In the UK, ratification has no direct impact upon the domestic environment as the state maintains that any obligations entered into at international law remain international in nature and do not have domestic effect until Parliament has enacted specific legislation. The judiciary has adhered to this practice as explained in *Blackburn v. A-G* ([1971] 2 All ER 1380):

> Even if a treaty is signed, it is elementary that these courts take no notice of treaties as such. We take no notice of treaties until they are embodied in laws enacted by Parliament, and then only to the extent that Parliament tells us.

For individuals in the UK, an international human rights instrument cannot be seen as a source of legally enforceable rights until Parliament "has blessed it with legitimacy and a truly "legal" pedigree" (Hunt 1997, 8–9). The same holds true in the USA where Article 7 of the Constitution says treaties make up part of the "supreme Law of the Land" and judges are to be bound by them. However, the signature of a human rights treaty by the USA is often accompanied by a statement that the rights in the treaty are "non-self executing," meaning individuals will not have access to the international instrument until the federal government allows it through the ratification process.

These examples are telling because they involve democratic states who express a strong attachment to the legal protection of rights. However, this attachment only applies to legal measures from inside and little time is given to measures that originate from outside the state. The situation is no better in states that do not have a comparable tradition of domestic rights protection. Ratification allows states to determine the exact terms and conditions under which an international instrument will be part of the domestic legal system and accessible to the individual and at times, the result may not bear any resemblance to the original international instrument. International law's position on ratification allows states to sign up to international treaties in order to demonstrate support for the utopian view, but this does not automatically translate into the human rights in a treaty being accessible to those they are addressed to. An attempt by a state to ignore the relevance of obligations agreed to internationally to the domestic sphere was eloquently criticized by the New Zealand Courts in the following way:

> That is an unattractive argument, apparently implying that New Zealand's adherence to the international instrument has been at least partly window-dressing. … Legitimate criticism could extend to the New Zealand courts if they were to accept the argument that, because a domestic statute giving discretionary powers in general terms does not mention international human rights norms or obligations, the executive is necessarily free to ignore them (*Tavita v. Minister of Immigration* [1994] 2 NZLR 257).

Despite this the structure of the international legal arguments allows states to keep international obligations at a distance from domestic application, the place where they truly are necessary.

Reservations

At the time of signature, or during ratification, states are allowed to put forth reservations, declarations or interpretative statements of understanding that provide the state's view on the applicability of certain provisions. Again it is easy to see the primacy of state interest being accommodated as these measures may be utilized to distance, or completely exclude, individuals from accessing IHRL. The issue of reservations stands as a clear example of the primacy of sovereignty as it is solely self-referential based purely on state interests.

The ability of a state to utilize a reservation to prevent individuals and groups from relying upon IHRL can be demonstrated by the reservation France has lodged in relation to Article 27 of the ICCPR provides persons belonging to ethnic, religious or linguistic minorities the right to enjoy, along with other members of their group, "their own culture, to profess and practice their own religion, or to use their own language." France has declared "that Article 27 is not applicable so far as the Republic is concerned" since Article 2 of the French Constitution ensures the "equality of all citizens before the law, without distinction of origin, race or religion." In short France has declared that minorities, for the purposes of Article 27, do not exist in France as Article 2 of the Constitution ensures equality for all. France is a party to the Optional Protocol to the ICCPR allowing for individual petitions to be lodged before the Human Rights Committee (HRC) concerning alleged violations of the ICCPR. A number of applications to the HRC involving France and issues under Article 27 have been lodged and in each case the HRC had to declare the application inadmissible due to the reservation. This remains the case even though in the treaty's reporting procedures the HRC has expressed disagreement with France's position on Article 27 (Concluding Comments on France, UN Doc. CCPR/C/79/Add.80 (1997)) and individual committee members have expressed the view that the reservation is unacceptable (*T.K. v. France* communication no. 220/1987 and *H.K. v. France* communication no. 222/1987 Individual opinion of Rosalyn Higgins).

Despite these views the applicability of the reservation remains. In *Hopu and Bessert v. France* (Communication No. 549/1993) the application involved allegations, among others, of activities that were contrary to Article 27 ICCPR concerning the treatment of minority groups in Tahiti. This part of the application was declared inadmissible by the majority of the HRC due to France's reservation. Five individual members of the Committee did attempt to challenge the reservation based on distinctions made in the French Constitution concerning special legislative measures for overseas territories. The basis of the challenge was that France had separate laws for the overseas territories therefore the reservation would not be applicable to these regions unless expressly provided for (*Hopu and Bessert v. France*, opinions of Evatt, Quiroga, Pocar, Scheinin, Yalden). The validity of the reservation was not challenged on the fact that it completely excludes access to an entire provision of the treaty. The practical result being that it prevents individuals and groups from accessing the rights in the ICCPR. Even though France has obligated itself to the ICCPR, the legal impact of its provisions concerning minority rights has been excluded by the state and challenges to this position have been unsuccessful as state interests maintain primacy.

Reservations are seen as a necessary aspect of IHRL for they help to ensure more states will enter into a treaty regime. This view has its merits but it also demonstrates a clear position in favor of state values and interests to the detriment of human values. The Convention on the Rights of the Child (CRC) is commonly heralded as a success in IHRL as it entered into force in less than a year after it was open for signature and currently has the highest number of ratifications of any international human rights instrument with 192 states party to the treaty. That is only part of the story as over half of the states parties have made reservations of one form or another and a number of the reservations appear to be in direct conflict with the object and purpose of the treaty. For example, Indonesia has entered a reservation that states that ratification of the CRC does not imply the acceptance of any obligations beyond pre-existing constitutional guarantees (available at www.ohchr.org/english/law/crc. htm). The reservation of Malaysia is similar in saying that the government accepts the provisions of the CRC so long as "they are in conformity with the Constitution, national laws and national policies of the Government of Malaysia (available at ww.ohchr.org/english/law/crc.htm). Even though these states have signed and ratified the treaty they have clearly stated there is no intention of ensuring domestic law actually conforms (see the concerns expressed by the Committee of the Rights Child in its Concluding Observations on Indonesia, UN Doc. CRC/C/15/Add.25, 24 October 1994 and in General Comment No. 5, UN Doc. CRC/GC/2003/5, 27 November 2003, para. 15.)

The underlying rule in international law concerning the validity of a reservation is it should not be "incompatible with the object and purpose of the treaty" (Vienna Convention on the Law of Treaties, Article 19(c)). There is considerable difficulty in determining object and purpose and there is the even more contentious issue as to who has the authority to determine the compatibility of a reservation. States are of the view that the process of determining the compatibility of reservations is one reserved to inter-State relations. It is difficult to see how this can be effective for even though States have often lodged statements indicating that it is felt a reservation by another state is incompatible this does appear to have any impact on the applicability of the reservation in actual practice. This is illustrated by the reservations of the USA to the ICCPR involving the application of the death penalty to juveniles (31 *International Legal Materials* (1992) 645). In short the USA's reservations completely exclude the applicability of the ICCPR with regard to obligations concerning the death penalty. Over ten states have lodged statements indicating that they feel the reservation is contrary to the object and purpose of the ICCPR but this has not changed the US position. The HRC has also made clear that the US reservation is not acceptable (Concluding Observations 3 October 1995, UN Doc. A/50/40).

One way to resolve the massive imbalance in the reservation process would be to empower a treaty monitoring body with the authority to determine the compatibility of reservations. The HRC has attempted to put forth proposals indicating that it is an authoritative body for determining the compatibility of reservation to the ICCPR (General Comment 24, UN Doc. CCPR/C/21/Rev.1/Add.6). This has been met with rather stern resistance from states such as the USA (3 *International Human Rights Reports* (1996) 265), the UK (3 *International Human Rights Reports* (1996) 261) and France (4 *International Human Rights Reports* (1997) 6). Furthermore, treaty-monitoring bodies realize that extensive pressure on a state to change its reservation may lead the state to renounce the treaty or no longer actively participate in the treaty regime (Schabas 1994, 44). Reservations remain a legitimate legal tool utilized by states to modify or minimize the domestic application of international obligations. Academics and commentators may expound at length as to how a reservation is incompatible with the object and purpose of a treaty but this will have a minimal impact upon individuals and groups trying to overcome the obstacles created by a reservation.

Derogations

A further aspect of IHRL that demonstrates a bias toward state values is the existence of derogation provisions that allow for the suspension of particular rights in emergency situations. As with reservations, derogation provisions are seen as necessary because states must have available to them certain courses of action in order to respond to emergency situations when the life of the nation is under threat. If IHRL prohibited any suspension of treaty guarantees, the argument goes, than states would not sign up to the treaty. However, the use of derogations demonstrates the primacy given to the interests of the state at the expense of human rights.

Derogations involve exceptional measures deemed necessary by a state in order to respond to some particular threat or emergency which in itself constitutes an extraordinary situation. By definition derogations are a deliberate act by a state that is contrary to obligations accepted under IHRL in response to some extraordinary, but temporary, circumstances (Marks 1995, 85). Derogations represent a significant site of tension between the ability of IHRL to regulate state behavior and the sovereign prerogative of states. The main purpose of a state is to provide for the security of the population and territory, and in certain circumstances this may mean placing limitations on human rights. When there is an attempt to use IHRL in order to regulate state behavior in these circumstances, the domestic authorities will argue that they are better placed to determine when an emergency exists and what measures are needed in response. The idea of what constitutes a threat to the life of the nation is one of the most contentious points surrounding derogations as it brings into question the position of the domestic authorities in determining a threat to the security of the state. This does not necessarily mean that governments are free to act wholly without restraint, but it does indicate that the central element in determining the legitimacy of derogation falls within the apologist position based on sovereign prerogative of states (*Ireland v. UK*, Series A No. 25 (1970) para. 207).

The current threat of international terrorism and the response of the UK demonstrate the limitations of IHRL in attempting to regulate state behavior in what are considered emergency situations. In response to the terrorist attacks in the US on 11 September 2001, the UK stated that it now faced an emergency situation where the life of the nation was under threat. As a result the UK lodged derogations to its obligations under the ECHR and ICCPR with regard to the right to liberty. In response to the terrorist threat perceived by the UK, the Anti-Terrorism, Crime and Security Act 2001 was passed into law that provided for the indefinite detention of non-UK nationals who were suspected to be involved with international terrorism. The measures have been justified based on providing security for the state and necessary for protecting the human rights, in particular the right to life, of individuals living in the UK. The UK was the only member of the Council of Europe to enter a derogation to the ECHR. A number of individuals were detained under this legislation and spent up to three years in prison. The House of Lords, the highest domestic judicial authority, eventually ruled that the measures were contrary to the UK's human rights obligations because they are disproportionate and discriminatory ([2004] UKHL 56). However, individuals detained under the offending law remained in jail as the Government maintained they were a threat to the nation and could not be released (*BBC* News online, "Act on detention ruling, UK urged" 18 December 2004, available at http://news.bbc.co.uk/1/hi/uk_politics/4107299.stm).

The position of the UK government was argued on the belief that the sovereign right of a state to provide security for the population and territory takes precedent over human rights obligations or concerns. The UK is not alone in asserting this view as the war on international terrorism appears to be evolving into a "permanent emergency" that is threatening the security of states. In this sort of environment it becomes difficult to question the ability of states to pursue acts designed to preserve the security of the population by asserting obligations of restraint based on IHRL. At the same time the threat from international terror cannot become an excuse for unhindered actions that purposely violate human rights, regardless of the classification of the individual concerned. The ability of international monitoring bodies to utilize IHRL in trying to offset the actions of states in the fight against international terror will have a major effect on the future credibility and effectiveness of IHRL. Even before the particular threat posed by international terrorism came to the fore the ability of international monitoring bodies to counter expressions of sovereign rights was heavily constrained due to the primacy of the state in international law (Marks 1995, 92).

International Human Rights Law: Moving to Utopia?

IHRL finds itself struggling in a world of contradictions; it may speak of the importance of human values but does much to preserve and protect state values. In the current international environment states are justifying abuses of human rights on the basis of preserving security and, ultimately, protecting human rights. However, a great deal of criticism has been leveled at the actions of states through appeals to the rhetoric and legal provisions of IHRL. At the same time, states can just as easily appeal to international law in support of their actions. As Koskenniemi has shown international law exists between two opposing poles and engages in continual movement between opposing positions. The apologist side of state interest has pretty much dominated international law since its inception but over time selfish state interest has had to give ground to the utopian aspirations of human rights based on human interests. The horrors of World War II made it clear that international law could no longer be just an instrument preserving the primacy of state power. For the most part, the IHRL that has emerged speaks of the importance of human values in the preambular statements of the treaties or in the general pitch and tone of the document. The UN Charter states that the founding principles of the organization include the desire "to save succeeding generations from the scourge of war" and the reaffirmation of "faith in fundamental human rights, in the dignity and worth of the human person." Similar statements exist in preambles of human rights instruments. Both the UDHR and ICCPR state that "recognition of the inherent dignity and of the equal and inalienable rights of all members of the human family is the foundation of freedom, justice and peace in the world." These aspects of IHRL are more rhetorical than substantial, for as discussed above, there remain a number of accepted legal techniques available for preserving state interests and for bypassing or minimizing legal obligations for the promotion and protection of human interests.

What then of the future for IHRL? If the power of IHRL is confined mainly to rhetorical pronouncements, is it possible to conclude that it will continue to have an impact in restraining state power? It is submitted that IHRL will continue to have an impact, a significant impact no less, on restraining the behavior of states and furthering the promotion and protection of human interests in the world. In the current "war on terror" the ability of IHRL to act as a check on state power has been limited, but it has not been wholly absent. International institutions, nongovernmental organizations, defense lawyers and concerned individuals have continued to assert the standards and obligations proclaimed by IHRL in response to a wide range of state behavior that fails to respect human freedom and dignity. IHRL will continue to provide standards by which behavior can be measured, evidence of obligations that have been agreed to, and statements of principles as to what sort of behavior is acceptable or not. This may not result in preventing all abuses of human rights but efforts to reinforce the importance of IHRL remain crucial in the promotion and protection of human rights in the world (Carter Center 2003, 7 and 13). While the appeal to IHRL may be rebutted by states through a variety of political proclamations and legal maneuvers, it is not possible to escape the rhetoric inherent in IHRL, and which has taken hold in the international system, that proclaims the importance of protecting the values and interests of human beings against unbridled state power.

It is through the power of its rhetoric that IHRL will continue to have an impact and influence in the current crisis human rights finds itself in. For many, this may appear to be an overly optimistic assessment of the current world situation. However, there exist a number of reasons for taking some hope in the power of rhetoric in favor of human interests. First, even if the initial impact of IHRL is minimal, studies have shown how over time that once the rhetoric of human rights is publicly engaged, the behavior states begins to conform more closely with the rhetoric (Risse, Ropp, and Sikkink 1999). This is expected as states cannot continually espouse the importance of human rights in various international statements without expecting demands for substantive action based on the expressed rhetoric. Even where IHRL is manipulated by states for the pursuit of self-interest, the mere fact that principles and norms of behavior are being discussed openly contributes to the slow incremental process of furthering the promotion and protection of human rights.

Secondly, as discussed above the structure of the international legal argument is based on opposing positions and it is not possible for international legal rules to reside wholly on one side of the other. For this discussion this means that human rights standards have become an accepted part of the international system as it is not possible to maintain that state interests alone determine the focus and direction of international law and relations. Today we are witnessing very strong assertions of the primacy of state interests and the sovereign rights of states to act in support of their own interests, unconstrained by other concerns. However, the existence of IHRL cannot be completely denied or ignored and if states choose to take no notice of human rights standards there will be a variety of actors there to reassert the importance of human rights. The international legal argument may give a prominent place to state interests but it is not an exclusive place and other interests have taken hold. As IHRL continues to gather support the foundations of international law will need to evolve in order to accommodate the reality that human interests do matter (Falk 2000, 69).

Finally, and following on from the above point, it is possible to take solace from E.P. Thompson's analysis of the Black Act (Thompson 1975) which demonstrates that even when the powerful manipulate the law to serve their own interests, the rhetoric surrounding the law and its role in society can eventually act as a constraint upon the unbridled exercise of self-interested power and allow those in a weaker position to exert the importance of their own interests. The Black Act was a statute in English law enacted in 1723, with the purpose of protecting the property rights and economic interests of the wealthy through the creation of new offences, the extension of existing public order offences, a severe limiting of procedural rights for the accused and the imposition of the death penalty for those found guilty. The draconian measures of the Black Act were supposedly a response to an "overwhelming emergency" facing the country due to the actions of poachers and thieves who were terrorizing landowners and taking from the Royal lands (Thompson 1975, 23). The impact of the Black Act was overtly beneficial for the wealthy and those in power but detrimental to the lower classes and less powerful (Cole 2001, 180).

In his analysis, Thompson explains that it would be possible to view the Black Act as just another example of the powerful using law to support their own self-interest and to oppress those in a less advantageous position. However, Thompson goes on to explain that this is not the whole story as the law is much more complex than mediating simple class relationships. Inherent in our beliefs about the law is the idea that the law brings structure and order, as well as serving justice and preventing injustices. Thompson further explains that the law aspires to some form of universal application so that all those in society are in some way brought under its purview. This universality of the law means that those in a privileged position may be able to manipulate the law for their own interests but the discourse surrounding the law is not exclusive and others may strive to use it for the pursuit of their own interests (Thompson 1975, 264). Even though the law remains a tool for the powerful, it may also provide support for curbing the exercise of that power. As Thompson explained:

> [t]he rhetoric and rules of a society are something a great deal more than a sham. In the same moment they may modify, in profound ways, the behavior of the powerful, and mystify the powerless. They may disguise the true realities of power, but, at the same time, they may curb that power and check its intrusions (Thompson 1975, 265).

States will continue to use international law to support their own power and interests but it is not possible to evade entirely the public rhetoric of IHRL that proclaims that human interests are an important aspect of international law that is to be respected.

The actions taken by states in the fight against international terror demonstrate the fragility of IHRL in its ability to constrain state action. IHRL at present does not necessarily provide in all circumstances an effective mechanism for individuals and groups to address violations of obligations publicly agreed to by states. At the same time, it does provide a language that may be utilized for furthering the utopian views inherent in the human rights project. By signing up to, and participating in, IHRL states themselves have removed the barriers of exclusivity that had prevented appropriate considerations of human values. Even if, at the time, states believed that nothing would come from the various international documents and declarations agreed to, the mere existence of IHRL on paper has provided individuals and groups with a strong foundation for pursuing the promotion and protection of human rights through legal and non-legal means.

Works Cited

Cassese, A. (1986), *International Law in a Divided World*, Oxford: Clarendon.

Cassese, A. (1990), *Human Rights in a Changing World*, Oxford: Polity Press.

Carter Center (2003), *Human Rights Defenders on the Frontlines of Freedom: Protecting Human Rights in the Context of the War on Terror*, Conference Report, November 11–12, 2003, Atlanta.

Cole, D. (2001), "An Unqualified Human Good: E.P. Thompson and the Rule of Law," *Journal of Law and Society* 28:2, 117–203.

Daes, E. (1992), *Status of the Individual and Contemporary International Law: Promotion, Protection and Restoration of Human Rights at National, Regional and International Levels*, New York: United Nations.

Dinstein, Y. (1995), "Human Rights: Implementation through the United Nations System," *Proceedings of the American Society of International Law* 89, 242–247.

Donnelly, J. (1989), *Universal Human Rights in Theory and Practice*, Ithaca: Cornell University Press.

Falk, R. (2000), *Human Rights Horizons: The Pursuit of Justice in a Globalizing World*, London: Routledge.

Fitzpatrick, J. (2003), "Speaking Law to Power: The War against Terrorism and Human Rights," *European Journal of International Law* 14:2, 241–264.

Henkin, L. (1990), "Law and Politics in International Relations: States and Human Values," *Journal of International Affairs* 44:1 (1990) 183–208.

Henkin, L. (1995), *International Law: Politics and Values*, Dordrecht: Martinus Nijhoff.

Humphrey, J. (1967), "The UN Charter and the Universal Declaration of Human Rights," in E. Luard, ed., *The International Protection of Human Rights*, London: Thames and Hudson, 39–59.

Hunt, M. (1997), *Using Human Rights Law in English Courts*, Oxford: Hart Publishing.

Ishay, M. (2004), *The History of Human Rights: From Ancient Times to the Globalization Era*, Berkeley, University of California Press.

Jhabvala, F. (1997), "The Drafting of the Human Rights Provisions of the UN Charter," *Netherlands International Law Review* 44:1, 1–31.

Kelsen, H. (1964), *The Law of the United Nations*, London: Stevens.

Kirby, M. (1995), "The Impact of International Human Rights Norms: 'A Law Undergoing Evolution'", *Western Australia Law Review* 25:1, 30–48.

Koskenniemi, M. (1989), *From Apology to Utopia: The Structure of the International Legal Argument*, Helsinki: Finnish Lawyers Publishing.

Lauterpacht, H. (1945), *An International Bill of the Rights of Man*, New York: Columbia University Press.

Marks, S. (1994), "Nightmare and Noble Dream: The 1993 World Conference on Human Rights," *Cambridge Law Journal* 53:1, 54–62.

Marks, S. (1995), "Civil Liberties at the Margin: the UK Derogation and the European Court of Human Rights," *Oxford Journal of Legal Studies* 15:1, 69–95.

Pechota, V. (1981), "The Development of the Covenant on Civil and Political Rights," in L. Henkin, ed., *The International Bill of Rights: The Covenant on Civil and Political Rights*, New York: Columbia University Press, 32–72.

Reisman, M. (1990), "Sovereignty and Human Rights in Contemporary International Law," *American Journal of International Law* 84:4, 866–876.

Risse, T., Ropp, S. and Sikkink, K. eds, (1999), *The Power of Human Rights: International Norms and Domestic Change*, Cambridge: Cambridge University Press.

Schabas, W. (1995), "Invalid Reservations to the International Covenant on Civil and Political Rights: Is the United States Still a Party?" *Brooklyn Journal of International Law* 21:2, 277–325.

Simma, B. (1998), "Reservations to Human Rights Treaties – Some Recent Developments," in G. Hafner ed., *Liber Amicorium Professor Ignaz Seidl-Hohanveldern*, The Hague: Kluwer, 659–682.

Thompson, E.P. (1975), *Whigs and Hunters: The Origin of the Black Act*, London: Penguin, 1990 ed.

Chapter 5

Women's Human Rights in the Twenty-First Century: Crisis, Challenge, and Opportunity

Marsha A. Freeman

Introduction

If the twenty-first century is seeing human rights in crisis, the field of women's human rights is experiencing crisis times two. The dramatic accomplishments of the 1990s, placing women's human rights on the international agenda, are threatened with the fate of many social movements, supported by donors and institutions as long as they are seen as "cutting edge," but rapidly becoming yesterday's news when the excitement of discovery fades and the hard work of implementation and institutionalization still lies ahead. The legal and policy obligations are enshrined in numerous documents; the principle has been formally established that "women's rights are human rights." These accomplishments cannot be taken away. But the twenty-first century challenge is to make them permanently meaningful, implemented from the halls of parliaments to the huts of remote villages.

The crisis is twofold, political and financial. First, it encompasses frustration over the lack of implementation of and accountability for the rights that once seemed to be close to attainment. The happy perception of success was based on the global acknowledgment, made at the 1993 World Conference on Human Rights, that human rights specifically and generally include what had been designated "women's rights," followed immediately by the recognition of women's human rights and empowerment as critical to managing population issues (International Conference on Population and Development 1994), and the accomplishments of the Fourth World Conference on Women (Beijing 1995). But these successes now feel like distant history, as the government commitments have elided into the broader Millennium Development Goals,[1] with less and less direct commitment to particular goals and

---

1 The Millennium Development Goals (MDGs) are derived from the United Nations Millennium Declaration, adopted in 2000 by 189 countries. The MDGs represent a global consensus of the most important development goals and the intent to achieve them by 2015. The MDGs include a gender equality goal. However, the content of the equality goal is vague. Indicators are extraordinarily and disappointingly simple (comparative literacy rates, participation in parliaments etc). In an attempt to be overarching, the MDGs lose all nuance with respect to discrimination against women. They do not include any reference to rights, thereby dismissing all the international human rights commitments, and the linkage of human

less accountability than even the limited framework of the world conferences. In addition, since 2000, funding to support women's human rights and development work has declined dramatically throughout the globe, compounding the perception of a massive loss of momentum.

The momentum of women's human rights is a local as well as a global issue. International human rights standards are only as valuable as the political will to implement them, and political will is created by the applied energy and skills of civil society. In the last decades of the twentieth century, thousands – perhaps millions – of women learned to use human rights language and processes to multiply their voices for political and social impact. The fourteen thousand women who participated in the Nongovernmental Forum at the 1985 Third World Conference on Women (Nairobi), and the thousands more with whom they worked at home before and after the World Conference, knew that the time had come to claim women's space in their families, their communities, and their nations, as a matter of rights. In the following fifteen years, and particularly in the 1990s, women's organizations and some other groups successfully advocated for changes in constitutions and laws relating to marriage and divorce, violence against women, property ownership, and educational and employment equality, based on the fundamental international human rights principles of equality between women and men. The global sense of possibility that both fostered and resulted in these changes has also diminished with political changes and the decline in resources.

The Trajectory of Success

The recognition of equality between women and men and the elimination of discrimination against women as integral and necessary to achievement of both human rights and development is the result of a very long process. Research and action on these principles began generations before they became commonly recognized as the key to women's status and rights (Fraser 2002). However, the actors most involved in developing international human rights law – traditional international human rights organizations, academics, governments, and United Nations and regional bodies and experts – consistently failed to recognize either sex discrimination or gender-based human rights violations as human rights issues under international law until almost the end of the twentieth century.[2] These actors considered status of women issues in the global South (developing countries) largely under the rubric of development.[3] Even in Western industrialized countries, the establishment of domestic equality

---

rights to development, that were key accomplishments of the 1990s. For further information see, www.un.org/millenniumgoals.

2   The conversation was broken open in academic and expert circles by the award-winning article, Charlesworth, Chinkin, and Wright 1991.

3   A very large literature now exists examining women's role in development and the failures of development policy to address status of women issues. This WID (women in development) research began in the 1960s, and the WID literature began to mushroom in the 1970s. While the research and terminology focused on women in developing countries, status of women issues were hardly confined to the global South. As Arvonne Fraser, the first WID

laws in the 1960s and 1970s was hard fought and remains incomplete. The artificially imposed "equality" standards of the Soviet bloc collapsed with the fall of the Berlin Wall and remain rubble to this day.

The history of legislation relating to violence against women illustrates the hard-fought and very recent battles for recognition of women's rights as human rights. While the United States and the United Kingdom pioneered legislation against domestic violence in the 1970s – Minnesota adopted the first US legislation in 1979 – in most countries (including European countries) violence against women was not publicly discussed at all until well into the 1980s. The international recognition of violence against women as a human rights issue began with studies for the United Nations in the 1980s. Violence against women in the family, as it was called in the 1980s, was acknowledged as a complex and significant global issue in the report of the Third World Conference on Women, the *Nairobi Forward-Looking Strategies to the Year 2000* (Third World Conference on Women 1986, p. 60, para. 258). Following upon the Nairobi Conference and resolutions of the UN Commission on the Status of Women and other bodies, the United Nations held an Expert Group Meeting on Violence in the Family, with Special Emphasis on its Effects on Women, in Vienna in December 1986. The report of that meeting, *Violence against Women in the Family*, is the first study of the issue that attempts to place it on the international agenda "as a world issue rather than as an issue that is confined to one country or cultural system" (United Nations 1989, p. i).

The new willingness to acknowledge and discuss violence against women led to the specific articulation of this issue in 1992 under the Convention on the Elimination of All Forms of Discrimination against Women (the CEDAW Convention). In the 1960s and 1970s, when the CEDAW Convention and its predecessor Declaration[4] were drafted, violence against women was not widely acknowledged and certainly was not considered an aspect of discrimination. Rather than attempting to amend the 1979 Convention, in 1992 the Committee adopted a General Recommendation that articulated the necessity of addressing violence under most of the articles of the Convention and instructed States Parties to do so. Significantly, the initial discussion and drafting of this General Recommendation were promoted by an NGO, the International League for Human Rights, in collaboration with the International Women's Rights Action Watch. Firm and formal integration of violence against women into the international agenda was achieved the next year, as the 1993 World Conference on Human Rights specifically addressed the topic (World Conference on Human Rights 1993, *Declaration* para. 18; *Programme of Action* Sec. 3).

Beyond this particular accomplishment, until well into the 1990s the sole international arena in which women's human rights have been consistently articulated and where governments have been held accountable, has been the UN Committee on the Elimination of Discrimination against Women (CEDAW Committee), which is

director at the US Agency for International Development, has said repeatedly, "*in terms of women, the whole world is developing.*"

4 The United Nations Declaration on the Elimination of All Forms of Discrimination against Women was adopted in 1967. GA res.2263 (XXII), 7 November 1967. The Declaration was a statement of principles that ultimately were enshrined in the CEDAW Convention.

specifically charged with monitoring and reviewing implementation of the CEDAW Convention. The CEDAW Convention developed out of the work of the United Nations Commission on the Status of Women (CSW) which was created in 1948. The CSW is not itself a human rights body and was not constituted to provide for accountability. However, CSW commissioned the study that resulted in adoption of the 1967 Declaration on the Elimination of All Forms of Discrimination against Women and was the drafting body for the CEDAW Convention and its Optional Protocol.

The CEDAW Convention was adopted by the UN General Assembly in December 1979, having been drafted in record time upon recommendation by the governments participating in the First World Conference on Women (Mexico City 1975). The governments and nongovernmental organizations participating in that conference acknowledged that development could not proceed without equality, and equality could not be achieved without recognition that discrimination against women is a human rights issue. The CEDAW Convention was opened for signature at the Second World Conference on Women in 1980 (Copenhagen), and the CEDAW Committee was established in 1981, when twenty governments had ratified the treaty. Again, however, until well into the 1990s, the CEDAW Committee labored under a number of conceptual and practical constraints that hindered its identification as a human rights body, and many governments and nongovernmental organizations saw its work as somehow separate from "real" human rights activity.

In what seemed originally to be a triumph of women's advocacy and political skills, the CEDAW Convention was identified from its inception until quite recently as being about "women" rather than about human rights. Because it came out of a women's conference (the First World Conference on Women in 1975), and out of the Commission on the Status of Women as drafting committee, a narrow view of the CEDAW Convention as by, for, and solely about women rather than about human rights, became almost inescapable. The Convention's status as a human rights instrument, and the CEDAW Committee's status as a human rights body, suffered from their location for UN servicing in the Division for the Advancement of Women (DAW). For many years the offices of the DAW (which until the late 1980s was a lower-level "Branch" rather than a UN division) were in the Vienna International Centre while all the other treaty bodies were serviced out of the Geneva-based Office of the High Commissioner for Human Rights. The CEDAW Committee met alternately in New York and Vienna for many years, until the meetings were moved permanently to New York in the mid-1990s; all the other treaty bodies meet in Geneva. Membership (23 experts) has been almost entirely female. A number of years ago the Government of China noted, during the review of China's CEDAW implementation, that it considered the CEDAW review to be different from a human rights review because this was about women.

When the Third World Conference on Women was held in Nairobi in 1985, the language of rights had just begun to seep into the global discussion of "equality, development, and peace" that were the themes of that conference. The *Nairobi Forward-Looking Strategies to the Year 2000* included numerous references to rights. After Nairobi, the pace of discovery and accomplishment increased. Fourteen thousand women from nongovernmental organizations throughout the globe had participated in the NGO Forum that was held parallel to the government conference, and they were not going to go home and be quiet. Several workshops on the CEDAW Convention drew standing-room-only crowds, and participation in the countless other workshops and informal gatherings indicated very clearly that a global women's movement, focused on rights and development, was gathering steam.

Several key organizations focusing on rights grew out of the Nairobi experience. The International Women's Rights Action Watch was organized in 1985, as a result of conversation at Nairobi between a half dozen activists from five countries. It was based in the US because one of the American founders had the most viable base of operation. From its inception IWRAW focused on raising awareness of the potential for using the CEDAW Convention to promote and establish women's human rights and on building NGO capacity to advocate for rights. Three regional networks (Asia-Pacific, Latin America, Africa) were established out of workshops held at Nairobi by the Washington-based program, Women, Law and Development, to promote the linkage of law, rights, and development. Women from the developing world organized the Development Alternatives for a New Era (DAWN) network specifically to provide a voice, a network, and a research agenda for women from the global South, whose voices generally were not heard – or respected – in many international venues. Countless local organizations were started or strengthened on the basis of participation in the Nairobi conference and its resonance.

The women's human rights movement gained momentum from 1990, as preparations for the 1993 World Conference on Human Rights provided a space for making the point that women's rights are human rights and for emphasizing the universality of human rights. Many other women's groups, from South and North, held workshops and otherwise staked out both physical and intellectual territory in the Vienna conference venue – to such an extent that the major media gave the bulk of their coverage to the phenomenon of the women's presence in the conference (Riding 1993).

From the US, the Center for Women's Global Leadership (established 1989 at Rutgers University, New Brunswick), the Human Rights Watch Women's Rights Project (established 1992), the women's project of the International League for Human Rights, and the women's program of the International Human Rights Law Group played key roles in the organizing and lobbying that resulted in the inclusion of a section on women's human rights in the Vienna Declaration and Programme of Action. The American NGOs benefited from proximity to the UN in New York during the lead-up to the conference; they also enjoyed ready access to the official US delegation during the conference. Those conditions, combined with the leading role of the Clinton Administration at the conference, combined to grant a prominence to American NGOs at Vienna that caused controversy among the other NGOs. Despite including global empowerment in their mission statements, the US-based groups dominated the conference, and they carried major responsibility for the NGO work on official conference documents.

The Vienna Declaration recommended the appointment of a Special Rapporteur on Violence against Women, its Causes and Consequences. The breadth of this mandate was a victory in itself. The Conference delegates wrestled over the language of the mandate, with conservatives arguing to limit the mandate only to "violence." Such language would have allowed only for reporting on the incidence of violence and on programs to address it. The broader language that was finally adopted, which included the term "causes and consequences," allowed for a much deeper look at all the circumstances that place women in a position of vulnerability to violence as well as changes to provide them with the means to avoid it and to rebuild their lives. This broader language allowed the mandate to address discrimination, culture, family and social systems, as well as resource allocations.

The 1994 World Conference on Population and Development (ICPD, Cairo), organized by the UN Fund for Population Activities (UNFPA or the Population Fund), was designed to focus specifically on the issues of dealing with population in an era in which "fertility control" programs, dictated by donors and governments for execution by bureaucrats and medical workers who saw women as objects of rather than participants in the process, clearly were no longer an option. Not only were such programs frequently unsuccessful, but the role of women in making their own decisions was increasingly becoming an issue. As a result of enlightened leadership in the Population Fund and in many government delegations (again, the accessibility and attitude of the US delegation was notable), and very effective lobbying by well-organized NGOs, the Cairo Declaration recognized the primacy of women's choices – their human rights – in dealing effectively with population issues (International Conference on Population and Development 1994).

The preparatory period for the Fourth World Conference on Women began in 1992 when the UN Commission on the Status of Women adopted a resolution announcing the conference. The UN Division for the Advancement of Women, the secretariat for the Commission and CEDAW, headed into high gear. NGOs that had been working with the Commission and CEDAW did the same. Three years did not seem enough time to plan, particularly with two other world conferences on the agenda prior to Beijing, but it was all there was.

The formal Beijing conference process started with regional preparatory meetings that included NGO fora as well as official government meetings. Having the benefit of experience from the 1992 World Conference on Environment and Development, the 1993 World Conference on Human Rights, and the 1994 ICPD, a number of NGOs organized to have an impact on the outcome of the regional government meetings as well as engaging in the usual NGO program of workshops, panels, and networking events. The Asia Pacific regional meeting, held in Manila in November 1993, the European/US regional meeting, held in Vienna in October 1994, and the African regional meeting, held in Dakar in November 1994, were particularly successful in this respect. The official declarations from these meetings were the basis for the draft global Platform for Action to be finalized at Beijing, and well-prepared NGOs had a significant influence on the language of the regional declarations. The Dakar Platform in particular included an entire section on the girl-child that was provided by the NGOs. This was the only regional Platform that included a section on this topic, and it ultimately was included in the Beijing Platform.

In preparation for the Beijing conference, a coalition of American NGOs met for over a year, monitoring the development of the Platform for Action and pursuing a strategy to place human rights at the heart of it. Many of the US NGOs were working with networks of NGOs in other countries, particularly the global South, which were planning their own strategies for working the conference. Everyone tried, not always successfully, to maintain communications across regions. The US coalition meetings were held in Washington, with NGOs from outside the DC area joining by conference call. At least one meeting was held with New York-based NGOs. The moving force behind this coalition was a passionate Maryland-based activist, Leah Browning, although many coalition members took on specific tasks.

In Beijing, the US coalition formed a core for daily strategy meetings that expanded with the presence of many NGO representatives from other countries, meeting in a hotel until the official conference began, and then meeting on the site of the government conference when that venue opened. The organization of the strategy sessions, both in the US and in Beijing, was not without conflict and controversy; indeed, conflict between some US-based NGOs emerged prior to the Beijing conference, and on site the conflict was exacerbated by the stressful circumstances of the conference. The North-South tensions were perhaps inevitable given the resource inequality, difficulties with accommodations, and communications issues within Beijing and between the site of the government conference and the nongovernmental forum over an hour away in Huairou. In acknowledgment of these resource and access inequalities, several US-based NGOs, including IWRAW, facilitated travel and participation by Southern NGOs. Despite the stress and strains, the strategy meetings proved successful. NGOs had unprecedented access to the official meeting; they were prepared to lobby effectively; many NGOs were on their government delegations, and there was a great deal of communication between them and the others.

Immediately after the Fourth World Conference on Women a sense of energy, accomplishment, and possibility permeated the international women's movement. The Platform for Action, with all its contentious and unwieldy language, was based on a human rights framework (Fourth World Conference on Women 1995). The Platform recommended universal ratification of the CEDAW Convention by 2000 and the drafting of an Optional Protocol providing for individual complaints to the CEDAW Committee. The energy and enthusiasm of this era manifested in the explosive growth and ambition of NGOs working within their own countries and regionally to promote women's human rights.

Post-Beijing the international human rights treaty monitoring system became much more receptive and attentive to women's human rights. The Office of the High Commissioner for Human Rights (UNOHCHR) had established a gender focal point in the mid-1990s and shortly before the Beijing Conference held an Expert Group for Mainstreaming Gender Perspectives into the Work of the (then) Centre for Human Rights (UN OHCHR 1995a). The Chairpersons of the Human Rights Treaty Bodies (HRTB) adopted recommendations based on the Expert Group report in September 1995 and in September 1998 noted the usefulness of *Assessing the Status of Women*, a manual produced by the International Women's Rights Action Watch for monitoring and implementing CEDAW obligations, as a guide for use by all the treaty bodies in monitoring women's human rights (UN)HCHR 1995a; UNOHCHR 1995b; UNOHCHR 1998). Several of the treaty bodies adopted General Comments (interpretive statements on the content and meaning of treaty language) on States Parties' obligations with respect to equality in enjoyment of the rights in the respective treaties (UN HRC 2000; UN CERD 2000; UN CESCR 2005). The CEDAW Committee undertook significant changes in its working methods, including a process for adopting Concluding Observations to give States Parties clear directives for compliance. Governments began to work on the Optional Protocol to CEDAW, and it was adopted in 2000.

Five years after the Fourth World Conference, at the Beijing + 5 special session of the General Assembly, the glow was wearing off. Certain enlightened governments (still including the US), supported by the women's human rights and development NGOs, expended a great deal of time and resources to prevent major backsliding from the language of the Beijing Platform for Action. Another five years down the road, in preparation for the Beijing + 10 review, numerous NGOs documented persistent government failure to live up to the commitments of Beijing (for example see Equality Now 2005, which lists discriminatory statutes that should have been revised after Beijing). The Bush Administration delegation to the Beijing + 10 review session in March 2005 undermined the discussion by attempting to pass a resolution redefining "human rights" and insisting on a "clarification" of the Platform for Action's approach to abortion – and, having made its point to satisfy its domestic constituencies, backed off after wasting an entire week of the delegates' time (Hoge 2005; New York Times 2005; Freeman 2005). The United Nations Population Fund had decided simply to avoid holding a ten-year review of the International Conference on Population and Development in 2004 – speaking volumes about the current politics of reproductive rights. In view of the lack of a public review, three powerhouse reproductive rights organizations – the Washington, DC-based Population Action International, the London-based International Planned Parenthood Federation, and the New York-based Family Care International – published a comprehensive overview, *ICPD at Ten: Where Are We Now?* (2004). The publication was launched with major events in London and in the US in the fall of 2004, as part of the Countdown 2015 Initiative, which links the promises and subsequent government actions of the International Conference on Population and Development (Cairo 1994), with the Millennium Development Goals.

On the domestic level, the human rights momentum of the 1990s and the increasingly sophisticated approach of the NGOs has had a significant impact on law and policy throughout the globe. Some African countries adopted laws to increase women's property rights in divorce and inheritance and to outlaw female genital mutilation. In Nepal, the inheritance code was held to be discriminatory and a new one ordered to be enacted, and abortion was made legal. In Egypt, family law was changed to allow women to bring an action for divorce. In a number of Eastern European countries, domestic violence is now against the law. In most of the Gulf States, women can now vote. Chile has finally provided for divorce, and Turkey has adopted a new family code that provides for equality in family relations and divorce.

But every one of these changes has been hard fought for years, and now implementation is a major challenge. All of these policy changes will remain merely laws on the books until women have the power to seek and obtain enforcement, until administrative and judicial authorities are trained to understand that it is their duty to deal respectfully with women, and until the role of culture and tradition in reinforcing fundamental power imbalances are seriously addressed. And in many places even minimal legal change remains a dream.

The women's human rights activity of the last fifteen years has resulted in the establishment of an enormous global knowledge base and a dramatic increase in the number and advocacy capacity of NGOs in the global South and former Soviet bloc. With shifts in political winds and funding priorities, these groups are losing resources and the ear of their governments at the critical moment of institutionalizing change.

Money – the Moving Target

The work of both US-based and overseas NGOs depended on the involvement of a relative handful of donors. In the US, the John D. and Catherine T. MacArthur Foundation and the Ford Foundation were the two largest consistent donors and provided grants in the nature of general operating funds. Two smaller foundations provided smaller but consistent grants: The Moriah Fund and the Shaler Adams Foundation, a family foundation whose president was passionate on the subject. The Sigrid Rausing Trust, based in London, funded a number of the US NGOs for several years. IWRAW received considerable support from the Carnegie Corporation, specifically for work on women's rights to health and education in Commonwealth sub-Saharan Africa.

MacArthur funds came from its Population Division, headed by Carmen Barosso, who put in place a funding portfolio that clearly linked reproductive rights and population issues with women's human rights. Ford funds came largely from the portfolio that funded women's rights activities in the US and abroad (and not from its human rights portfolio). Both provided multi-year grants to the American groups in the form of general operating funds, in amounts of up to $150,000 per year. The smaller donors' grants were generally in the $20,000–25,000 range, frequently annual and sometimes project-designated. MacArthur, Carnegie, Shaler Adams (through the Tides Foundation) and Moriah also funded overseas directly. Ford funded some overseas projects directly from New York and more broadly through its regional offices.

European development agencies have been the primary source of funding for NGOs in the global South and Nations in Transition. The Nordic countries and the Netherlands are the most generous. Switzerland, the European Union, the British government, and large international NGOs such as Oxfam affiliates and Action Aid (which receive government funds) also have been key donors. Few US groups regularly obtained overseas development money, with the exception of IWRAW, which was funded for many years by the Swedish International Development Cooperation Agency and in some years by the Dutch, Norwegian, Danish, and Swiss agencies. Many Eastern European groups came to rely on the Soros Foundations, established in-country by George Soros and related programmatically to (but not funded by) Soros's New York-based Open Society Institute. OSI generally did not and still does not fund international work by US-based groups.

One of the more notable aspects of the funding equation is the relatively small size of the NGOs. None of the US-based groups had budgets of over $1,000,000 during the 1990s, and several were considerably less. Most do not have huge staffs, ranging from five to sixteen in peak activity years. Many overseas groups are even smaller. The scale of accomplishment is truly remarkable in view of the relatively small scale of the enterprise.

Since approximately 2000, funding for international women's human rights work by NGOs based in the United States has declined dramatically. While casual observers may attribute the decline to market conditions or current US politics, many of the events and decisions affecting funding of US-based NGOs are unrelated to economic issues and occurred before the 2000 elections. They are unlikely to be changed by market improvements or election results. The field is in a major funding crisis. The US situation can be summed up as "the perfect storm." The MacArthur Foundation leadership changed in 1998, and its focus changed to eliminate support for the connection between reproductive health and population issues and women's human rights; Carmen Barosso and staff have departed, and the program focus has narrowed considerably. The Ford Foundation no longer has a funding allocation for overseas work by US-based women's NGOs and is directing more funding to overseas NGOs and other priorities. The Carnegie Corporation also changed leadership, and with a total reorganization of its human resource development area to focus on development of African universities, the program that funded IWRAW disappeared. The Shaler Adams Foundation ceased funding international women's human rights projects in 1998, and it is now focusing on building awareness of international human rights in the US. And the Rausing Trust began several years ago to focus less on funding in the US and more on developing a human rights infrastructure in Europe.

The decline of funding for work on women's human rights and development is a global phenomenon, experienced by NGOs in the global South and Nations in Transition as well. With political and economic changes, a number of European donor agencies are moving away from funding international organizations such as UNIFEM, IWRAW and other global networks. These agencies are primarily focused on economic development and poverty alleviation, with human rights, rule of law, and gender components seen as part of the solution. When they decide that rule of law or targeted gender projects or international organizations – the latter always a hard sell – do not sufficiently support their primary poverty alleviation focus, they cut off the funding.

The funding issue was much discussed in a number of NGO and donor venues at the March 2005 Beijing + 10 gathering in New York. IWRAW has documented the funding issue for US-based organizations. The Association for Women's Rights in Development (AWID), an international organization based in Canada, commissioned a study of the global trends and issues that was released in 2005 and updated in 2006. The results indicate that the global crisis is real (AWID 2006). AWID reports that a mere 0.6 percent of all overseas development assistance provided by the members of the Organization for Economic Development and Cooperation – thirty donor democracies and the European Union – in 2003, was allocated to programs that indicate gender equality as a principal objective (AWID 2006, 22–23). The women's human rights programs and NGOs would be included as a small component of this figure – a grim picture indeed. Additionally, NGOs in EU accession countries have taken a triple hit. Pre-accession programs and funding in most cases did not deal with gender (Reisen 2005b, 30–31, 37). Since accession they cannot be funded by OECD/DAC donors because they now are seen as part of the "developed" EU, despite their countries' lagging economies and lack of tradition of internally funding NGOs. Finally, the Soros Foundation offices in Eastern Europe have cut back their activities, including funding of women's groups, as those countries' democratic systems become more established and, in some cases, join the European Union (private communication 2005; http://www. soros.org/initiatives/regions/central-eastern_europe (accessed February 7, 2008)).

The Impact of Mainstreaming

The concept of gender mainstreaming, adopted as an operational and substantive policy by many funding and development agencies, is a key factor in international funding. In the view of many experienced observers, the policy has resulted in evaporation of focused and accountable attention to women's human rights, development, and equality issues. Funds have been denied to organizations with experience and programs in women's human rights, empowerment and development, and granted to programs that attempt to "mainstream gender" – with little understanding of what that means or how to account for the impact of the programs on women, girls, and equality between the sexes (for further discussion see AWID 2004).

Conceptually, "mainstreaming" refers to integration of gender perspectives into all programming by an agency or entity. Ideally, mainstreaming would result in requirements that all actors and all funding recipients ascertain that programs fully recognize gender roles, differences and disadvantages, develop and fund programs on the basis of that recognition, and include realistic and accurate gender impact assessment in their evaluations. The term has been adopted for programmatic use within the United Nations and most development agencies. Agencies' websites include elaborate definitions and indicate that "gender" is to be "mainstreamed" in their programs (i.e., see Canadian International Development Agency 2006; and Swedish International Development Cooperation Agency 2005). However, the results to this point are a net loss of specific focus on women's human rights and development, and little or no profit.

The currency of "gender mainstreaming" is largely a product of the Beijing process. NGOs, development experts, and some UN staff pressed for adoption of gender mainstreaming language during the Beijing preparatory phase and in the conference. The Platform for Action endorses the idea and encourages governments to "mainstream gender" in all aspects of development. Ten years later, however, NGOs are seeing mainstreaming as a prime example of the adage, "be careful what you wish for."

A primary cause of this loss is the failure of definition, which is essentially a failure of vision. Despite all efforts, few agencies or experts have clearly understood that the word "mainstream" is itself a problem; the concept is well-taken, but we need a different term. "Mainstreaming" suggests that women somehow lie outside of a primary reality into which they must be brought. This assumed primary reality is clearly framed in male terms. As it has evolved in practice, "mainstreaming" offers women opportunities designed for men, which frequently fail to account for practical and attitudinal issues that keep women from taking advantage of the proffered opportunity, or simply offers women lesser or no opportunities. This operational frame fails entirely to acknowledge, for example, that 70 percent of the world's poorest people are women, and thus poverty alleviation and economic development must be about women's realities in the first place.

The definitional issue extends to the term "gender." Gender is universally acknowledged to refer to cultural expectations and assumptions about the behavior, attitudes, personality traits, and physical and intellectual capacities of men and women, based solely on their identity as men or women. Conceptually, practically, and grammatically, it is impossible to "mainstream" a role expectation. It may be possible to insist on examining and accounting for assumptions and role expectations in program design and development. It may be possible to plan and account for women's full participation in all programs. Giving credit to the good will of those who use the term "gender mainstreaming," it fails to capture the essence of the problem or its potential solutions.

A second, and equally significant, issue is the failure to apply adequate evaluation tools to determine the impact of "mainstreamed" programs. Proper evaluation goes beyond counting heads (process evaluation; a "metric") to understanding outcomes. It requires qualitative and longitudinal as well as quantitative approaches. Mainstreaming also requires framing and holding to budget priorities that can be identified to promote women's human rights and status. Tools for determining budget priorities as they relate to women have been developed and applied by activists in a number of countries, beginning in the global South.[5] But neither expertise nor funding has been dedicated globally to adequate evaluation of budget and program outcomes for women.

Donor agencies take on faith alone the premise that mainstreaming will benefit women. Several expert analyses indicate that this assumption is not true, or at least has not been validated. Instead, in the name of gender mainstreaming, funding and program priorities targeting women's human rights and development have disappeared, with no evidence that mainstreaming has produced significantly beneficial results for women (Reisen 2005a and 2005b).

A New Mainstreaming Issue: The Human Rights Treaty Bodies' Expanded Common Core Document

The women's human rights community recently has had to deal with the potential impact of a new effort to mainstream women's human rights throughout the treaty system. The Secretary General's reports on UN reform indicated quite strongly that treaty monitoring must be harmonized in some fashion to eliminate duplicated effort and the burdens placed on States Parties by the requirement of frequent and multiple reports (see UN Secretary General 2005, para 147). The Office of the High Commissioner for Human Rights initially responded by offering a set of guidelines for expanding the currently required Common Core Document (a

---

5   A very large literature exists on gender budgeting. An excellent overview can be found on the Gender Budget Group Web site, http://www.wbg.org.uk/GBA.htm. See also the resource collection in Bridge Project 2003.

single report containing basic information on a country, to be used by all treaty bodies in their reviews), which reflected a series of recommendations made by the Chairpersons of the Human Rights Treaty Bodies since the mid-1990s.[6] The expanded Common Core Document would require reporting on issues of equality and nondiscrimination in all sectors and under all treaties. All the treaty monitoring bodies thus would have before them a comprehensive description of efforts to deal with sex discrimination and equality, content that frequently is missing from States Parties' reports to bodies other than CEDAW.[7]

This would seem to be a boon to women, as attention to sex discrimination in the enjoyment of human rights should be on the agenda of every treaty body for every country review and frequently is not. However, as originally constructed in 2004, the proposed guidelines undermined the special expertise of the CEDAW Committee while failing to account for the uneven expertise in the other treaty bodies and the lack of time to do justice to all the gender issues in States Parties' human rights implementation. In other words, there was a distinct possibility that women's human rights issues could be mainstreamed into oblivion in the treaty system.

This dire outcome was averted by a well-focused Working Group that the Chairpersons of the Human Rights Treaty Bodies established to revise the guidelines. As proposed in 2006, the revised guidelines for the Common Core Document require reporting on all laws and enforcement frameworks pertaining to discrimination, as well as on remedies for violations of human rights (UNOHCHR 2006). The Chairpersons have provisionally adopted these guidelines, suggesting that all the treaty monitoring bodies require their use, with a review at the 2008 Chairpersons meeting.[8]

The new Common Core Document guidelines clearly indicate that attention to sex discrimination is within the purview of all the treaty monitoring bodies, that these bodies cannot ignore the issue, and that States Parties must attend to equality issues as an obligation under each of the treaties. Under the new guidelines women's human rights advocates have a mechanism for multiplying their voices and drawing increased attention to their issues by using the treaty monitoring system strategically. Unlike development planning and programming, treaty implementation review provides a

---

6   The Chairpersons of the seven human rights treaty monitoring bodies meet annually in Geneva to review matters of common concern to all the treaty bodies. Since 2002, an Inter-Committee Meeting, the working session to deal substantively with the issues, has immediately preceded the Chairpersons Meeting. It includes the chairpersons and two other members of each body.

7   The drafts of the expanded Common Core Document guidelines and comments on them can be found at http://www.ohchr.org/english/bodies/treaty/reform.htm. In 2005 the High Commissioner also launched an initiative to establish a single "unified" treaty monitoring body. This proposal is highly controversial and could be very problematic for women. Many governments, including key States Parties, as well as most NGOs and the UN Specialized Agencies (UNICEF, UNESCO, etc.) have unequivocally objected to the proposal. As of this writing (2006), it remains under review. A meeting of States Parties on the proposal was supposed to have been held some time in 2007.

8   United Nations, Report of the Chairperson of the Human Rights Treaty Bodies (2006). A/61/385 (18 September 2006).

venue and a clear process for accountability. In this setting "mainstreaming" can be a positive development, if NGOs learn to steer it.

Conclusion: Opportunities among the Challenges

The women's human rights movement is far from dying, or even slowed down, but it may look quite different in ten years. The trends of the last few years have resulted in a coalescence of purpose. During the Beijing + 5 review period in 2000, a concern over losing ground engendered broader alliances for monitoring and lobbying. Since then, growing concern over funding issues; over conservatism and fundamentalisms, including the role and legacy of the Bush Administration in the US, the UN, and the globe; and over issues of NGO continuity in a difficult environment, have led NGOs to talk more with each other, document the issues they have been perceiving, and become proactive in addressing them. While many of the NGO workshops and presentations at the Beijing + 10 review in 2005 referred to problems and abuses of women's human rights, a considerable number of NGOs also participated in productive discussions and planning to confront the issues with donors and governments. Most heartening, some of these sessions included donors who listened and participated.[9]

The question of legacy looms for many of the activists who founded the national and international NGOs that had such a dramatic impact on the establishment of women's human rights in the 1990s. While some organizations have already seen a change in leadership, a number are still headed by founders. The decline in funding certainly has made succession planning difficult, and some groups may merge or cease to exist. But a younger generation of activists, from current students to practitioners in their thirties and forties, has been visibly seeking opportunities to move the international women's human rights agenda. Some will find spaces as the current generation of leadership retires. Many will find spaces in existing organizations that are not specifically dedicated to women's human rights. This could be seen as a defeat – or, as this author prefers to think – as an opportunity to broaden the perspective of existing organizations and to make the movement global conceptually as well as geographically.

Women's human rights advocates must also generate and take advantage of opportunities to work with organizations and systems that have not traditionally been targeted to or used by women. Men can be allies as well as obstacles. And as long as women dedicate their efforts largely to systems that are labeled "women," they will lose opportunities to make their point and to multiply their voices in places where decisions are made. In short, we must and can claim the entirety of the human rights enterprise.

The women's human rights movement is characterized by a stubborn determination. Having built a global knowledge base and accomplished more than anyone could have dreamed fifteen years ago, women are not about to stop in their tracks and retreat, defeated, to the kitchen. As one NGO leader from a European

---

9   The Ford Foundation was among the most involved, hosting an invitational session on funding issues that was opened by Ford President Susan Berresford.

Union accession country declared,[10] describing loss of funding and a sense of local hostility to human rights, "if we have to move into the basement, where we started from, we will do it, and keep fighting."

Works Cited

Association for Women's Rights in Development (AWID) (2004), *Spotlight*, No. 3, November.

Association for Women's Rights in Development (AWID) (2006), Where is the Money for Women's Rights? Assessing the resources and the role of donors in the promotion of women's rights and the support of women's rights organizations. Rev'd ed., February 2006 <http://www.awid.org/go.php?pg=where_is_money>, accessed March 22, 2007.

Bridge Project (2003), Gender and Budgets: Supporting Resources Collection <http://www.snvworld.org/cds/rgGEN/Chapter%203/bridge2.pdf> accessed March 21, 2007.

Canadian International Development Agency (2006), "Frameworks for Integrating Gender Equality" <http://www.acdi-cida.gc.ca/CIDAWEB/acdicida.nsf/En/8525711600526F0A852571370070A406?OpenDocument> updated 1 December 2006, accessed March 21, 2007.

H. Charlesworth, C. Chinkin, and S. Wright (1991), "Feminist Approaches to International Law," 85 *American Journal of International Law*, 613–645.

Convention on the Elimination of All Forms of Discrimination against Women (1979), GA Res. 34/180, U.N. Doc. A/34/46.

Equality Now (2005), Words and Deeds: Holding Governments Accountable in the Beijing+10 Review Process <http://www.equalitynow.org/english/wan/beijing10/beijing10_en.pdf> accessed March 23, 2007.

Fourth World Conference on Women, *Platform for Action*, U.N. Doc. A/CONF.177/20 (17 October 1995).

Fraser, Arvonne S. (2002), "Becoming Human: The Origins and Development of Women's Human Rights," *Human Rights Quarterly* 21:4.

Freeman, Marsha (2005), Private communication with a delegate from Belgium, New York, March 7.

Hoge, Warren (2005), "Panel Backs Women's Rights After U.S. Drops Abortion Issue," *New York Times*, March 5 <http://select.nytimes.com/search/restricted/article?res=F20D13FB3A>.

International Conference on Population and Development, Cairo, Egypt, 5–13 September 1994, *Declaration and Programme of Action*, A/CONF.171/13.

New York Times (2005), "The Bush Team's Abortion Misstep," *New York Times*, March 5 < http://nytimes.com/search/restricted/article?res=F2013FB3A>.

Population Action International, International Planned Parenthood Federation, and Family Care International (2004), *ICPD at Ten: Where Are We Now?* (Washington DC, London, and New York: self-published).

---

10 At the Ford Foundation meeting, 7 March 2005 (see fn. 11).

Private meeting with NGOs and Donors, Ford Foundation, New York, March 2005.

Riding, Alan (1993), "Women Seize Focus at Rights Forum," *New York Times*, 16 June 1993 <http://select.nytimes.com/search/restricted/article?res=F00614FF3F5>.

Riesen, Mirjam van (2005a), *Accountability Upside Down: Gender equality in a partnership for poverty eradication*, Eurostep and Social Watch.

Riesen, Mirjam van (2005b), *To the farthest frontiers: Women's empowerment in an expanding Europe*, Eurostep, WIDE, Social Watch, Karat Coalition.

Soros Foundation, http://www.soros.org/initiatives/regions/central-eastern_europe.

Swedish International Development Cooperation Agency (2005) <http://www.sida.se/sida/jsp/sida.jsp?d=429&a=1414&language=en_US&searchWords=gender%20mainstreaming> last updated December 5, 2005, accessed March 21, 2007.

Third World Conference on Women, 15–26 July 1985, *Nairobi Forward-Looking Strategies to the Year 2000: Report of the World Conference to Review and Appraise the Achievements of the United Nations Decade for Women: Equality, Development and Peace*, U.N. Doc. A/CONF.116/28/Rev.1 (1986), p. 60, para. 258.

United Nations (1989), *Violence against Women in the Family*, UN Sales No. E.89.IV.5.

United Nations Committee on Economic, Social and Cultural Rights (2005), General Comment No. 16: *The Equal Right of Men and Women to the Enjoyment of All Economic, Social and Cultural Rights*, E/C.12/2005/4 (11 August 2005).

United Nations Committee on the Elimination of Discrimination against Women (1992), *General Comment No. 19: Violence against Women*, G.A. Doc. A/47/38 (29 January 1992).

United Nations Committee on the Elimination of Racial Discrimination (2000), *General Comment No. XXV on Gender-Related Dimensions of Racial Discrimination*, G.A. Doc. A/55/18, annex V.

United Nations Human Rights Committee (2000), *General Comment No. 28* (Article 3, Equality), CCPR/C/21/Rev.1/Add.10.

United Nations Office of the High Commissioner for Human Rights (1995a), *Expert Group Meeting on the Development of Guidelines for the Integration of Gender Perspectives into Human Rights Activities and Programmes*, E/CN.4/1996/105 (20 November 1995).

United Nations Office of the High Commissioner for Human Rights (1995b), *Report of the Sixth Meeting of Persons Chairing the Human Rights Treaty Bodies*, A/50/505 (4 October 1995).

United Nations Office of the High Commissioner for Human Rights (1998), *Report of the Persons Chairing the Human Rights Treaty Bodies on Their Tenth Meeting*, A/53/432 (25 September 1998).

United Nations Office of the High Commissioner for Human Rights (2006), *Harmonized guidelines on reporting under the international human rights treaties, including guidelines on a common core document and treaty-specific documents*, http://daccess-ods.un.org/access.nsf/Get?Open&DS=HRI/MC/2006/3&Lang=AHRI/MC/2006/3 (10 May) http://daccessdds.un.org/doc/UNDOC/GEN/G06/419/42/PDF/G0641942.pdf?OpenElement.

United Nations Secretary General (2005), *In Larger Freedom: Towards Development, Security and Human Rights for All*, U.N. Doc. A/59/2005 (21 March 2005).

Women's Budget Group <http://www.wbg.org.uk/GBA.htm> (home page), accessed March 23, 2007.

World Conference on Human Rights, *Declaration and Programme of Action*, U.N. Doc. A/CONF.157/23 (12 July 1993), Declaration para. 18; Programme of Action Sec. 3.

PART III
Pursuing Human Rights and Prosecuting Violators

Chapter 6

The Center for Justice & Accountability: Holding Human Rights Abusers Responsible in the United States and Abroad

Matt Eisenbrandt[1]

A. Introduction

In handing down its ruling at the end of the trial of top Nazi officials at Nuremberg, the International Military Tribunal observed, "Crimes against international law are committed by men, not by abstract entities, and only by punishing individuals who commit such crimes can the provisions of international law be enforced."[2] The tribunal's words provide a guiding principle for the Center for Justice & Accountability (CJA), a human rights law organization based in San Francisco. Since its inception in 1998, CJA has endeavored to hold responsible those who violate human rights and break the impunity they enjoy. CJA has won several victories on behalf of survivors of torture and other abuses in civil actions in US courts. In addition, CJA has played a key role in the criminal prosecution of human rights abusers in Spain, deportations of persecutors from the United States and efforts of home countries to criminally prosecute those who have been deported. Initially, most of CJA's cases concerned abuses in Latin American and Caribbean countries, in part due to the large number of human rights abusers and refugees from those regions in the United States. The results of those cases include winning four multi-million dollar jury verdicts,[3] enforcing a landmark foreign human rights judgment in the United States, providing critical evidence leading to the deportation and potential prosecution of a military intelligence commander, collecting over $1 million from two defendants,

---

1   Consultant and former Legal Director for the Center for Justice & Accountability.

2   *Opinion and Judgment of the International Military Tribunal for the Trial of German Major War Criminals* (1946), available at http://www.yale.edu/lawweb/avalon/imt/proc/judlawch.htm.

3   Appeals courts have upheld the verdicts in two of the cases. See *Romagoza Arce v. Garcia*, 434 F.3d 1254 (11th Cir. 2006); *Cabello v. Fernandez-Larios*, 402 F.3d 1148 (11th Cir. 2005). The third case, *Chavez v. Carranza*, 407 F. Supp. 2d 925 (W.D.Tenn. 2004), is currently on appeal. The fourth case, *Jean v. Dorelien*, No. 03-20161-CIV-KING/GARBER (S.D.Fla.), has not been appealed as of the writing of this chapter.

and obtaining a judgment holding an individual liable for one of the most notorious assassinations in Latin America.

There are several areas where CJA's work has made an impact, offering a measure of legal accountability for those who commit human rights abuses and presenting important opportunities for fact-finding and truth-telling that uncover new information about abuses. CJA's civil cases also have shaped US jurisprudence on several legal issues, including the law of command responsibility, liability for conspiracy and aiding and abetting, and the validity of crimes against humanity as a claim in US courts. This chapter details the diverse contributions CJA has made to the international movement against impunity and demonstrates that CJA has taken a unique and versatile approach to hold human rights abusers responsible for their crimes.

B. Accountability

CJA is the only non-governmental organization in the United States primarily dedicated to investigating and holding responsible individual human rights violators. CJA seeks to end the impunity enjoyed by human rights abusers in several concrete ways: (1) providing an important measure of accountability through the filing of civil lawsuits and collection of assets in the United States; (2) participating in criminal prosecutions in Spain (see section B(2) of this chapter and Stephens 2002); (3) encouraging the US Department of Justice to bring criminal charges for human rights abuses; (4) supporting and providing assistance in the deportation of perpetrators from the United States when there is a strong possibility that they will be criminally prosecuted in their home countries; (5) supporting extraditions to other countries for criminal prosecution; and (6) building the capacity of foreign nations to effectively prosecute human rights cases.

1. CJA's Civil Cases

CJA has filed fourteen civil lawsuits against fifteen human rights abusers since 1998. The principal legal mechanisms on which CJA relies are the Alien Torts Claims Act (ATCA, also known as the Alien Tort Statute) and the Torture Victim Protection Act (TVPA) (28 USC § 1350 and note). These laws allow US federal courts to hear civil claims against persons allegedly responsible for severe human rights abuses. The ATCA, adopted in 1789, provides jurisdiction to federal district courts over cases brought by non-citizens for torts committed in violation of "the law of nations." The history of the ATCA and the reasons for its passage by the first Congress are disputed. Nonetheless, according to the case *Sosa v. Alvarez-Machain*, it appears that the ATCA was originally intended to give US courts the ability to handle disputes of an international, rather than purely domestic, character that, if not addressed, could have led to problems in US foreign relations (Bradley 2002 and Dodge 1996). Beginning with the 2nd Circuit Court of Appeals' groundbreaking decision in *Filartiga v. Peña-Irala*, US courts have held that conduct that violates the "law of nations" under the ATCA includes human rights abuses prohibited by norms of "customary international law."

In June 2004, the Supreme Court in *Sosa* upheld the validity of the ATCA. The court determined that, in passing the ATCA, Congress intended for federal common law to "provide a cause of action for [a] modest number of international law violations." The Court limited the common law claims that can now be brought under the ATCA to those that rest on a "norm of international character accepted by the civilized world and defined with a specificity comparable to the features of the 18th-century paradigms" the Court recognized – namely violation of safe conduct, infringement of the rights of ambassadors and piracy.

Although the majority opinion did not expressly invoke the concept of "universal jurisdiction," Justice Breyer, in his concurrence, confirmed that this is the standard underlying the ATCA. The principle of universal jurisdiction allows any state to prosecute certain offenses of international law that are of global concern, even when neither the perpetrator nor the victims are nationals of the prosecuting state, and the violations occurred in another country (Restat 3d of the Foreign Relations Law of the US, § 404; Orentlicher 2004, 1057 and 1059). This principle is enshrined in the Convention Against Torture, which states "The State Party in the territory under whose jurisdiction a person alleged to have committed any offence referred to [in the treaty] is found shall … if it does not extradite him, submit the case to its competent authorities for the purpose of prosecution (Convention Against Torture 1984). The Geneva Conventions assert, "each High Contracting Party shall be under the obligation to search for persons alleged to have committed, or to have ordered to be committed, such grave breaches, and shall bring such persons, regardless of their nationality, before its own courts" (Geneva Conventions 1949).

The Supreme Court decision in *Sosa* cited with approval *Filartiga* and other cases which have permitted claims for violations of "specific, universal and obligatory" international norms. The court cited *Tel-Oren v. Libyan Arab Rep.* for the language, "definable, universal and obligatory," and *In re Estate of Ferdinand Marcos, Human Rts. Litig.*, for the language, "specific, universal and obligatory." It remains to be seen which torts claims can go forward under the Supreme Court's definition, but the list is likely to include torture, extrajudicial killing, forced labor, slavery, war crimes, crimes against humanity, and genocide (see Stephens 2004; *Mujica v. Occidental Petroleum*; *In re "Agent Orange" Product Liability Litigation*; *Doe v. Saravia*).

The TVPA, passed by Congress in 1992, extended the ATCA by providing a cause of action to US citizens and non-citizens alike for extrajudicial killing and torture. The legislative history and the Supreme Court's decision in *Sosa* indicate that the TVPA did not replace the ATCA, but rather reinforced it (see S. Rep. No. 102–249 (1991), p. 4; H. Rep. No. 102–367 (1991)). However, the TVPA only applies to torture and extrajudicial killing, and is only applicable against an "individual" who acts "under actual or apparent authority, or color of law" of a "*foreign* nation" (28 USC § 1350 note § 2(a), emphasis added). Therefore the TVPA has expanded upon the ATCA by providing a remedy to US citizens while simultaneously restricting that remedy to only two types of abuses and potentially limiting their recourse against US officials and non-individuals, such as corporations.

All of the defendants in CJA's civil suits were served with process while in the United States. Of the fifteen abusers sued by CJA, thirteen were living in the United States and two were visiting from abroad at the time of service. In most cases, the defendants had been leading quiet lives here, having essentially escaped their bloody pasts. In several situations, the filing of lawsuits by CJA disrupted that tranquility by exposing their location, publicly presenting evidence of their responsibility for abuses and subjecting them to legal liability. The following sections summarize several of CJA's cases in the United States beginning with the three lawsuits involving El Salvador.

Because CJA is a non-profit organization with a limited budget and staff, CJA co-counsels with a private law firm on each of its civil cases; all references to actions by CJA in the context of civil suits should be taken to include both CJA and the co-counsel firm.

a. Romagoza Arce v. Garcia   In May 1999, CJA and co-counsel James Green[4] filed a civil lawsuit in West Palm Beach, Florida against former Salvadoran Ministers of Defense José Guillermo García and Carlos Eugenio Vides Casanova on behalf of three torture survivors from El Salvador. García and Vides Casanova both came to the United States in 1989 after heading the Armed Forces of El Salvador that were responsible for thousands of civilian deaths during a prolonged period of repression and civil war in the 1980s (Commission on the Truth for El Salvador 1993, and Stanley 1996). In 2002, following a four week trial, a federal jury found the generals legally responsible for the torture of CJA's clients and ordered them to pay $54.6 million. Vides Casanova has been forced to relinquish over $300,000 of his own funds which, although the amount is only a small fraction of the total damages to which the plaintiffs are entitled, is an important step. A federal judge has also found that transfers of over $110,000 by Vides Casanova to his relatives were fraudulent and that the money should be turned over to CJA's clients. The successful collection represents one of the first times in US history in which victims in an ATCA case have recovered money from those found responsible for abuses. In 2005, a Bush Administration official said that the generals could be placed in deportation proceedings (Chardy 2005).

CJA's success in the *Romagoza Arce* case relied on vital groundwork in a prior, unsuccessful attempt to hold García and Vides Casanova liable for the 1980 rape and murder of four US churchwomen by the Salvadoran Security Forces (*Ford v. Garcia*). In 1999, the Lawyers Committee for Human Rights (now Human Rights First) filed suit against García and Vides Casanova on behalf of the families of the churchwomen. While the suit did not result in victory at trial, the decision of the appeals court was critical in confirming the viability of the law of command responsibility in US courts. CJA worked closely with the *Ford* attorneys to address potential difficulties with the claims of command responsibility in CJA's case. In contrast to the *Ford* case, at the *Romagoza Arce* trial a former Argentine colonel testified as an expert witness and explained to the jury how a military chain of command functions and described the ways in which García and Vides Casanova exercised effective control over their troops, including those responsible for the torture of CJA's clients.

---

4   Morrison & Foerster LLP joined the legal team as *pro bono* co-counsel after the filing of the case.

b. Doe v. Saravia   Another Salvadoran perpetrator, Alvaro Saravia, had been living in Modesto, California for over a decade when CJA and co-counsel Heller Ehrman LLP served him with a lawsuit in September 2003. The complaint alleged that Saravia was responsible for coordinating the assassination of revered Salvadoran Archbishop Oscar Romero in March 1980. Saravia has not been seen in Modesto after the filing of the suit, although it is not clear whether he disappeared as a result of the lawsuit or if he had fled immediately beforehand (Reyes 2006, Arax 2004, Dada 2005). Nonetheless, in 2004, Judge Oliver Wanger found that Saravia had been properly served with the complaint, and the case moved forward. In an extensive written decision, Judge Wanger found Saravia liable for the assassination and entered a $10 million judgment against him (*Doe v. Saravia*). The evidence presented in CJA's case led the US Bureau of Immigration and Customs Enforcement to issue an arrest warrant for Saravia and to place him on its Most Wanted list (Immigration and Customs Enforcement).

c. Chavez v. Carranza   In its third El Salvador case, CJA, along with co-counsel Bass Berry & Sims PLC, initiated a lawsuit in December 2003 against Colonel Nicolás Carranza on behalf of eight victims of repression (although the cases of only five plaintiffs were presented at trial). Carranza served with General García as Vice-Minister of Defense in 1980 and under General Vides Casanova as director of the notorious Treasury Police from 1983–4. He has been living in Memphis, Tennessee since moving to the United States in 1985 and became a US citizen in 1991. After hearing testimony for two weeks, a jury in November 2005 found Carranza responsible for torture, extrajudicial killing and crimes against humanity on the claims of four of CJA's clients. The jury could not reach a unanimous decision on the fifth plaintiff. The entire verdict against him was $6 million. On August 15, 2006, Carranza's motion for judgment notwithstanding the verdict and for a new trial was denied.

d. Cabello v. Fernández-Larios   Former Chilean secret police agent Armando Fernández-Larios moved permanently to the United States in 1987 as part of a plea agreement with US federal prosecutors in which he pled guilty for his role in the 1976 Washington D.C. car-bombing that killed former Chilean ambassador Orlando Letelier. After serving only five months in prison, Fernández-Larios was released and entered the federal Witness Security Program. However, the family of Winston Cabello, a Chilean economist killed in 1973 shortly after the coup that brought Augusto Pinochet to power, knew that Fernández-Larios was also responsible for Cabello's murder as part of the "Caravan of Death" (on Pinochet's regime see Kornbluh 2005, Dinges 2005, and Constable and Venezuela 1993; on the Caravan of Death see Verdugo 2001). After Fernández-Larios was located in Miami, CJA filed a lawsuit against him on behalf of the Cabello family.[5] Fernández-Larios sat through a three week trial at the end of which the jury found him liable for the killing and ordered him to pay $4 million in damages. The governments of Chile and Argentina

---

    5   Wilson Sonsini Goodrich & Rosati and Kerrigan, Estess, Rankin & McLeod, LLP later joined the case as *pro bono* co-counsel.

have both asked the United States to extradite Fernández-Larios to face criminal charges in their countries (*La Nación* 2006).

e. Mehinovic v. Vuckovic   Kamal Mehinovic, a torture survivor from Bosnia-Herzegovina, came to the United States as a refugee in 1995 after enduring brutal torture at the hands of, among others, Bosnian Serb guard Nikola Vuckovic (for background see Gutman 1993, and Rohde 1998). In 1998, Mehinovic contacted CJA when he discovered that Vuckovic was living in the Atlanta area. Shortly thereafter CJA filed its first case, alleging that Vuckovic was responsible for widespread abuses during the civil war in the former Yugoslavia.[6] In 2001, after Vuckovic failed to appear for trial, Judge Marvin Shoob ruled him in default and held a bench trial on the merits (*Mehinovic v. Vuckovic*). Judge Shoob found Vuckovic liable for torture, arbitrary detention, war crimes, crimes against humanity and cruel, inhuman or degrading treatment, and ordered him to pay $140 million in damages to Mehinovic and three other CJA clients. The court did not reach the issue of whether Vuckovic was liable for genocide. It is believed that Vuckovic has returned to Bosnia-Herzegovina.

f. Doe v. Constant   While most perpetrators have maintained low profiles in the United States, the location and culpability of other defendants was already well known to the public before CJA cases were filed against them. Emmanuel "Toto" Constant was perhaps the most notorious perpetrator in Haiti during the repressive military regime that ruled that country from 1991–4 (for background see Commission Nationale de Vérité et de Justice 1995, and Bell and Danticat 2001). He headed the paramilitary unit called the Front for the Advancement and Progress of Haiti (FRAPH). Although Constant snuck into the United States on Christmas Eve of 1994, his presence here became nationally known when he was arrested by immigration authorities and went on the 60 Minutes news program to complain that the US government, which had worked closely with Constant through the Central Intelligence Agency, had betrayed him (Grann 2001). After this pronouncement, the US government released him from detention. Constant returned to Queens, New York where he was subjected to numerous protests by members of the Haitian community expressing their disgust at the fact that Constant was permitted to live freely in their neighborhood (Grann 2001).

This sentiment was continually expressed to CJA, which, along with the Center for Constitutional Rights (CCR), filed a lawsuit against him in December 2004 on behalf of three women who had been brutalized by FRAPH.[7] The case was intended to counteract the impunity that Constant had enjoyed and to disrupt the freedom he had felt. While CJA's case was still pending, Constant was arrested and indicted for grand larceny, forgery and falsifying business records in an alleged mortgage fraud scheme in New York (Hays 2006). CJA provided evidence to the New York Attorney General's office to show that Constant was a flight risk and helping to keep him in

---

6   Several attorneys contributed to the case in a *pro bono* capacity. The plaintiffs were represented at trial by CJA, the ACLU of Georgia and Paul Hoffman of Schonbrun DeSimone Seplow, Harris & Hoffman LLP.

7   Sonnenschein, Nath & Rosenthal LLP later joined the case as *pro bono* co-counsel.

prison. In CJA's case, Constant failed to defend, and after an evidentiary hearing on damages was held in August 2006, Judge Sidney Stein ordered Constant to pay $19 million in damages.

g. Jean v. Dorélien   In another Haiti case, CJA recovered nearly $900,000 belonging to Carl Dorélien, a former member of the Haitian High Command during the period when FRAPH and the Haitian Armed Forces combined to carry out widespread atrocities. Like Toto Constant, Dorélien came to Florida after the United States invaded Haiti in 1994 to force the military regime out of power. While Dorélien was living in the United States, he won over $3 million in the Florida lottery. In January 2003, CJA filed suit in federal court in the Southern District of Florida against him for his responsibility in the notorious 1994 Raboteau massacre.

After the filing of the case, Dorélien attempted to sell off his rights to annual lottery payments in exchange for a lump sum. CJA, in conjunction with co-counsel law firm Holland & Knight and solo attorney John Thornton, successfully intervened before the Florida state court hearing the lottery case and opposed the deal, arguing that Dorélien's attempt to convert his yearly payments into a lump sum constituted a fraudulent transfer that sought to keep his assets out of the reach of his creditors, including CJA's client. CJA obtained an order from the state court permitting the deal to go through, but preventing Dorélien from receiving the lump sum of nearly $900,000. Instead, the judge ordered that the money be paid into an escrow account under the court's control.

Dorélien, like Constant, was convicted *in absentia* in Haiti in November 2000 for conspiracy and complicity in murder and other crimes in connection with the Raboteau massacre. In addition to his guilty conviction, Dorélien, along with his co-defendants, was ordered to pay the Raboteau victims 1 billion *gourdes*, or approximately $24 million. CJA domesticated the Haitian judgment, which is now enforceable in Florida. On August 17, 2006, based on the validity of the Haitian judgment in Florida, the state court judge ordered the lottery money being held in escrow to be made available to CJA's client.

When Dorélien was deported to Haiti in 2003 during the presidency of Jean Bertrand Aristide, he was placed in detention immediately upon his arrival in Port au Prince. However, during the 2004 uprising that removed Aristide from power, Dorélien and others were released from prison (Daniel and Nesmith 2004). He remains at large. Nonetheless, it is clear that CJA's case against Dorélien has had an impact. After a Haitian newspaper ran a story stating that the Florida state court had allowed CJA's client to recover his lottery money, Dorélien wrote a letter to the newspaper, which was published, stating that the Florida court was wrong and denying that any judgment exists against him in Haiti (Dorélien 2006).

2.   *Criminal Prosecutions in Spain*

While civil lawsuits for human rights abuses have been the norm in the United States, criminal prosecutions have been more common in Europe, particularly in Spain. Under the universality principle, Spanish courts have jurisdiction to hear cases of genocide and other international crimes regardless of the nationality of the perpetrator or victims and regardless of where the crimes took place (Article 23.4, Ley Orgánica 6/1985, de 1 de julio, del Poder Judicial). In December 1999, in the wake of the arrest in London of former Chilean dictator Augusto Pinochet, Nobel Prize laureate Rigoberta Menchú and a group of Spanish and Guatemalan victims filed a criminal case in the Spanish National Court (SNC) against several former Guatemalan government officials, including former president Efraín Ríos Montt, who oversaw the slaughter of thousands of civilians in the 1980s (on Pinochet see Roht-Arriaza 2005, and HRW, "Pinochet"; on Guatemalan genocide see Schirmer 2000 and Comisión para el Esclaracimiento Histórico 1999). Due to CJA's record of success on other Central America human rights cases, CJA attorney Almudena Bernabeu, who is licensed in Spain, was asked to join the complaint as a private prosecutor in 2004.

In a groundbreaking decision, on September 26, 2005, the Spanish Constitutional Court, the country's highest judicial body, reversed a lower court decision and held that Spain can, in fact, exercise universal jurisdiction over crimes of international importance, including genocide (Sala Segunda del Tribunal Constitucional 2005). Following this ruling, investigating judge Santiago Pedraz, accompanied by Ms. Bernabeu, traveled to Guatemala to take testimony from the defendants located there under the auspices of a rogatory commission. Upon their arrival, lawyers for the defendants filed several appeals forcing the Guatemalan Constitutional Court to indefinitely suspend the proceedings. In response, Judge Pedraz issued arrest warrants for all eight defendants and an order to freeze their assets (Llorca 2006).

3. Criminal Prosecution in the United States

The US government has the capacity to criminally prosecute some human rights abusers. In 1994, Congress passed a statute designed to implement some of the United States' obligations under the Convention Against Torture (18 USC § 2340A). The law criminalizes torture committed outside the United States if the perpetrator is a national of the United States or is physically present in the United States. However, the US Attorneys' Manual only permits prosecutions that are authorized by the Assistant Attorney General of the Criminal Division at the Department of Justice rather than an individual US Attorney (United States Attorneys' Manual, section 9–2.136). Despite the presence of hundreds of torturers in the United States, prior to 2006 the Department of Justice had never indicted anyone under this statute.

Criminal statutes also permit prosecution of perpetrators found in the United States for genocide and war crimes, but these laws are limited. War crimes charges may be brought only when the perpetrator or the victim "is a member of the Armed Forces of the United States or a national of the United States" (18 USC. § 2441). Similarly, genocide is criminally punishable only when "the offense is committed within the United States; or the alleged offender is a national of the United States" (18 USC. § 1091). The US Department of Justice has never filed charges under these laws.

CJA has contacted the Department of Justice and the Immigration and Naturalization Service (now the Bureau of Immigration and Customs Enforcement) regarding the presence of various human rights abusers in the United States, including known Peruvian torturer Tomás Ricardo Anderson Kohatsu. In March

2000, in response to CJA's request, the FBI detained Anderson Kohatsu in the Houston airport. However, in a dubious decision, the State Department intervened and asserted that Anderson Kohatsu had diplomatic immunity (DeYoung and Adams 2000). He was released, and he immediately returned to Peru.

In part due to encouragement by CJA, the US government filed its first ever torture prosecution in 2006 against Chuckie Taylor, the son of Charles Taylor and the former head of the Liberia's brutal Anti-Terrorism Unit. (*US v. Belfast*, 06-20758-CR-ALTONAGA (S.D.Fla)). The case is set to go to trial in 2008.

4. Deportation

In analyzing opportunities to hold perpetrators responsible, CJA also considers whether a deportation action brought by the US government will provide a possibility for accountability. CJA maintains a policy of analyzing potential deportations on a case-by-case basis and supporting removal when there is a strong possibility that they will be criminally prosecuted in their home countries under conditions assuring the defendant's due process rights. Without the potential for prosecution, deportation may actually help perpetuate the impunity that many perpetrators enjoy.

Two defendants in CJA cases, Carl Dorélien and Juan López Grijalba, have been deported from the United States. Dorélien was deported independently of CJA's case (*Dorélien v. Ashcroft* 2003). More deportations are foreseeable due to the Intelligence Reform Act of 2004. This law allows deportation of aliens who have "committed, ordered, incited, assisted, or otherwise participated in the commission of" genocide, torture or extrajudicial killing (Intelligence Reform and Terrorism Prevention Act of 2004, Public Law No. 108–458).

López Grijalba, the former chief of military intelligence in Honduras and a leader of the infamous Battalion 316 death squad, was arrested by the then-named Immigration and Naturalization Service in April 2002. CJA filed a case against López Grijalba shortly thereafter on behalf of two torture survivors and the relatives of two men who disappeared in Honduras in the early 1980s. In the immigration proceedings, INS argued that López Grijalba was ineligible for the Temporary Protected Status that legalized his presence in the United States because he had been responsible for persecution in Honduras. López Grijalba put on a vigorous defense, claiming that he had not been a persecutor. CJA worked very closely with immigration authorities and provided critical evidence for the case. CJA facilitated the testimony of five witnesses, three of whom were cited by the Immigration Judge in his written opinion holding that López Grijalba was, in fact, a persecutor. One of CJA's witnesses testified that López Grijalba was present at a raid which resulted in the torture of the witness and two of CJA's clients.

López Grijalba was deported to Honduras in October 2004 (Morris 2004). In his absence, CJA and co-counsel Carlton Fields presented evidence of López Grijalba's responsibility for torture and disappearances before a federal court in Miami. Judge Joan Lenard found López Grijalba responsible for the abuses in the case and issued a default judgment against him for $47 million. Even prior to his removal CJA maintained close communications with the Honduran Special Prosecutor for Human Rights to lay the groundwork for his prosecution. He now faces possible criminal charges in Honduras based on the US judgment and the evidence developed by CJA linking him directly to the torture and disappearances in the case (Isaula 2006a, Isaula 2006b). His indictment would be the first serious attempt to prosecute a senior military official in Honduras for human rights violations.

5. Extradition

CJA seeks to contribute to transnational justice by working to get perpetrators extradited from the United States to other countries, whether their home nations or third countries, for criminal prosecution. Through its extensive contacts, especially in Latin America, CJA is often well-positioned to assist in this effort. In the Guatemala case in Spain, CJA has pursued the arrest of the one defendant known to be outside Guatemala. After more than a year of searching, investigators working with CJA located Donaldo Alvarez Ruiz, the Minister of Defense from 1976 to 1982, in Mexico. Alvarez Ruiz lived in Miami in the 1980s, but left the United States in February 1999 after the US Embassy in Guatemala revoked his visa in response to his indictment in Spain. Although an arrest warrant and extradition request were properly issued for his arrest by the Spanish authorities, Mexican officials allowed Alvarez Ruiz to escape (Cevellos 2004).

CJA also played a key role in the arrest of Vittorio Orvieto Teplinzky, a Chilean doctor alleged to have treated tortured prisoners during the Pinochet regime to ensure that they did not die in order that their torture could continue. CJA learned that he was a permanent resident of the United States living in the Miami area and contacted a Chilean judge who then requested that INTERPOL transmit an international arrest warrant and issue a special alert. When Orvieto attempted to return to Chile using an Egyptian passport, Chilean police took him into custody based on the special INTERPOL alert (Chardy and Steinback 2005).

6. Prosecutions in Home Countries

Criminal prosecution in a perpetrator's home country is often considered the preferred mechanism for accountability rather than proceedings elsewhere based on universal jurisdiction (Roht-Arriaza 2005, 193–196). The TVPA requires US courts to "decline to hear a claim … if the claimant has not exhausted adequate and available remedies in the place in which the conduct giving rise to the claim occurred" (28 USC § 1350 note § 2(b)). However, in many situations, the domestic courts of countries where widespread abuses occur are not willing to prosecute human rights violators. When a country does not have "adequate and available" remedies, the case may be able to go forward in the United States (see the discussion in section D(5) of this chapter). As a result, CJA continues to pursue cases that will have a broad impact in the countries at issue and will be likely to contribute to a change in those countries that will lead to domestic prosecutions.

This situation is most acute in El Salvador. The three El Salvadoran cases CJA has pursued (as described previously) were covered extensively in the Salvadoran media, and the combination of all three cases has drawn the attention and wrath of former Salvadoran officers (Miranda 2004, Fagoaga 2005). Current Minister of Defense Otto Romero lashed out at the human rights efforts in the United States:

> CJA does not understand our situation. We defended the democratic system that they are using to do these trials. These people are trying to take money from people who do not have money. Thanks to Carranza, García and Vides Casanova we are not communists in this country (Fagoaga 2005).

Salvadoran President Tony Saca expressed similar distaste for CJA's case against Carranza:

> We lived through a war and a campaign that tried to take power through the armed route, that did not respect human rights, and that's why there were Armed Forces, to defend our sovereignty. That is why I hope that Colonel Carranza does well, I wish him much success, because he is a hero of our country's democracy (Grégori 2004).

While Salvadoran military and government officials disagreed with the pursuit of CJA's cases, religious authorities and human rights defenders were much more receptive. Key representatives of the Catholic Church, the head of the Lutheran Church and the Human Rights Prosecutor called for the repeal of the country's blanket amnesty law and a reopening of the investigation into Archbishop Romero's assassination (Cordova 2004, Fuentes and Zometa 2003). Father José Maria Tojeira, President of the Universidad Centroamericana "José Simeon Cañas" (UCA), explained:

> These Salvadorans brought their case in the US not to hurt El Salvador, not for propaganda, but to help construct an El Salvador that is based on the truth. To fail to pursue the commanders endangers the rule of law and the foundation of our society.

The current Archbishop of San Salvador stated that the *Saravia* case should help the beatification process underway to consider Archbishop Romero for sainthood (Buncombe 2004).

CJA's cases involving Haiti have the potential to have an impact similar to its work in the Honduras (see above sections B(1)(f) and (g)). In 2000, prior to the filing of CJA's cases against Toto Constant and Carl Dorélien, the government of Haitian president Rene Preval initiated a landmark prosecution of military and paramilitary leaders for their involvement in the 1994 Raboteau massacre. The trial resulted in convictions of many of the defendants, including *in absentia* convictions of some who were not present, like Dorélien and Constant (Tribunal de Premier Instance des Gonaives 2000). While the civil compensation component of the case has been enforced against Dorélien's assets in Florida, the criminal convictions remain in effect in Haiti.

Although Dorélien is still on the lam, Rene Preval was elected president for the second time in 2006. Hope remains high that his government will carry out the Raboteau judgment and arrest the top perpetrators who are now on the loose. According to the Florida state court, the Raboteau judgment remains in force against those defendants who were convicted *in absentia*, despite attempts by Dorélien to have his indictment invalidated. CJA will also deliver its judgment and evidence against Toto Constant to the Preval government. CJA hopes that the US judgment will provide the impetus for the Haitian government to seek Constant's extradition or deportation for future prosecution in Haiti after he serves any criminal sentence in the United States on the mortgage fraud charges.

C.   Finding and Exposing New Information about Abuses

One of the major advantages to bringing human rights cases in the form of civil lawsuits in the United States is the broad discovery power that parties possess in US courts. Discovery rules are designed to bring as much evidence as possible to light prior to trial. Parties have the largely unfettered ability to submit to other parties written questions and requests for production of documents. Plaintiffs and defendants alike can be forced to testify in depositions. The testimony is under oath and subject to the penalty of perjury. Although human rights cases involve criminal acts, when they are brought under the ATCA and TVPA they benefit from the truth-finding mechanisms inherent in civil jurisprudence, and defendants do not necessarily benefit from some of the constitutional protections they would enjoy in criminal cases.

1.   Defendant Testimony and Admissions

Six perpetrators have testified in CJA's cases, leading to admissions that had either not been made before or were critical in CJA's later efforts to prove the defendants' responsibility. Nicolás Carranza, who testified in a deposition and at trial, made several admissions about allegations that had always been denied by Salvadoran officials. The most important of these admissions concerned Carranza's relationship with the CIA. In a pre-trial deposition, Carranza acknowledged under oath that he received money from the CIA during his career. He had previously denied such accusations when they surfaced in 1984 (Taubman 1984; Drudge 1984). At trial, former US Ambassador to El Salvador Robert White testified that Carranza was a paid informant for the CIA during the time he was Vice-Minister of Defense and a member of the High Command in 1980. At that time White asked the CIA station chief in El Salvador to remove Carranza from the CIA payroll because of his deplorable human rights record but no action was ever taken. Later in the trial, Carranza confessed that he had been receiving money from the US government since 1965.

  Another of Carranza's important admissions was that ANTEL, El Salvador's national telecommunications company, regularly tapped the phones of Salvadoran citizens. Carranza acknowledged that when he was president of ANTEL from 1981–2, he and the President of the Republic received daily reports about intercepted conversations. Carranza further testified that José Guillermo García, as Minister of Defense in 1980, controlled the repressive Security Forces directly, subverting the normal, legal chain of command. García had already been found liable for torture in 2002 (see above, section B(1)(a)). Finally, Carranza testified that he assisted the infamous general José Alberto Medrano with the establishment of ORDEN, a paramilitary and vigilante group responsible for numerous human rights violations in the 1960s and 1970s.

In several other CJA cases, defendants have made important admissions that helped establish their responsibility for abuses. Armando Fernández-Larios, who was found liable for the killing of Winston Cabello as part of Pinochet's Caravan of Death, testified that he might have been the only member of the Caravan to carry a *corvo*, a short, curved knife. Another Chilean officer testified that that the inner curve of the *corvo* can easily slit a person's throat. This testimony, combined with that of the doctor who examined the corpse of Winston Cabello and saw a gash that ran from the ear to the throat, helped to prove that Fernández-Larios was responsible for the murder.

In the *Lopez Grijalba* case, CJA alleged that Manfredo Velásquez, the brother of plaintiff Zenaida Velásquez, had disappeared and was killed by the DNI police force in 1981. In his deposition, López Grijalba testified that when he was chief of the DNI, one of his subordinates was a man named José Isaias Vilorio. In a prior case before the Inter-American Court of Human Rights, a Honduran officer had testified that Isaias Vilorio was one of the DNI agents who had been involved in the abduction of Velásquez (Inter-American Court of Human Rights 1988, ¶ 113). Thus, López Grijalba's own testimony provided a key link showing that he was the commander of the troops responsible for Velásquez's disappearance.

Although Alvaro Saravia did not testify in the case against him, CJA's judgment led to Saravia's public admission that he was involved in the assassination of Archbishop Romero. On the 26th anniversary of Romero's murder, Miami's *El Nuevo Herald* newspaper published an article in which Saravia admitted his role in the killing and asked forgiveness from the Catholic Church (Reyes 2006a). During those 26 years, Saravia had never spoken publicly about his involvement in the assassination. In the article, Saravia stated that he has been living in hiding in Central America because, in September 2004, he read a newspaper article about CJA's verdict against him (Reyes 2006b). According to *El Nuevo Herald*, "Although [Saravia] does not admit it, it is clear that he feels beset by a phenomenon that hangs in the air – being closed in on by a discrete legion of people uncovering injustices who are dedicated to hunting down torturers, violators of human rights and war criminals to the farthest corners of the earth" (Reyes 2006b). Saravia said that he would meet with the Archbishop of San Salvador and ask for forgiveness (Reyes 2006a). He admitted that he knows the identity of the actual assassin who shot Romero, and that many other important people were involved in the murder, including people who financed the operation (Reyes 2006b).

2. *Uncovering Evidence and Witnesses*

CJA's civil cases often lead to the discovery of new evidence and witnesses. Although torture survivors can testify about the abuses they suffered, there are often few witnesses to murders and disappearances, and those that exist were either involved in the killing or are too afraid to come forward. In cases involving extrajudicial killings, CJA must link the defendants to the murders just as a prosecutor would do in a criminal probe. Although CJA works closely with very capable private investigators, much of the investigation is carried out by CJA's own attorneys. In-country field work has been carried out by CJA lawyers in at least 12 countries, including Ethiopia, Somalia, El Salvador, Honduras, Haiti, Guatemala, Peru and Kuwait.

CJA has met with numerous witnesses whose recollections had never before been made public. Julio Vásquez was an eyewitness to the raid in Tegucigalpa, Honduras in July 1982 in which CJA clients Oscar and Gloria Reyes were abducted. Vásquez himself was detained during the raid and tortured by the military. He is also the only person who has publicly testified that López Grijalba was present at the raid and gave orders to soldiers. Vásquez's testimony was cited by the Immigration Judge in his ruling ordering López Grijalba deported from the United States. Only through an intensive search was CJA able to locate Vásquez, who had been in hiding outside of Honduras at the time CJA made contact with him. Today he and his family live in safety.

A similar situation arose with respect to another Honduran witness, Leopoldo Aguilar. He previously provided testimony in 1988 before the Inter-American Court of Human Rights in a case brought by Zenaida Velásquez. In that case he testified that while he was in a DNI detention center in 1981 he spoke with Manfredo Velásquez (Inter-American Court of Human Rights 1988 ¶ 115). He is the only known person, other than DNI agents themselves, who had contact with Velásquez while in custody. By utilizing nearly every member of an extensive Honduran network, CJA eventually found Aguilar and secured his testimony for its case.

The case against Armando Fernández-Larios was built almost entirely on the testimony of Chileans who had never spoken publicly about the events they observed. Through several trips to Chile, CJA client Zita Cabello managed to secure their agreement to testify under oath in depositions. They included Victor Bravo, the military doctor who was forced to examine the bodies of Winston Cabello and twelve other prisoners murdered with him; Juan Morales, a colonel in the Chilean military who witnessed Fernández-Larios beating a prisoner and putting checkmarks on a list of detainees, and who was ordered to drive the dump truck containing the corpses to a mass grave and to take fingerprints of the dead men; Leonardo Meza, who was ordered by the military to help move the thirteen bodies from the truck into the mass grave; and Enrique Vidal, a lieutenant in the Chilean Army, who saw Fernández-Larios carrying a flail with a spiked steel ball attached and heard him say he was going to use it to "caress the little pigeons," in reference to the prisoners.

CJA undertook an equally dramatic investigation to find an eyewitness to the assassination of Archbishop Romero in El Salvador. Although several people were inside the church where Romero was killed, only one person was a witness to the shooter firing the bullet: Amado Antonio Garay. In 1987 Garay testified before a judge in El Salvador about the assassination and then disappeared. In a dubious and politically-motivated decision, the Salvadoran Supreme Court eventually ruled that Garay's testimony was unreliable because it had been given several years after the assassination. CJA searched for nearly three years for Garay, who had served as Alvaro Saravia's personal driver. Finally, CJA obtained information about Garay's hometown. During a visit to the town, CJA learned that Garay was in the Witness Security Program in the United States.[8] After another long wait and several

---

8   How Garay ended up in the Witness Security Program in the United States is not entirely clear. El Salvador's president at the time of Garay's testimony in 1987 was Napoleon Duarte, a Christian Democrat who had defeated the ARENA party's founder, Roberto D'Aubuisson, in the 1984 elections. In 1987, Duarte – who was strongly backed by the US

conversations with the Witness Security Program, one of the attorneys on the legal team received a phone call from Garay. Eventually Garay agreed to provide testimony in the case. He testified that Saravia had ordered him to drive a man and follow his directions, that they arrived at a church where the man shot Romero, that the man reported back to Saravia after the shooting, and that several days later Saravia told death squad leader Roberto D'Aubuisson that the mission had been completed. Thus, Garay's testimony was the key link between Saravia and the assassination.

As a result of this case, Saravia himself finally admitted his responsibility in the assassination and stated that he is prepared to disclose the names of others who were involved (see the foregoing discussion in section C(1)).

D. Developing US Law

CJA's civil lawsuits have been at the center of the development of US law on several issues under the ATCA and TVPA. These topics include accomplice liability (conspiracy, aiding and abetting), command and superior responsibility, statute of limitations, exhaustion of remedies, state action and crimes against humanity.

1. Accomplice Liability

In the case against Fernández-Larios, the District Court ruled that the ATCA and TVPA permit suits to proceed against defendants alleged to have conspired with or aided and abetted those who were the hands-on perpetrators of human rights abuses (*Cabello v. Fernandez-Larios* 2002). In 2005, the 11th Circuit Court of Appeals upheld the jury's verdict that Fernández-Larios was responsible for Winston Cabello's killing as an aider and abettor and a co-conspirator (*Cabello v. Fernandez-Larios* 2005). Similarly, the District Court in *Saravia* held that the ATCA and TVPA encompass liability for conspiracy and aiding and abetting (*Doe v. Saravia*). The court stated that both domestic and international law have long recognized theories of accomplice liability. The court then found Alvaro Saravia liable as a co-conspirator, as an aider and abettor, and also as a directly liable participant, in the assassination of Archbishop Romero. The decisions in both cases, and in *Mehinovic*, have been cited widely in judicial opinions, particularly in lawsuits against corporations (*Mujica v. Occidental Petroleum Corp.*; *In re Agent Orange*).

---

government – was facing the prospect of legislative elections in 1988, which the Christian Democrats lost badly to ARENA, and another presidential election in 1989, which he lost to ARENA's Alfredo Cristiani (Ramirez 1988). *El Nuevo Herald* hints that Duarte publicized Garay's 1987 testimony connecting Saravia and D'Aubuisson to the assassination because of his political rivalry with D'Aubuisson (and consequently ARENA) (Reyes 2006a). Although the implication is that the US government assisted Duarte by admitting Garay to the Witness Security Program after his testimony, the author cannot find any concrete evidence at this time to confirm such an arrangement.

2. Command and Superior Responsibility

CJA's jury verdict against Generals García and Vides Casanova in 2002 was one of the first in the United States based on the law of command responsibility. This doctrine holds commanders legally responsible for a human rights violation when (1) there is a superior-subordinate relationship between the commander and the perpetrator of the crime; (2) the commander knew or should have known, owing to the circumstances at the time, that his subordinates had committed, were committing, or planned to commit abuses; and (3) the commander failed to prevent the commission of the crimes, or failed to punish the subordinates after the commission of the crimes (*Ford v. Garcia*).

The law of command responsibility has a long history in US and international law (Van Schaack 2003). It was used after World War II in the trials of German and Japanese officials (Van Schaack 2003). The US Supreme Court upheld the conviction of Japanese General Tomoyuki Yamashita based on his failure to prevent the atrocities committed by his subordinates in the Philippines (*In re Yamashita*). In so doing, the court held that "the law of war presupposes that its violation is to be avoided through the control of the operations of war by commanders who are to some extent responsible for their subordinates" (*In re Yamashita*). More recently, the international criminal tribunals for Rwanda and the former Yugoslavia, as well as the International Criminal Court, have incorporated the law of command responsibility into their statutes (UN Doc. S/25704 1993, Article 6(3); UN Doc. S/Res/955 1994; and UN Doc. A/CONF.183/9 1998).

CJA reinforced the validity of the law of command responsibility with successful verdicts against Nicolás Carranza and Carl Dorélien. CJA also received a favorable judgment against Liu Qi, the former Mayor of Beijing, for his role in overseeing the torture of Falun Gong practitioners. In 2004, the District Court for the Northern District of California issued a ruling holding Liu liable for torture as a civilian superior with authority over the police who had abused CJA's clients (*Doe v. Liu Qi*). Applying the test for military command responsibility to Liu as a civilian superior, the court found that Liu knew or should have known that the Beijing police were committing abuses and failed to prevent the abuses or punish those responsible (*Doe v. Liu Qi*).

3. Crimes Against Humanity

A crime against humanity is "one of a number of defined acts when committed as part of a widespread or systematic attack directed against any civilian population, with knowledge of the attack" (*Doe v. Saravia*). Murder and torture are two of the enumerated acts. Due to the difficulties of proving this claim, few cases in US courts have alleged crimes against humanity. CJA has made a priority of proving crimes against humanity in its cases because the claim puts the plaintiffs' individual claims in the wider context of large scale abuses. The 2002 judgment in *Mehinovic* was one of the first published decisions to hold a perpetrator liable for crimes against humanity (*Mehinovic v. Vuckovic*). Two years later, CJA won its trial against Armando Fernández-Larios. The verdict in that case represents the first jury verdict in the United States holding a defendant liable for crimes against humanity in a contested case. Another key aspect of the verdict is that it reflected a judgment by the jury that a single murder is sufficient to qualify as a crime against humanity, so long as it took place in the context of a widespread or systematic attack on a civilian population.

This important precedent was reinforced a year later by the judgment against Alvaro Saravia. The *Saravia* court also held that a single murder – that of Archbishop Romero – was a crime against humanity (*Doe v. Saravia*). The judgment against Saravia was of special importance because it was issued after the Supreme Court's decision in *Sosa v. Alvarez-Machain* and supported the notion that a single act can constitute a crime against humanity after *Sosa*.

The jury verdict against Nicolás Carranza in 2005 was the first in the United States against a commander for crimes against humanity. The *Carranza* jury found that the torture of Daniel Alvarado and the assassination of Manuel Franco, one of six pro-democracy opposition leaders of the Frente Democrático Revolucionario (FDR), took place in the context of a widespread or systematic attack on the civilian population of El Salvador.

4. Statute of Limitations

The TVPA requires that lawsuits be brought within ten years after the abuses at issue occurred (28 USC § 1350 note §2(c)). Courts have unanimously applied this requirement to the ATCA (*Cabello v. Fernandez-Larios* 2001). However, the start of the ten-year clock is often postponed under the doctrine of equitable tolling, allowing plaintiffs to file cases even after ten years have passed. Such grounds for tolling have included the defendant's absence from the United States and fear of reprisal by plaintiffs or witnesses (*Hilao v. Estate of Marcos* 1996).

In 2005 and 2006, the 11th Circuit issued three important decisions tolling the statutes of limitations in CJA's cases, upholding jury verdicts in two instances and overturning a lower court's dismissal in the third. In 2005, two weeks after initially ruling against CJA in its case against Generals García and Vides Casanova – a ruling that was later vacated[9] – the 11th Circuit ruled that the filing of the suit against Fernández-Larios was timely even though it came 26 years after the death of Winston Cabello (*Cabello v. Fernandez-Larios* 2005). The court held that equitable tolling is appropriate only where there are "extraordinary circumstances." Such circumstances may be demonstrated where the defendant misleads the plaintiff or when the plaintiff has no reasonable way of discovering the wrong perpetrated against her. Because the Chilean government actively concealed the facts about Winston Cabello's death, including sending three conflicting death certificates to the family, until his body was

---

9   In February 2005 the 11th Circuit initially overturned the jury verdict against García and Vides Casanova (*Romagoza Arce v. Garcia* 2005). In that decision, the court ruled that the statute of limitations would not be tolled during the time the defendants were absent from the US nor during the duration of El Salvador's civil war. However, in June 2005, the 11th Circuit issued a letter acknowledging factual errors in its prior ruling and asking the parties to submit briefs concerning whether the case against Vides Casanova was in fact filed in a timely manner. In August 2005, the 11th Circuit vacated its prior ruling which had overturned the verdict. Then, on January 5, 2006, the 11th Circuit issued a new ruling tolling the statute of limitations and upholding the jury verdict in its entirety (*Romagoza Arce v. Garcia* 2006).

finally exhumed in 1990, the court tolled the statute of limitations until that date and found the filing of the case in 1999 timely.

In December 2005, the 11th Circuit again ruled in CJA's favor in *Jean v. Dorelien*. The court first held that the statute of limitations must be tolled while a defendant is outside the United States. Then, applying the "extraordinary circumstances" test, the court found that the "pattern and practice of torture, mass murder, intimidation and reprisals against perceived opponents of the government during the military regime in Haiti" constituted sufficient circumstances to toll the statute of limitations until Dorélien left his position in the military. Importantly, the court noted that "every court that has considered the question of whether a civil war and a repressive authoritarian regime constitute 'extraordinary circumstances' which toll the statutes of limitations of the ATCA and TVPA has answered in the affirmative."

Lastly, in January 2006, the 11th Circuit held that the filing of *Romagoza Arce v. Garcia* was also timely (*Romagoza Arce v. Garcia* 2006). As in *Dorelien*, the court affirmed that Congress intended for the statute of limitations to be tolled while defendants are outside the United States. The court also held that "exceptional circumstances" allowed for the tolling of the statute of limitations until the end of the civil war in El Salvador in 1992:

> Justice may also require tolling where both the plaintiff and the defendant reside in the United States but where the situation in the home state nonetheless remains such that the fair administration of justice would be impossible, even in United States courts. Absent regime change, those in power may wish to protect their former leaders against charges of human rights abuses. The quest for domestic and international legitimacy and power may provide regimes with the incentive to intimidate witnesses, to suppress evidence, and to commit additional human rights abuses against those who speak out against the regime. Such circumstances exemplify "extraordinary circumstances" and may require equitable tolling so long as the perpetrating regime remains in power.

The 11th Circuit's decision follows the rulings of two other courts that had applied equitable tolling to CJA's other El Salvador cases. In *Carranza*, although most of the abuses in that case occurred in 1980 – 23 years before the case was filed – the court tolled the statute of limitations until March 1994 when the first elections were held after the civil war (*Chavez v. Carranza*). Importantly, the court found that a fear of reprisal against the plaintiffs' families in El Salvador, even when the plaintiffs were no longer in El Salvador, constituted "extraordinary circumstances" that warrant equitable tolling. In *Saravia*, due to the extreme danger the plaintiff faced as a result of the high profile nature of the case, the court tolled the statute of limitations through the date of filing of the complaint in 2003 (*Doe v. Saravia*).

5.   *Exhaustion of Remedies*

Plaintiffs are required by the TVPA to exhaust "adequate and available remedies" in the country where the abuses took place (28 USC.. § 1350 note §2(b)). That is, plaintiffs are not required to pursue legal options when they are "unobtainable, ineffective, inadequate, or obviously futile" (*Doe v. Saravia*). As on the issue of statute of limitations, CJA has obtained favorable rulings on exhaustion in several cases. In

Dorelien, the 11th Circuit found as a preliminary matter that the TVPA's exhaustion requirement does not apply to the ATCA. Also, the court held that exhaustion is an affirmative defense under the TVPA, so the defendant has the burden of proof. The district court had dismissed the claims of CJA's client, reasoning that her participation in the Raboteau trial in Haiti showed that she had remedies available to her there. However, the 11th Circuit said that the district court improperly overlooked the fact that the Haitian government that had brought the case had since been overthrown by some of the very same people who had been prosecuted in that trial, and that Dorélien was let out of jail and is now living freely in Haiti.

At the district court level, CJA has also obtained favorable rulings regarding exhaustion of local remedies in El Salvador. In *Saravia*, in particular, the court conducted an extensive analysis of the lack of legal options available to the plaintiff in El Salvador and found that, due to danger and the preclusive effect of the country's sweeping amnesty law, there were no adequate and available remedies to be exhausted. The *Carranza* court similarly cited the amnesty law as evidence that there are not adequate or available remedies in El Salvador.

6. State Action

Under the TVPA, plaintiffs asserting claims for torture or extrajudicial killing must show that the defendant acted "under actual or apparent authority, or color of law of any foreign nation" (28 USC § 1350 note §2(a)). This is commonly known as the "state action" requirement. In many of CJA's cases, this requirement is easily met because the defendants were active members of the military at the time they committed the abuses at issue. However, some of CJA's cases have expanded the scope of what is considered state action to include abuses committed by those who were not themselves government officials.

Alvaro Saravia was no longer a member of the Salvadoran military at the time he organized the Romero assassination. Similarly, Roberto D'Aubuisson had also left military service when he masterminded the killing. Nonetheless, the court found that Saravia acted with the apparent authority and under color of law of the Salvadoran government (*Doe v. Saravia*). The court offered two tests for determining state action: if the defendant "acts together with state officials" or "acts with significant state aid," or if there is a "substantial degree of cooperative action" between the defendant and the government.[10] In ruling that Saravia's actions met those tests, the court cited the fact that the Salvadoran death squads were often made up of active members of the military, that the death squads frequently carried out joint operations with the Armed Forces, and that the National Police, rather than investigating the Romero assassination, contributed to the cover-up and tried to murder the judge assigned to the case.

Whereas *Saravia* examined the state action requirement in terms of cooperation with a legally constituted government, *Mehinovic* dealt with the issue of what constitutes

---

10 *Doe v. Constant* implicates similar issues, in that Constant was a non-governmental actor as the head of a paramilitary group, but he worked very closely with the Haitian government. See the previous discussion in section B(1)(f).

a "foreign nation" under the TVPA. Vuckovic was a soldier in the military forces of *Republika Srpska*, the self-proclaimed Serb republic in Bosnia during the civil war. The court found that *Republika Srpska* possessed *de facto* governmental authority and therefore met the definition of a "foreign nation" under the TVPA (*Mehinovic v. Vuckovic*). Once the court made that determination, it was clear that Vuckovic, as a member of the military forces of *Republika Srpska,* acted under color of law.

7.   Enforcement of Subpoenas

In June 2006, the D.C. Circuit Court of Appeals ruled in CJA's favor that the US government is required to comply with subpoenas for documents in private lawsuits even when the government is a third party not involved in the case. In *Yousuf v. Samantar*, CJA's lawsuit against Mohamed Ali Samantar, who served as Prime Minister and Defense Minister of Somalia during the 1980s, the court rejected the US government's claim that it is not bound by the provisions of Federal Rule of Civil Procedure 45 governing the enforcement of subpoenas. The government argued that it is not a "person" under Rule 45 and did not have to comply with the subpoena, but the D.C. Circuit strongly disagreed with this reading of the rule. The court stated that the drafters of the rule on subpoenas "underestimated the creativity of the United States" when they concluded that the rule was "so simple that it did not need any discussion." The court concluded, "That creativity notwithstanding, we hold the United States is a 'person' within the meaning of Rule 45 – as it has been held to be under every Rule thus far litigated."

E.   Conclusion

CJA continues to pursue a wide range of activities designed to make an impact in pursuing and punishing human rights abusers in the United States and abroad. In civil cases under the ATCA and TVPA, CJA has developed domestic case law and won several important victories. CJA has also branched out beyond the world of civil litigation to undertake and assist in criminal prosecutions in Spain, deportations, extraditions, and efforts to facilitate prosecutions in countries where abuses occur. Through these various actions, CJA seeks to impose a measure of accountability on human rights abusers and help bring an end to impunity.

Works Cited

Amnesty International, *Universal Jurisdiction Cases* http://web.amnesty.org/pages/ uj-cases-eng.

Arax, M. (2004), "El Salvador Slaying Case to Open in Fresno," *Los Angeles Times*, 24 August B1.

Bell, B. and Danticat, E. (2001), *Walking on Fire: Haitian Women's Stories of Survival and Resistance*, Ithaca: Cornell University Press.

Bradley, Curtis A. (2002), "The Alien Tort Statute and Article III," *Virginia Journal of International Law*, 42, 587–648.

Buncombe, A. (2004), "The archbishop, the death squad and the 24-year wait for justice," *The Independent*, 24 August.

Cevallos, D. (2004), "Net Closes Around Ex-Torturer in Mexico," *Inter Press Service News Agency*, 13 December.

Chardy, A. (2005), "Rights-Abuse Suspect Targeted for Deportation," *The Miami Herald*, 5 January 6A.

Chardy, A and Steinback, R.L. (2005), "Torture suspect is arrested in Chile," *The Miami Herald*, 9 April 4B.

Commission Nationale de Vérité et de Justice (1995), *Si M Pa Rele* http://www.haiti.org/truth/table.htm.

Commission on the Truth for El Salvador (1993), *From Madness to Hope: the 12-year war in El Salvador: Report of the Commission on the Truth for El Salvador* http://www.usip.org/library/tc/doc/reports/el_salvador/tc_es_03151993_toc.html.

Comisión para el Esclaracimiento Histórico (1999), *Memoria del Silencio* http://shr.aaas.org/guatemala/ceh/mds/spanish.

Constable, P. and Venezuela, A. (1993), *A Nation of Enemies: Chile Under Pinochet*, New York: W.W. Norton & Company.

Convention against Torture and Other Cruel, Inhuman or Degrading Treatment or Punishment (1984), S. Treaty Doc. No. 100–20, 1465 U.N.T.S. 85.

Cordova, R. (2004), "Tutela de Arzobispado pide derogar Ley de Amnistía," *Diario Co Latino*, 7 September.

Dada, C. (2005), "Álvaro Saravia: El primer condenado," *elfaro.net*, April 4.

Daniel, T. and Nesmith, S.A. (2004), "Abusers Back in the Streets," *The Miami Herald*, 15 March 11A.

DeYoung, K. and Adams, L. (2000), "US Frees Accused Torturer; Human Rights Groups Decry Ruling on Peruvian," *The Washington Post*, 11 March A1.

Dinges, J. (2005), *The Condor Years: How Pinochet and His Allies Brought Terrorism to Three Continents*, New York: New Press.

Dodge, William S. (1996), "The Historical Origins of the Alien Tort Statute: A Response to the 'Originalists'," *Hastings International and Comparative Law Review*, 19, 221–258.

Dorélien, C. (2006), "Lettre de Carl Dorélien a M. Max Chauvet," *Agence Haitien de Presse*, 21 July.

Drudge, M.W. (1984), "Police Chief Denies Charges He Worked With CIA," *United Press International*, 22 March.

Fagoaga, C.C. (2005), "Presidente Saca defiende a ex viceministro Carranza," *elfaro.net*, 14 November.

Fuentes, L. and Zometa, J. (2003), "Critican demanda por caso Romero," *La Prensa Gráfica*, 27 September.

Hays, T. (2006), "Ex-Haitian strongman gets $50,000 bail in Long Island case," *The Associated Press*, 7 July.

Human Rights Watch, *The Pinochet Precedent* http://www.hrw.org/campaigns/chile98/index.html.

Geneva Convention Relative to the Protection of Civilian Persons in Time of War (1949), 6 UST 3516, 75 UNTS 287.

Grann, D. (2001), "Giving 'The Devil' His Due," *The Atlantic*, June 54–71.

Gutman, R. (1993), *A Witness to Genocide*, London: Element Books Ltd.

Immigration and Customs Enforcement, *ICE Most Wanted Fugitive – Rafael Alvaro Saravia* (updated March 17, 2006) http://www.ice.gov/pi/investigations/wanted/rafael_saravia.htm.

Intelligence Reform and Terrorism Prevention Act of 2004, Public Law No. 108–458 (2004).

Inter-American Court of Human Rights (1988), "Judgment of July 29, 1988," *Velásquez Rodriguez Case*, Ser. C, No. 4.

International Military Tribunal (1946), *Opinion and Judgment of the International Military Tribunal for the Trial of German Major War Criminals* http://www.yale.edu/lawweb/avalon/imt/proc/judlawch.htm.

Isaula, R. (2006), "Piden proceder contra Grijalva," *El Heraldo*, 5 May 5. ("Isaula 2006a")

Isaula, R. (2006), "De visita abogada española que llevó caso contra López Grijalba," *El Tiempo*, 5 May. ("Isaula 2006b")

Kornbluh, P. (2005), *The Pinochet File: A Declassified Dossier on Atrocity and Accountability*, New York: New Press.

La Nación (2006), "Suprema da luz verde a extradición de Armando Fernández Larios," 12 July.

Ley Orgánica (1985), 6/1985, Article 23.4, de 1 de julio, del Poder Judicial < http://noticias.juridicas.com/base_datos/Admin/lo6-1985.l1t1.html>.

Llorca, J.C. (2006), "Montt Says He Was Unaware of Atrocities," *The Associated Press*, 13 July 13.

Miranda, E. (2004), "Militares en retiro respaldan a Saca," *El Diario de Hoy*, 14 Feb.

Morris, R. (2004), "Death squad suspect deported from Miami to Honduras," *Sun-Sentinel*, 22 October 3B.

Orentlicher, D.F. (2004), "Whose Justice? Reconciling Universal Jurisdiction with Democratic Principles," *Georgetown Law Journal*, 92, 1057–1134.

Ramirez, S. (1988), "Duarte says opposition seeking his ouster," *United Press International*, 25 July. ("Reyes 2006a").

Restatement (Third) of the Foreign Relations Law of the United States (1987), Philadelphia: American Law Institute.

Reyes, G. (2006), "Pide perdón el acusado del asesinato de Monseñor Romero," *El Nuevo Herald*, 24 March A1 ("Reyes 2006a").

Reyes, G. (2006), "Monseñor Romero: la verdad se abre paso," *El Nuevo Herald*, 26 March 23A ("Reyes 2006b").

Rohde, D. (1997), *Endgame: The Betrayal and Fall of Srebrenica, Europe's Worst Massacre Since World War II*, New York: Farrar Straus Giroux.

Roht-Arriaza, N. (2005), *The Pinochet Effect*, Philadelphia: University of Pennsylvania Press.

Rome Statute of the International Criminal Court, U.N. Diplomatic Conference of Plenipotentiaries on the Establishment of an International Criminal Court (1998), U.N. Doc. A/CONF.183/9.Schirmer, J. (2000), *The Guatemalan Military Project: A Violence Called Democracy*, Philadelphia: University of Pennsylvania Press.

Stanley, W. (1996), *The Protection Racket State*, Philadelphia: Temple University Press.

Statute of the International Criminal Tribunal for the Prosecution of Persons Responsible for Genocide and Other Serious Violations of International Humanitarian Law Committed in the Territory of Rwanda and Rwandan Citizens Responsible for Genocide and Other Such Violations Committed in the Territory of Neighbouring States (1994), U.N. Doc. S/Res/955.

Statute of the International Tribunal for the Prosecution of Persons Responsible for Serious Violations of International Humanitarian Law Committed in the Territory of the Former Yugoslavia Since 1991 (1993), U.N. Doc. S/25704.

Stephens, B. (2002), "Translating Filartiga: A Comparative and International Law Analysis of Domestic Remedies For International Human Rights Violations," *Yale Journal of International Law*, 27, 1–57.

Stephens, B. (2002), "Sosa v. Alvarez-Machain: 'The Door Is Still Ajar' For Human Rights Litigation in US Courts," *Brooklyn Law Review*, 70, 533–568.

Taubman, P. (1984), "Top Salvador Police Official Said To Be C.I.A. Informant," *The New York Times*, 22 March, A1.

United States Attorneys' Manual (2007), http://www.usdoj.gov/usao/eousa/foia_reading_room/usam/title9/2mcrm.htm#9-2.136.

Van Schaack, B. (2003), *Command Responsibility: The Anatomy of Proof in Romagoza v. Garcia*, U.C. Davis Law Review, 36, 1213–1260.

Verdugo, P. (2001), *Chile, Pinochet and the Caravan of Death* (Miami: North/South Center Press).

Cases Cited

Cabello v. Fernandez-Larios, 402 F.3d 1148 (11th Cir. 2005).

Cabello v. Fernandez-Larios, 205 F. Supp. 2d 1325 (S.D.Fla. 2002).

Cabello v. Fernandez-Larios, 157 F. Supp. 2d 1345 (S.D.Fla. 2001).

Chavez v. Carranza, 407 F. Supp. 2d 925 (W.D.Tenn. 2004).

Doe v. Liu Qi, 349 F. Supp. 2d 1258 (N.D.Cal. 2004).

Doe v. Saravia, 348 F. Supp. 2d 1112 (E.D.Cal. 2004).

Dorelien v. Ashcroft, 317 F.3d 1314 (11th Cir. 2003).

Ford v. Garcia, 289 F.3d 1283 (11th Cir. 2002).

Hilao v. Estate of Marcos, 103 F.3d 767 (9th Cir. 1996).

In re "Agent Orange" Product Liability Litigation, 373 F. Supp. 2d 7 (E.D.N.Y. 2005).

In re Estate of Ferdinand Marcos, Human Rts. Litig., 25 F.3d 1467 (9th Cir. 1994).

In re Yamashita, 327 US 1 (1946).

Jean v. Dorélien, 431 F.3d 776 (11th Cir. 2005).

Mehinovic v. Vuckovic, 198 F. Supp. 2d 1322 (N.D.Ga. 2002).

Mujica v. Occidental Petroleum Corp., 381 F. Supp. 2d 1164 (C.D.Cal. 2005).

Romagoza Arce v. Garcia, 434 F.3d 1254 (11th Cir. 2006).

Sala Segunda del Tribunal Constitucional (2005), 237/2005, de 26 de septiembre de 2005 http://www.tribunalconstitucional.es/Stc2005/STC2005-237.htm.

Sosa v. Alvarez-Machain, 542 US 692 (2004).

Tel-Oren v. Libyan Arab Rep., 726 F.2d 774 (D.C. Cir. 1984).

Tribunal de Premiere Instance des Gonaives (2000), *Extrait Plumitif d'Audience Criminelle du jeudi*, 16 November.

Yousuf v. Samantar, 451 F.3d 248 (D.C. Cir. 2006).

Chapter 7

Human Trafficking and Migration

Dina Francesca Haynes

Human rights are violated during periods of crisis, when people are most vulnerable and their worlds have been turned upside down. Events such as civil war, political upheaval, genocidal behaviors, extreme economic disparity, and environmental disasters trigger migration, and it is during these periods of personal or externally created chaos, that those who are already vulnerable may choose to migrate, be displaced or be forcibly relocated. Unlike displacement and forcible relocation, migration has an element of volition to it, despite the fact that the will to move may derive from such extreme necessity that one effectively has no choice. The migrating individual, perhaps in recognition of his or her inherent human dignity, determines to move on, in order to tap opportunities and resources that exist elsewhere. Both groups however, those who determine to move and those who are forced, are particularly vulnerable to certain types of human rights violations that involve exploitation of the particular kind of vulnerability created during the transitional period of migration. During this vulnerable period of physical, cultural, social, and economic relocation, when people exist in between state protection mechanisms, human rights protections become crucial, to ensure that migrating persons do not fall in between the cracks of sovereignty.

In the last twenty years, ethnic conflict and civil war across Southeastern Europe, much of Northern, West and Central Africa, and parts of Southeast Asia, exacerbated by increasing pockets of poverty in Africa, Eastern Europe, Latin America and Asia, combined with the increasing accumulation of wealth of the Northern and Western Hemispheres, has spurred massive migration from the South and East to the West and North.

Whether spurred by external geopolitical factors (war, genocide, ethnic discrimination) or local and personal factors (poverty, family crisis, the desire to improve or expand one's existence), migration is almost always a chaotic passage for the individuals undertaking it. Migrants are not only likely to be economically and emotionally vulnerable but also exist, in fact if not always in law, between state protection mechanisms. In other words, they often cannot rely on the protection of the state they have left behind, which might be unable (as a weak or failing state) or unwilling (due to state-sponsored discrimination or unwillingness to fight for the rights of someone seeking to relocate) to protect them. At the same time, they have not yet, and may not ever, procure the protection of the state in which they hope to land (UN 1951).

Once a migrant arrives in a country in which she hopes to remain, assuming she is able to enter, she may become a prospective immigrant, and is subject to that country's immigration laws, policies and practices, and societal attitudes towards migrants. Among the many laws that govern immigration, three types of claims are recognized as, and as a matter of law are handled as, human rights issues: asylum, human trafficking, and torture. Each offers a form of immigration relief recognizing, respectively, the particular need of persons who have been persecuted; persons who have been exploited during migration; and those who are likely to be tortured if returned to their home country. States create categories of immigrant status, in compliance with international law, which recognize that some types of migration should be seen and responded to through a human rights framework.

This differentiation – between those who supposedly have no volition in their movement and those who seem to have more choice in the matter – presents an incongruous picture of present day preferences in immigrants. Immigration benefits governed by a human rights framework are granted to those who are at risk of imminent physical and emotional harm, while those who are at risk of "only" economic, social, or cultural harm enjoy no such benefits. A Twenty-first Century Statue of Liberty would offer refuge in the United States to the persecuted, the exploited, the tortured, the extraordinarily skilled, and those willing to enter the low-wage workforce, but only if the refugee was careful not to mention that he was "yearning to breathe free." Today's immigration laws make it risky to acknowledge that individual agency and purpose drove the decision to move on and improve one's life. The legal fiction is that one can either be a victim or a capable person of free will, but not both.

The modern US domestic legal interpretation of these rights that derive from international human rights law prefers a simple victim story to one that is complicated by a parallel story about the desire to leave behind economic and cultural malaise. The oft-cited justification for this preference is the "fear of opening the floodgates." For its part, the United States, for instance, only wants "real victims," not "economic refugees." For this feared flood of migrants to appear, however, three preconditions would also need to be true: 1) that people everywhere want to move to the United States, and 2) that these same prospective immigrants have a desire to "be an American" so great they would rather migrate and "become Americans" than remain and contribute to the long term improvement of their countries of origin, given the choice, and 3) that they are willing to put themselves in harm's way in order to get here.

Whatever the motivation, hundreds of millions of people migrate each year (UN 2005). Most vulnerable during migration are those who are already the most disenfranchised: women, children, minorities, and people with disabilities (US DOS 2005). Human rights protections can be crucial within this sphere – in lieu of (or in spite of) sovereign protection. When governments are either incapable of or unwilling to protect their citizens, and when people exist between States, we turn to the human rights described in various international instruments, to determine what, if any, protection mechanisms may be available to them.

One of the human rights abuses inflicted on the most vulnerable during these periods of chaos is human trafficking, in which people are exploited and forced, coerced or tricked into becoming human commodities for the profit of the trafficker, in the form of sex workers, spouses for sale, domestic laborers, and indentured servants trapped in debt peonage. Adding to the indignity and rudderless state of being that comes of statelessness or "rightless[ness]," these people in motion, treated like "the scum of the earth" by States they hope to enter are also prey to traffickers looking for people just like them; rightless and devalued in fact and as a matter of law (Arendt 1966). This devalued state renders migrants perfect prey.

While the impetus to identify and fight against the phenomenon of human trafficking as a distinct crime came from human rights organizations which saw the act of trafficking for what it is, a massive violation of human rights, both domestic and international laws tackle the problem as a law enforcement matter.

What is "Trafficking in Human Beings"?

Trafficking involves the transportation, harboring or receipt of persons by means of threat, coercion, abduction or fraud, for the purpose of exploitation. The current international legal standard, from which many domestic definitions of trafficking are also derived, is the *Protocol to Prevent, Suppress and Punish Trafficking in Persons, Especially Women and Children*, a protocol to the *United Nations Convention Against Transnational Organized Crime*, commonly referred to as the Palermo Protocol (UN 2000). The Palermo Protocol defines trafficking as:

> (a) … the recruitment, transportation, transfer, harbouring or receipt of persons, by means of the threat or use of force or other forms of coercion, of abduction, of fraud, of deception, of the abuse of power or of a position of vulnerability or of the giving or receiving of payments or benefits to achieve the consent of a person having control over another person, for the purpose of exploitation (UN 2000).

According to this definition, then, a victim of human trafficking could for instance be Ahn, who was sold by her father to be the third concurrent wife of a man who in turn sold her to people who told her they would find her work and a better life outside of China. Instead, they sent her off traveling through twelve countries, confiscated her passport so that she could not flee and made her understand that since she was already significantly in debt to them for the cost they incurred by transporting her, she would work for them whenever and however they told her to, for as long as they found her useful to repay that debt. A different type of human trafficking victim could be Carlos, who paid ten thousand dollars to an international company claiming to help him secure a visa to teach in the United States, but who was then confined to a hotel room for three months upon arrival in the US and told that because there was in fact no job for him, he would have to pay them more and do what the company told him to or he would be deported. Some trafficking victims are literally taken, kidnapped, sold or enslaved. More often they are people who set off in search of a better life, an economic opportunity, an adventure, the ability to provide for their families back home, but discover that the very desire to improve their lives and the lives of their families has been turned on its head and exploited by traffickers.

The Palermo Protocol (UN 2000) was the first point at which trafficking became defined as a matter of international law, expanding upon and linking together pre-existing individual crimes such as abduction, kidnapping, forced prostitution, and slavery. Essential to the crime of trafficking is the intent to exploit and control another human being, and defining and criminalizing trafficking as a specific crime validated the fact that, as to the level of egregiousness, the whole of trafficking in human beings is greater than the sum of its parts. Trafficking in human beings is a specific and a specifically egregious crime because those who do it set out to exploit people during their most vulnerable periods, for personal profit, often in exceptionally abusive ways.

Reliable statistical information is extremely hard to find when it comes to quantifying almost any aspect of trafficking, from the number of people trafficked to the amount of money earned by traffickers; and yet, it is important to offer some statistical information in order to put the issue into perspective and demonstrate the perceived magnitude of the problem. It is presumed, for instance, that trafficking in human beings is an *extremely* lucrative business, although there is virtually no empirical data to substantiate the estimates of 5 to 10 billion dollars earned per year by traffickers (UNICEF 2002).

Statistics as to the number of persons trafficked are similarly elusive. Until 2005, statistics ranged anywhere from 700,000 to 4 million new victims worldwide per year (US DOS 2002, 2003, 2004, 2005). These statistics can not be confirmed, of course, but are based on estimates, often made by people who may have their own agenda in offering the figures. In 2005, the US Department of State offered a new estimate of 600,000 to 800,000 as the number of people trafficked across international borders annually, adding that 80 percent of victims are women and 50 percent are minors, while the US Department of Justice lowered the estimated number of persons trafficked into the United States each year to 17,500 (US DOS 2005; US DOJ 2006). The same year, the International Labor Organization estimated that, at any given time, there are 12.3 million people in the world enslaved in forms of involuntary servitude (ILO 2005).

One aspect that attracts traffickers to trafficking in human beings, as opposed to arms or drugs, for instance, is that people can be sold and resold and are typically forced to pay back their purchasers for the costs incurred in their transport and purchase, in addition to whatever they will earn within the context of the labor they are ultimately forced or coerced to perform. Again, statistical data is weak, but a study commissioned by the CIA in the mid-1990's estimated that traffickers earn about $250,000 (a quarter of a million dollars) for each woman trafficked for sex slavery (Caldwell 1997). In Austria alone, for instance, for one year (1999) an estimated 40,000 persons trafficked into Austria earned traffickers $100 million (Caldwell).

What is known is that trafficked persons originate where the conditions are ripe for exploitation: where there is structural (economic, social) pressure on the victims to migrate; where there are few educational or employment opportunities; where there is an unstable family structure (perhaps also due in part to economy, political, or social structure); and where gender/racial/caste stigma or marginalization exists. Traffickers are getting smarter and know how to target both the most vulnerable and least visible people. They understand how to exploit the fundamental desire, born of human dignity, to improve one's life. And they know how to make their fingerprints in the process virtually invisible.

Current Approaches to Combating Human Trafficking

Governments tend to approach trafficking from a law-enforcement perspective (as opposed to a victim protection or human rights perspective), and are concerned primarily with protecting borders, preventing unwanted migration and attacking organized crime and now terrorism. Because governments are founded on principles of state sovereignty, and laws are passed by governments, this approach may be natural; yet focusing on crime prevention, rather than on human rights and human protection, may actually reduce the chance of success in prosecuting traffickers. Traffickers cannot be prosecuted without proof, and proof most often comes in the form of witness testimony. Nevertheless, governments regularly fail to require victim protection or preventative programs that focus on potential victims, as a matter of law. Those laws that do contain victim protection measures generally condition that protection on the extent to which the victim will be able to assist with the prosecution of the traffickers.

Two examples of law enforcement-oriented laws combating trafficking are those adopted in the European Union and the United States. The EU harmonization process, the process by which EU countries come into relative conformity in terms of their transnational laws, produced a wholly law-enforcement motivated and sovereignty focused set of laws to address trafficking that "exhibit an almost exclusive focus on crime control" (Spijkerboer 2004) Article 8, 1(b) of the Council of Europe's Directive on trafficking, for instance, provided that only victims of human trafficking *who have shown a clear intention to cooperate* with prosecutors shall be considered for issuance of a temporary residence permit (Council of Europe 2004). Renewal of the permit is then conditioned upon the "opportunity presented by prolonging his/her stay ... for the investigations or the judicial proceedings" (Council of Europe 2004). The benefit of protecting the victims by providing immigration status is seen as only relevant to the prosecution of the traffickers, rather than as a concern for protecting the victims from further harm.

As it is the nature of governments to protect their sovereignty, the EU is exceedingly conscious of stepping on the individual sovereignty of Member States. Government and sovereignty are mutually dependent, and any government supra-structure, like the EU or even the UN Crime Commission, that is dependent on the "buy-in" and acceptance of its constituent governments will be hyper-sensitive to encroaching on state sovereignty. Nevertheless, the exclusive focus on crime control fails to consider that providing security, protection and rehabilitation to victims can also work in the fight against trafficking, by reducing the likelihood of repeat victims and increasing the incentives for victims to come forward and testify against their traffickers.

For its part, the United States adopted the Trafficking Victims Protection Act in 2000 [TVPA], which was reauthorized (and supplemented) in 2003 and again in 2005 (US Congress 2000). While also clearly a law enforcement oriented piece of legislation, aimed primarily at prevention of trafficking and prosecution of traffickers, it does contain provisions geared at protecting trafficked persons. Nevertheless, those provisions are also strictly limited in specific ways which clearly demonstrate that the primary objective is to prosecute traffickers, rather than protect the victims.

The TVPA permits trafficked persons to attempt to remain temporarily in the United States, and ultimately apply to adjust to lawful permanent resident status, with several conditions. A trafficked person can apply for a T-visa (a visa reserved for victims of trafficking) if she can establish that she was the victim of a "severe form of trafficking," and provided that she cooperate in the prosecution of her traffickers. She can then apply to adjust her status to that of lawful permanent resident if she can further establish that her removal from the United States would result in an "extreme hardship" to herself (US Congress). In practice, law enforcement officials who are in a position to certify that a victim cooperated with them, therein allowing her to apply for a T-visa, will refuse to do so, even when she provided information to them, because they – the law enforcement officials – *choose* not to launch an investigation, *choose* not to prosecute the traffickers, or worse, insist on seeing the victim herself as a criminal.

In addition to the "certification" authority given to the Department of Justice to certify that a victim is indeed a victim, the TVPA also has a reporting component, in which the US Department of State reviews the attempts of other countries to curtail trafficking. The DOS Trafficking in Persons Report [TIP Report] annually ranks countries by tiers, with those in 3rd Tier subject to economic sanctions by the United States. Fears that the rankings and attendant sanctions might be susceptible to political manipulation having to do with factors other than success with anti-trafficking initiatives appear to be well-founded. The countries placed in Tier 3 in 2004, for instance, were Burma, Cuba, United Arab Emirates, Venezuela, Ecuador, Qatar, Jamaica, Saudi Arabia, Cambodia, Kuwait, and Sudan (US DOS 2004). Of the 23 countries ranked Tier 3 in 2003, only Burma, Cuba, and North Korea were sanctioned (US DOS 2003).

Perhaps not surprising, some of the "good practices" encouraged in the TIP Report, the adoption of which could assist a foreign country in moving up to Tier 2 or Tier 1 and thus enable them to receive US aid and financial assistance, are not included in the TVPA. Furthermore, in the year 2003, the Trafficking in Persons office at the Department of State put out a "Model Law," which could be used as a guide by other countries as they drafted their anti-trafficking legislation.[1] This Model Law had substantially more of a victim protection approach to trafficking than does the TVPA itself. In other words, the right hand (the Executive branch, through the US Department of State), asks other countries to provide more than the left hand (the legislative branch, through Congress) requires of the United States.

The stark polarity in approach between the anti-trafficking legislation passed by governments and intergovernmental bodies (such as the UN Crime Commission), which are largely law enforcement oriented, and the anti-trafficking initiatives proposed by NGO's and UN agencies that emphasize victim protection, reflects the differing agendas and motivations of sovereign bodies, which view the issue as a law enforcement matter through the lens of border control, from that of NGOs and human rights organizations which view the issue as a human rights issue, through a

---

1   The Model Law has since been removed from public circulation. Copy on file with author.

human rights framework.[2] The proposals of the NGOs emphasize opportunities for trafficked persons to find some immediate medical and psychosocial attention, the necessity of immigration benefits for victims (beyond that of repatriation to the home country), and the importance of witness protection in order to promote prosecution as well as to protect survivors from further harm. After all, why would a witness want to testify against her traffickers if her reward were deportation or repatriation without even victim protection?

A larger issue too is raised here, one too complex to be addressed in this chapter, and that is: in *legislating* for the end of a harm such as trafficking in human beings, will we always lose the human focus on protecting victims? In countering a harm with a law, will the focus always shift to combating crime, rather than rehabilitating the victims of those crimes, because the framework is legal in nature? If the answer is affirmative, we must return to considering the alternative human rights framework. Human rights laws may be perceived as weak or soft because they do not always come with enforcement mechanisms built in, yet human trafficking is ultimately a massive violation of human dignity, at the very least. It is a crime, to be sure, but it is imperative to view the totality of the tragedy from beginning to end. Rather than working backwards to punish the perpetrators after the fact, as much or more attention must be paid to understanding the motivations of the victims – the fundamental human desire to improve one's life – that ultimately provide such a ripe opportunity for exploitation in the first place. How are young women (primarily) all over the world being lured into exploitative situations again and again and again?

Critiques of Approaches to Combating Trafficking

Some scholars have commented that trafficking has been discussed enough; that like female genital mutilation (FGM) before it, it has had its moment in the spotlight and it is now time to move along to the next trendy issue. Exposés have been written, special features have aired on television, regular television series incorporate human trafficking into the weekly plot line, movies have been made, legislation has been passed and every agency within the Executive branch of the US government has a Task Force hard at work on the issue. Why, then, is trafficking still such a problem? Why can't women and men who are exploited at their most vulnerable moments find the protection of law enforcement officials, and the sympathy of the broader public? Or rather, why is it that only the victims who look like the victims on television are able to illicit the sympathies of the broader public while those who have the characteristics of real victims of human trafficking are not even recognized as such?

One dimension of this problem is that in defining the issue for the public, politicians and the media have played on the more lurid and debased aspects of the crime. A person new to the issue would believe trafficking to be only about the woman rescued in a police raid after being found chained to a bed in a brothel. While this scenario is indeed one possible manifestation of the crime, there are many others.

---

2   The primary victim-protection model law was prepared by the Global Alliance Against Trafficking in Women (GAATW), *Human Rights Standards for the Treatment of Trafficked Persons* (January 1999).

While we are still arguably in the phase of educating law enforcement officials about how to identify and properly treat a victim of human trafficking, post-modernist critics of human rights advocacy have already come full circle and called upon human rights advocates and activists to avoid re-victimizing persons who have been trafficked by focusing solely on the "victim" aspect of the story (Kapur 2002). They ask that rather than focusing exclusively on the gruesome details of the trafficking, we see these people holistically for the totality of who they are (Haynes 2006). For example, Ahn is not only a human trafficking victim, but a migrant, a woman with the intention and individual will to change her life, a person seeking more lucrative employment, and, we hope, a survivor. The critics suggest, rightly I think, that we be willing to acknowledge and accept that trafficked persons are not always totally unwilling participants who have been "duped" into trafficking but can also be people with the intention of participating in at least part of the process (migrating, finding a job as a hostess, seeking a different life, and even by resorting to illegal migration to accomplish it), whose express goals are then exploited and transformed into a coercive situation. In order to understand the phenomenon of trafficking we must first understand trafficked persons as whole humans, with history, culture, hopes, and dreams, rather than reducing them to the one dimension of their personhood defined by having been trafficked.

One troubling aspect of laws geared towards protecting victims of trafficking is that when these laws are invoked to secure "benefits" for trafficked persons, the trafficked person must present herself as a victim, rather than a survivor. That is, she must see herself as a "victim," and be willing and able to describe herself in those terms. She must tell the victim story. For instance, a trafficked person who wishes to secure a T-visa in the United States or temporary residence in Europe must prove that she was a *victim* of a severe form of trafficking and must tell that story to law enforcement officials.[3] If they believe her *and* if they find the information she provides useful towards investigating and prosecuting the trafficker, law enforcement can, but are not required to, "certify" her as a victim of trafficking. She may then receive some benefits (shelter, food, sometimes psychological and medical assistance) geared towards stabilizing her as a potential witness for the prosecution. If she wishes to try to remain in the United States, she must tell the compelling victim story again to the Department of Homeland Security which may choose to grant her a T-visa (US Congress). To secure the benefit she seeks, she must prove up the victimhood nature of her situation. The law itself forces the victim to offer herself up as an easily identifiable "victim subject," without the clutter and complication of a story in which the "victim" also had some agency in her decision. Carlos, for instance, was denied a T-visa when DHS determined that he was not "exploited enough," while Ahn was denied when DHS determined that she, the

---

3   Similarly, a woman wishing to seek asylum on the basis of FGM or domestic violence, must prove, among other things, that she was persecuted or will be persecuted and that she fears returning to her home country. The law is not only not interested in her "survivor" story, the story about her power to leave her country and seek asylum or a T-visa can work against her, but presenting the survivor story can work against her, as she will then be perceived as a economic migrant with a choice, not a victim of persecution or abuse without choice.

victim, bears the burden of proving her traffickers' intent, and that she was not able to supply enough evidence to conclusively prove that the intent of her traffickers was to exploit her (Haynes 2007).

What is useful to take from the post modernist critique is that we would be in a better position to assess the reasons why and the ways in which people become susceptible to traffickers if trafficked persons were permitted or even encouraged, as a matter of law, to express all of the reasons they wound up as trafficking victims. The reasons are complex and often involve more than simple coercion, fraud, or force. Instead, they involve more subtle forms of exploitation in which the agency and desire to migrate and improve one's life is itself the very quality the trafficker was able to exploit in the person. By focusing wholly on the victim aspect of the crime, as required to receive any benefits or protections that come with the label "victim," we miss the opportunity to identify what actually might be driving the cycle of exploitation.

Another critique of current approaches to human trafficking is that offering up this type of "victim subject" works to the detriment of securing social and economic rights for the same groups of people who are choosing to migrate. Instead of thinking broadly about the economic, cultural and social rights lacking to migrants in their countries of origin, which if repaired could serve to significantly reduce migration, we focus on the lurid sexualized aspects of the crime of trafficking. Stories of forced sex and abuse are generated for the mass media, rather than the more broadly applicable, but more subtle stories about lacking economic rights and equality and dignity. Stories we hear on television, in movies, and in books, after all, are most often about sexualized forms of exploitation – sex slavery, forced marriage and child pornography – and are seldom about agricultural workers forced into indentured servitude to repay their traffickers and in debt to the "company store" for their daily food and shelter. In other words, a story about forced prostitution reaches the mass media, while a story about an agricultural worker in debt peonage does not. A story about trafficking for domestic servitude is not as "sellable" as a story about a domestic worker forced to have sex with her employer. Sex sells; "simple" indentured servitude does not, even while the fix is rooted in rectifying the economic injustices that drove the worker to indentured servitude in the first place.

Most of the discussion about trafficking focuses overwhelmingly on trafficking for purposes of sexual exploitation, regardless of whether rudimentary statistics are now revealing that the majority of trafficking seems to be carried out for indentured servitude and sweatshop labor (Anderson, B.; O'Connell Davidson, J. 2002). The critique is that some anti-trafficking activists and the media focus disproportionately on abuses that contain an element of sex, sexuality, and gender because sex "sells."[4]

---

4 During a "Roundtable Session on Human Rights Programs," hosted by Harvard University, Upendra Baxi noted, accurately, I think, that the "less romantic" answer to the question as to why we are more interested in human rights today than 20 years ago is that "human rights and suffering have become a mass media commodity that serve a function in the growth of capitalistic mass media throughout the world." "The Role of the University in the Human Rights Movement," an Interdisciplinary Discussion held at Harvard Law School, September 1999.

Multi-culturalist critiques point out that in selling the sex and victimization aspects to the public, we risk further "essentializing and "othering" the victims (Kapur 2001; Gunning 1991). That is, we are reducing the victims, usually women from the southern or eastern hemispheres, to stereotypes based on race and gender, and those stereotypes are further conflated with the sexualized nature of the crime. Then we are setting "them," the victims, at a distance from "us," the general public.

Certainly it is true that foreign women, and in particular women from the southern and eastern hemispheres, are most often the victims of trafficking. There are a multitude of reasons that could account for this: these are the women seeking to migrate to improve their economic situations and secure jobs elsewhere; they are particularly sought after by traffickers who perceive them as more easily exploited (because they cannot speak a language in the new country (Anderson, B., O'Connell Davidson, J. 2003),[5] do not have access to or understand the legal or social mechanisms available to them), and are presumed to be more compliant and less likely to flee (because of the foregoing as well as the need to improve their economic situation) (Anderson, O'Connell Davidson 2003);[6] and they are sought after by potential users (of brothels and by "employers" who also view them as more submissive and compliant because of their lack of understanding of their rights) who also view women from these regions as compliant, submissive, and sexualized (Kapur; Anderson, B., O'Connell Davidson, J. 2003).[7]

Research on the demand side of trafficking suggests that some users of prostitutes and sex workers (who may or may not also be trafficked) view migrant sex workers as less desirable for these very same reasons: they do not share the user's language, they may have been forced into the work or have no other choice, and are generally perceived as being the "cheap end of the market" (Anderson, B., O'Connell Davidson, J. 2003). However, the same research also supports the conclusion that racism, prejudice, and "othering" allow users to convince themselves that such practices are justified because trafficked persons are the "'natural' ... occupants of the lowliest positions" (Anderson, O'Connell Davidson 2003).

In the context of domestic labor, stereotypes abound regarding the value of employing particular castes or minority groups (Anderson, O'Connell Davidson

---

5   The authors of the IOM Pilot Study quoted a 21-year-old Indian businessman commenting that Nepali girls who had been sold into brothels "are especially nice when they are new to the area. They don't talk too much and are more helpful to the client. You can control them." Countering this view, however, they quote a Thai police officer who had paid for sex work who stated, "It's hard to have sex without talking, because if you can't talk, you lose the feeling" (Anderson and O'Connell Davidson 2003, 25 and 22).

6   Anderson and O'Connell Davidson found some empirical support for these opinions. Among men who admitted buying sex from foreign sex workers, a "substantial number" believed that migrant prostitutes were "cheaper and more malleable than local women" (2003, 21).

7   Anderson and O'Connell Davidson offer the explanation of one interviewee, a married man from India, who valued the qualities of unhappiness and isolation in unfree or trafficked sex workers, because it might make them seek warmth, support and care from their clients (2003, 25).

2003).[8] Migrants in particular are valued by potential employers of domestic servants for being "more flexible" about the amount of hours they will work and the fees they will charge because of their vulnerability and perceived need (Anderson, O'Connell Davidson 2003).[9] In fact, some employers specifically sought out the "otherness" of a migrant worker to resolve the discomfort of having someone sharing their house, acknowledging that they felt more comfortable having someone from an entirely different race working in the house, because it makes the gap between servant and employer less embarrassing and more manageable (Anderson, O'Connell Davidson 2003).[10] Still other employers appreciate the power they have over their employee precisely because of the power dynamic inherent in employing someone without immigration status (Anderson, O'Connell Davidson 2003).[11] The vulnerability and "otherness" work together, as exemplified through this comment of an employer speaking of the ideal domestic servant:

> They're foreign and they're illegal and they're scared and timid, and so they're not going to take up space. They're going to be very, very small, and that is generally easier to live with than someone who feels that this is their home. They're in a really bad situation ... they're terrified (Anderson, O'Connell Davidson 2003).[12]

Employers who hire someone to work in their home prefer a servant who is virtually invisible.

Why are women most often victims of trafficking? In many parts of the world (arguably in all parts of the world) women exist in or are perpetually relegated to the "private sphere," where it is easier to be bought, sold, and manipulated without anyone noticing. The private sphere is the home, the family, the culture, the religion, and the cumulative effects of the foregoing, as opposed to the public sphere in which government and sovereignty reign.[13] Sex work and domestic service exist almost

---

8   For example, Indians valued tribal Christians for their perceived work ethic. Swedes prefer Baltic women whom they perceive as needing social and economic aid and avoid Roma or gypsy employees whom they perceive as unreliable. Generally valued in domestic help are the qualities of being cheap, hardworking and obedient (Anderson, O'Connell Davidson 2003, 30).

9   Local employees were also perceived as being spoiled or demanding while migrants were perceived as grateful and enthusiastic.

10   See, e.g. comment of a British expatriot employer in Hong Kong, employing a Filipino: "It's difficult having someone working for you from the same race because we have this idea of social class in our minds, don't we? And that would be uncomfortable in your house. Whereas when it's somebody from a different country, you don't have all that baggage ... There's not any of that middle-class, upper-class thing, ... it's just a different race."

11   For example, a Dutch employer working employing domestic workers in Singapore and Thailand comments, "the system [here in Singapore and Thailand] is wonderfully organized from an employer's perspective. The employer gets to hold the Filipino maid's passport, and the maid has to pay to leave. The employer pays the government, it's all official, but the maid is totally dependent on the employer ... they can't just quit" (Anderson, O'Connell Davidson 2000, 31).

12   Citing Bott 2003 [comments of a British female employer of domestic labor in London].

13   For distillation of "private sphere," in feminist jurisprudence see Higgins, T. (2000) 'Reviving the Public/Private Distinction in Feminist Theorizing, in Symposium: Unfinished Feminist Business' (*Chicago-Kent Law Review*).

wholly within the private sphere, and in a sense, the US government has relegated agricultural and sweat shop work to the private sphere, as well. While employers, by law, are required to hire documented workers with work authorization, the US government has taken a "don't ask, don't tell" type of approach for years, conspiring to further the US economy through the sweat of these virtually invisible people.

When it comes to discussing trafficking, the lines of feminism split. One branch, comprised of what I will call "free will feminists" and multiculturalists, would emphasize that women are neither less nor more likely to be "victims" due to their gender. They acknowledge that a woman may well have given consent to some part of the venture that resulted in her trafficking yet not be willing to be exploited or enslaved. They argue that women can and do consent to sex work (this view is prevalent where legalized prostitution presents a picture of sex work as a viable economic alternative and choice), but would conclude that even women who gave their consent to some part of the process should be considered eligible to receive the benefits available to those who have been trafficked if they were coerced or did not give consent *at any point* in the process.

The so-called "radical feminists" argue that all prostitution is non-consensual and always will be until women are no longer economically, politically, and socially marginalized (MacKinnon 1987). In other words, until and unless a woman has a choice among reasonable and available jobs – that is, until she can select Sex Worker or Teacher or Policewoman rather than choosing among Sex Worker or Unpaid Laborer or Unemployed Person – she effectively has no choice. She is unable to give any real consent because she has no viable economic alternative.

The split between these two lines of thought on the issue of consent has polarized the anti-trafficking movement and put prostitution in the spotlight. Politicians have picked up on this polarity and brought prostitution into the discussion and into the law, with the imposition of the Gag Rule, attacking prostitution along with trafficking where it suits their political agendas.[14]

Conflation of Human Trafficking with other Political Issues of the Moment

Before 9/11 some governments pursued anti-trafficking initiatives under the primary policy objective of preventing migrants from ending up in exploitative situations, but even before 9/11 the issue of trafficking had already been manipulated and hijacked by those with agendas that included eradicating prostitution or preventing illegal migration. These days, however, most governments squarely and unapologetically face the issue of trafficking through a filter of national security. "Combating" trafficking is conflated with the "war on terrorism," the goal of which is to keep out all undesirables and potentially harmful individuals by controlling borders and migration.

In 2002, President George W. Bush signed into effect *National Security Directive 22,* linking human trafficking to "terrorism and public health concerns." Whatever those specific links are founded on is unclear and inscrutable, as the "specific

---

14 "Gag Rule" refers to the provision in the 2003 Reauthorization of the TVPA, cutting funding to any NGO that assists prostitutes or does not affirmatively denounce sex work, while working with victims of human trafficking.

concerns" that allegedly link trafficking to terrorism are cloaked under classified status and cannot be released to the public (President G.W. Bush). Perhaps they deal with the facet of human trafficking that has been understood for a decade, which is that traffickers in human beings also traffic drugs and weapons, as once the route and players have been set up, it is easy to switch up the goods and commodities that are illegally trafficked, whether they are humans, drugs, or weapons. In the 2005 Reauthorization of the TVPA, an interagency task force was established to study the "relationship between trafficking and terrorism," thus continuing the funding that will be allotted to ensuring that the link between the two is found (US Congress).

Prostitution

As mentioned earlier, prostitution and trafficking are conflated in the United States in particular as part of our current administration's political agenda. For example, "gag rules" have been imposed upon all organizations working with victims of trafficking in the United States or abroad. In order to received US government funding, these organizations must overtly express their refusal to aid prostitutes or support prostitution in any way, including such measures as providing sexual health education in brothels that may host both trafficked women as well as consensual sex workers. As a result, the grassroots NGO working to assist sex workers by providing them with information about how to escape a coercive or abusive situation or slavery-like working conditions is no longer eligible to receive funding because some of those women may be "prostitutes." Thus, anti-trafficking work is co-opted by the agenda to abolish prostitution.

Illegal Migration

Much of the lack of implementation and the distortion of the law itself could be ascribed to the unspoken but palpably omnipresent fear of opening the floodgates. After all, as a journalist queried, "if the law allows a victim to become a citizen, won't everyone try to become a victim?"[15] The answer is no. Not only will few to no people willingly put themselves into the trafficking flow or present themselves to be violated in hopes of securing status somewhere down the road, but even if that were their goal it is exceptionally unlikely that they will be successful. After all, more than five years after the TVPA had entered into force in the United States, fewer than 600 T-visas had been granted (US DOS 2005).[16] This is in spite of the statistics offered by the US government claiming that either 17,500 or 30,000 to 40,000 (depending on which agency report you read) new victims of trafficking enter the United States each year.[17] Congress already had a fear of floodgates in mind when they limited, within the TVPA, the number of T-visas that could be granted each year to 5,000 (US Congress).

---

15 Chicago Tribune journalist to author in telephone interview.

16 As of July 2004, 584 victims had been granted T-visas.

17 Compare 2002 TIP Report 1 and 2003 TIP Report 7 and 2004 TIP Report 6 and 2005 TIP Report 7 with DOJ Report at 9.

From the statistics issued for 2005, it appears that less than 600 applications for T-visas were even received (US DOS 2005). To honor the intent of Congress and the Executive Branch, we should be asking how to reach more potential victims in order to secure their protection, health and safety, and to let them know that the T-visa option even exists, rather than worry about floodgates opening.

Furthermore, refusing to look carefully in order to identify and protect victims of trafficking for fear of being overinclusive and mistakenly offering benefits to someone who is "really" just an illegal migrant or a smuggled person is the wrong approach. As people comfortable with looking at the trafficking issue as one part of a larger whole that involves migration and exploitation of labor will attest, "[v]iolence, confinement, coercion, deception and exploitation can and do occur within both regular and irregular systems of migration and employment. ... abuses can vary in severity and thereby generate a continuum of experiences rather than a simple either/or dichotomy ... " (Anderson, O'Connell Davidson 2003). Refusing to recognize a victim of human trafficking for fear of granting a benefit to someone who was not abused or exploited *enough*, or insisting on haggling over the often quite fine distinctions between smuggling and trafficking only do a disservice to the population in need: people exploited during the migration process.

The distinction is a false one. If the goal is really to eradicate trafficking, in part by protecting victims and prosecuting traffickers, then the distinction between smuggling and trafficking is of little use. The real issue is the demand for labor and services from anyone "unable to freely retract from an exploitative situation because they are tied to their exploiter through some form of non-economic compulsion" (Anderson, O'Connell Davidson 2003) as will be discussed further, below. Migrants suffer easier and more severe forms of exploitation when their immigration status rests (in reality or perception) in the hands of their employers. The more the employer/user has the potential to wield personal control over the worker, and the less access the worker has to a support system, the higher the degree of exploitation.

It is clear that the users and employers understand that migrant and undocumented employees are cheaper, easier to control, and more exploitable specifically due to their lack of immigrant status. Expanding opportunities to immigrate and obtain status, ones that specifically do not tie legal status to the employer, could reduce the push to accept exploitative labor conditions.

The Root of the Problem – it's about Migration

In the decade or so during which the world has come to understand human trafficking as a distinct and significant crime, the attention of governments and lawmakers has been focused first on describing and then on identifying and combating the crime after the fact, not on the point of inception. This failure to focus funding and attention on the motivations that drive people to seek a better life is a crucial omission, as the victim's motivation to migrate contributes to her vulnerability to exploitation. There continues to be a false dichotomy applied to victims of trafficking: that one can either have some agency and will to improve one's life *or* be exploited and thus a "victim" of trafficking, but not both.

Law enforcement officials not only fail to see a victim if she also shows signs of having had a motivation to migrate, they also still perceive these exploited persons as criminals. Judges and immigration personnel still fail to understand both the distinctions between trafficking and smuggling or to acknowledge that concepts such as "exploitation," "coercion," and "consent" are subtle and may be culturally bound, or at least not universal in the black and white sense that adjudicators require. We must ask not only how traffickers operate and how we can prevent them from carrying out their nefarious business, but also why persons are vulnerable to this particular type of exploitation in the first place. We must acknowledge that a desire to improve one's life leads people to attempt to immigrate through both legal and illegal means and confront that fact head on, not mask it behind a rhetoric that suggests that agency and exploitation are mutually exclusive.

The Economic Rights Perspective

An emerging perspective on trafficking, more often discussed in Europe and among anthropologists than in the United States and among lawmakers, looks at the interrelationship between gender, migration, and economic disparity as a jumping-off point to discussing both the supply and demand sides of trafficking. This perspective asks whether trafficking flourishes, in large part, because all of the work done by trafficked persons is "private sphere" work – work that is hidden away or done in the home or on the margins of society. Even in countries where domestic violence laws and child abuse laws are thoughtfully written and implemented, the average citizen still feels that certain matters – those involving familial relationships or sex or matters in the home – are "private matters," governed not by the laws of the nation, so much as by the societal, religious, and cultural values of the population.

The economic rights perspective is unimpressed by the polarization among feminists over the issue of sex work and concludes that both of these perspectives start from the wrong premise. The correct starting point is recognition that the sex industry has expanded and diversified rapidly in the last two decades (Anderson, O'Connell Davidson 2003) and while there is no automatic correlation between the expansion in this market and the demand for trafficked persons, it does provide for legitimate concern that the demand for expansion and diversification in this largely unregulated industry is met by unfree workers.

Secondly, they point out that there is something unique to the type of labor trafficked persons are forced to do. Sex work and domestic labor are distinctive because *consumers* of such labor are interested in the *person* as well as in the actual labor output (Anderson, O'Connell Davidson 2003).[18]

The economic rights perspective also sheds further light on the complexities of the "private sphere" nature of the work. Employers of live-in migrant domestic labor and users of migrant or unfree sex workers imagine a personal relationship with the "employee," *because* the relationship takes place in the private sphere.

---

18 Thus, they conclude, sex work and domestic labor are "more closely related to the phenomenon of 'trafficking'/forced labour than in other sectors, such as the carpet or garment industries."

Because the domestic work and sex work is done in the home or in private, the employer can believe that the work done is governed not by the market or economic concerns, but by "mutual dependence and affective relations" (Anderson, O'Connell Davidson 2003). Unlike sex work, in which the users often want to believe that the sex worker is a free and equal participant in the act, however, the employers of a migrant domestic servant perceive the workers as "objects of, rather than subjects to, a contract," thus allowing them to see the "situation" of a trafficked domestic worker as "something quite external to their own role as employer" (Anderson, O'Connell Davidson 2003).[19] This phenomenon is further exacerbated when domestic labor is engaged through an agency (Anderson, O'Connell Davidson 2003).[20]

Anderson and O'Connell Davidson conclude that there are three factors key to explaining the exploitative conditions inherent in migrant sex and domestic work: 1) the unregulated nature of those markets, 2) the abundant supply of persons to be exploited, and 3) "the power and malleability of social norms regulating the behavior of employers and clients" (Anderson, O'Connell Davidson 2003).

From an economic rights perspective, we are all complicit in the existence of human trafficking because supply and demand do not simply exist; rather, they are created through action and inaction on the part of state actors and interest groups. Until there is what Anderson and O'Connell Davidson refer to as a "fundamental re-visioning" in society, in which migrants, sex workers, and domestic workers are truly fully recognized members of the public sphere – with full rights – they will be vulnerable to exploitation, and the society will be complicit in that exploitation (Anderson, O'Connell Davidson 2002).

Conclusion

The will to address human trafficking was manifested through the human rights movement and should continue to be tackled through a human rights framework, with emphasis on understanding and protecting the victims of trafficking. A significant aspect of understanding and stopping the phenomenon of human trafficking is understanding the victim. This in turn requires recognition that she is likely to have had a desire to migrate, and it is that very desire that was twisted and exploited by her traffickers. Very few trafficked persons are literally snatched from their homes or sold into slavery by their family members. Far more are acting on a desire or need to improve their economic existence and it is this need that is played upon by those who know how to exploit it.

The ultimate utopian solution to the problem would be to finally work together to eradicate the vast economic disparities around the world. We do not seem to be working towards this goal. A more realistic goal then might be that rather than viewing trafficking solely as an organized crime issue, and approaching it solely

---

19 The example provided by Anderson and O'Connell Davidson is of an Indian woman employing a 14-year-old girl who had been sold by her family into domestic service and who cried all of the time. Said her employer: "Not only did I have to do all the work, but I had to keep part-time help during that time as well."

20 See Note 11 in this chapter (Anderson, O'Connell Davidson 2003, 31).

from a law enforcement perspective, countries feel confident to discuss and respond to trafficking as a violation of human rights during and related to migration. Looking at the issue through the lens of migration, without tying it to fear tactics such as promoting the idea that unwanted migration deprives citizens of jobs and lets terrorists through sovereign borders, will allow us to identify what makes persons susceptible to traffickers at the point of origin when they begin to consider migration. Tackling human trafficking at its sources means understanding and responding to the particular vulnerabilities of its victims, and offering them solutions based upon recognition of their individual human worth and dignity.

Works Cited

Anderson, B., O'Connell Davidson, J. (2002), *Trafficking – a demand led problem?* 45, Sweden: Save the Children.

Anderson, B., O'Connell Davidson, J. (2003), *Is Trafficking in Human Beings Demand Driven? A Multi-Country Pilot Study*, IOM Migration Research Series No. 15.

Arendt, H. (1966), *The Origins of Totalitarianism*, New York: Harcourt.

Caldwell, G. et al (1997), *Crime and Servitude*, Washington D.C: Global Survival Network.

Council of Europe. Council Directive (2004), 2004/81/EC, Article 8 (COE).

Global Alliance Against Trafficking in Women (1999), *Human Rights Standards for the Treatment of Trafficked Persons*.

Gunning, I. (1991–92), "Arrogant Perception, World-Traveling and Multicultural Feminism: The Case of Female Genital Surgeries," 23 *Columbia Human Rights Law Review* 189.

Harvard Law School, "The Role of the University in the Human Rights Movement," an Interdisciplinary Discussion held at Harvard Law School, September 1999.

Haynes, D. (2004), "Used, Abused, Arrested and Deported: Extending Immigration Benefits to Protect Victims of Human Trafficking and to Secure the Prosecution of Traffickers 26, *Human Rights Quarterly* 2, Johns Hopkins.

Haynes, D. (2006), "Client-Centered Human Rights Advocacy," *Clinical Law Rev* (NYU).

Haynes, D. (2007), "(Not) Found Chained to a Bed in a Brothel," 21 *Georgetown Immigration Law J.* 3.

International Labor Organization (2005), Press Release (ILO).

Kapur, R. (2001), "Postcolonial Erotic Disruptions: Legal Narratives of Culture, Sex, and Nation in India," 10 *Columbia Journal of Gender and Law* 333.

Kapur, R. (2002), "The Tragedy of Victimization Rhetoric: Resurrecting the 'Native' Subject in International/Post-Colonial Feminist Legal Politics," 15 *Harvard Human Rights J.* 1.

MacKinnon, C. (1987), *Feminism Unmodified*, Cambridge: Harvard University Press.

President, Office of, National Security Presidential Directive, Memorandum Regarding Combating Trafficking in Persons, February 25, 2002.

Spijkerboer, T. (2004), Introduction to Reader: EC Directives on Immigration Law, prepared for "Gendered Borders, International Conference on Women and Immigration Law in Europe," *Vrije Universiteit*, Amsterdam.

United Nations, Convention Relating to the Status of Refugees (1951), U.N. Doc. A/Conf. 2/108 (entered into force April 22, 1954) (UN 1951).

United Nations, Protocol to Prevent, Suppress and Punish Trafficking in Persons, Especially Women and Children, Protocol to Convention Against Transnational Organized Crime (2000), G.A. Res. 55/25, Annex I, U.N. GAOR 55th Sess., Supp. No. 49, at 44, U.N. Doc. A/45/49 (Vol. 1), entered into force 29 September 2003 (UN 2000).

United Nations, Population Trends Division, Department of Economic and Social Affairs (2005), Trends in Total Migrant Stock: The 2005 Revision; available at: http://esa.un.org/migration (UN 2005).

United Nations Children's Fund (UNICEF) et al (2002), *Trafficking in Human Beings in Southeastern Europe*, xiii.

US Congress, United States Trafficking Victims Protection Act of 2000, Pub. L. No. 106-386, 114 Stat. 1464, Trafficking Victims Reauthorization Act of 2003, Pub. L No. 108-193, Reauthorization Act of 2005, H.R. 972, passed Dec. 14, 2005, signed January 2006.

Chapter 8

Doctors Without Borders and the Moral Economy of Pharmaceuticals

Peter Redfield

It is an old reporter's truism that not all deaths are equally significant or newsworthy. Although human rights and humanitarianism are by no means identical ethical genres – the first born from broadly legal assertion of principle and the second from a broadly medical response to suffering – in practice both oppose such media realism with a moral insistence on the equality of tragedy. Human rights groups and humanitarian organizations alike enumerate their claims through the violation and suffering experienced by the most ordinary of human bodies and lives, as presented in statistics as well as individual cases. Yet their efforts labor against a similar inertia to that of the newsroom, in that not all moments of human pain translate well to a given audience, and their comparison inevitably begs comparison to other examples present and past. Furthermore, both humanitarian and human rights movements fret over their own perceived relative state of crisis, occasioned by a combination of spectacular rhetorical success coupled with continuing practical failure. At the beginning of the twenty-first century claims to rights and humanitarian values have multiplied to the extent that even egregious violators commonly assert them, even as images of suffering only multiply.

This chapter addresses humanitarian parallels and alternatives to human rights discourse, focusing on the outspoken organization Doctors Without Borders/ Médecins Sans Frontières (MSF). Founded three decades ago as an alternative French medical response to humanitarian suffering, MSF has since grown into a complex and transnational fixture of global crises. Along the way it has also expanded its operation to include a wider range of medical problems, addressing "neglected diseases" as well as emergencies in an effort to confront human suffering. Here I examine how MSF's efforts to distance itself from recent military actions conducted in the name of humanitarianism parallel its increased engagement in struggles to advance pharmaceutical equity on a global scale. My suggestion is that these developments mark a potential redistribution in the "moral economy" of suffering and humanitarian values, one that renders the larger global infrastructure of health and life more visible, even while still revealing the continuing limits of humanitarian sensibilities in effecting systemic change.

Death in Northern Uganda

By the summer of 2003, Idi Amin was dying. The man who embodied the madness of dictatorship for a media generation of the 1970's now lay in a coma, clinging to the final thread of life in a Saudi Arabian hospital. In the northwest of Uganda, Amin's home district, rumors flew about his condition, and the possible return of his body, dead or alive, to the land of his birth. Unlike elsewhere in the country, popular sentiment here ran strongly in favor of this idea, presented as a moment of reconciliation with a slight whiff of redemption. Amid a landscape of rural poverty and both national and international neglect, the fallen dictator retained an aura of magnificence; while people admitted that he may have committed some crimes, he remained a native son grown larger than life – simultaneously local and extra-local in his sphere of recognition. His was a most remarkable demise, extending well beyond a single body.[1]

I was in northern Uganda for other reasons, however, visiting projects by Doctors Without Borders, internationally known as Médecins Sans Frontières, or MSF. One of these missions, an effort to combat sleeping sickness, was as dead as Amin for all except the most local adherents; the other, administering antiretroviral drugs to AIDS patients, was in full growth and flush with international significance. Both, however, focused on specific diseases and the medicines used to treat them, and traveling between the two in a matter of days offered a vision of the larger circulation of pharmaceuticals around the planet from the perspective of a Land Cruiser rather than a lab.

I will use this moment from the field (in its most classic composition) to frame a discussion about MSF's effort to launch a major new initiative targeting access to essential medicines and neglected diseases on a global scale. This effort has increasingly led the group into an advocacy role beyond its more historic field focus, as well as to a commitment to ambitious AIDS-related programs and even to the prospect of helping to coordinate and fund pharmaceutical research and development on behalf of less publicized diseases. In certain respects it has arguably brought the organization closer to the terrain of human rights issues, via legal issues of policy, intellectual property and international trade agreements.

Even while striking out in such new directions, however, MSF has also been fighting a rearguard campaign to defend its more traditional "humanitarian space" of action in emergency settings. The five years since the group first announced its medical initiatives have only witnessed new cycles of conflict and disaster, as well as conditions full of what are known in the soft euphemism of professional nonprofit discourse as "challenges." Chief among these was the reorientation of American foreign policy after September 11, 2001, which confirmed a longer trend of integration of humanitarian actors within military operations, and the incorporation of human rights rhetoric and humanitarian objectives into a larger geopolitical mission defined by national interest (Weissman 2004). Long iconoclastic, independent and outspoken, MSF has strenuously resisted this trend, first denouncing the association of food drops and bombing runs, then both criticizing efforts to deploy dire humanitarian

---

1   For a more comprehensive account of both the continuing crisis in northern Uganda and Amin's place in it, see Leopold (2005).

prophecy for antiwar ends on the one hand, and refusing to join any nonprofit coalition of the willing on the other. By the end of 2004 they had withdrawn from both Iraq and Afghanistan, the latter a particularly bitter retreat after over two decades of continuous presence following the murder of five staff members. At the same time they were deeply committed to projects in the Darfur region of Sudan (if wary of labeling that crisis genocide), and would soon halt fundraising for Tsunami relief in Southeast Asia in order to appeal for support for projects experiencing less publicity. In Uganda the disease specific missions now shared the billing with efforts to aid refugees from the country's shadowy northern war, which finally made it onto MSF-USA's annual top ten list of "underreported crises."

Viewed from the perspective of this particular organization, then, and its shifting portfolio of specific projects, medical humanitarianism would hardly appear a single or uniform endeavor. Instead, it struggles in several directions at once, alternately demanding or opposing state action depending on the context. Although some humanitarian figures increasingly make explicit reference to human rights discourse in their opposition to suffering (e.g. Farmer 2003), MSF scrupulously tends to avoid it. Warning against the expansion of humanitarian dreams beyond temporary solace, the critic David Rieff (2002) would still find much to approve in the group's outspoken claims to limits. Indeed, in opposing the state version of any humanitarian "right of intervention" into crisis settings, MSF was countering a trend partly anticipated by its own early history, and endorsed by its most prominent founding member, Bernard Kouchner. This apparent contradiction is far from anomalous. Although sharing a common acronym and charter, the constituent sections of MSF sometimes interpret their doctrine differently, and quite frequently debate specific actions and positions.[2] Even within any given section views are hardly settled, but rather the latest word in a continuing, internal argument.

Rather than defending any rights *per se*, the varied announcements and actions of MSF followed perceived dangers to the health and dignity of ordinary people. Thus the group could effectively discover a language of economic and policy critique in pharmaceutical discussions while rediscovering a discourse of political neutrality amid emergencies. For this reason I will use the term "moral economy" as an analytic frame for my discussion of its activities, and particularly the concern over the availability of medicines within them. By moral economy I wish to imply the circulation and distribution of moral sentiment at two interrelated levels. The first, analogous to the historian E.P. Thompson's (2001) use of the expression in his

---

2   The MSF acronym incorporates a loose federation of national sections, the five most central being in France, Belgium, Holland, Switzerland, and Spain. Although based in its country of origin, each of these sections is quite international in terms of volunteers and staff. MSF prides itself on a relatively equalitarian ethos that favors individual initiative and fosters debate over bureaucratic hierarchy, to the extent that some could express concern that the most recent international summit (known as "La Mancha") produced too little in the way of dispute. For purposes of this chapter, however, I will gloss over internal divisions except where directly relevant. Beyond formal references, this work draws on the author's ongoing ethnographic and historical study of MSF. The reader is also directed to the following relevant websites: www.msf.org; www.doctorswithoutborders.org; www.accessmed-msf.org and www.dndi.org.

analysis of eighteenth-century English crowds upset by grain prices, describes the feeling in and beyond MSF that the availability of goods such as medicines should not be governed solely by motives of profit. The second, analogous to historian of science Lorraine Daston's (1995) use of the term in her analysis of values embraced by practitioners of early modern science, describes the systemic distribution of principles across MSF's varied stands and endeavors, producing the ethical ground for a humanitarian position. Alongside an idealistic commitment to altruism and independence, exemplified by the group's opposition to the political expediency of "the sacrificial international order" (Bradol 2004), and a realist focus on immediate suffering and present conditions, exemplified by its insistence on the calculation of medical benefit "one person at a time," MSF also exhibits an egalitarian sense of prioritization, exemplified by the motto of its spin-off drug venture: "the best science for the most neglected."

Although the different component sections of the larger MSF movement, not to mention individual adherents, may interpret these principles differently in particular settings and argue forcefully among themselves, they maintain sufficient cohesion to articulate a common moral vision constructed around a secular commitment to the value of human life. Since the group maintains a distinctly global ambition in its response to worldwide health crises, and has grown to enjoy significant public support both throughout Western Europe, as well as Canada, the United States and Australia, I suggest that its shifting rhetoric and activities reflect structures of feeling about human suffering well beyond its immediate members. In this brief chapter I will consider MSF's turn to advocacy for medical access and direct involvement with problems of pharmaceutical production and distribution with reference to the particular landscape of Uganda. My suggestion will be that these developments mark a potential redistribution in the "moral economy" of suffering and humanitarian values, rendering the larger global infrastructure of health and life more visible. At the same time they continue to reveal the limits of humanitarian sensibilities in effecting systemic change.

Institutions and Neglect

First let me offer some brief background on both MSF and its drug crusade. At the beginning of the 1970s, two small groups of French doctors and a few journalists working for a medical review came together to establish a new humanitarian organization. Calling it *Médecins Sans Frontières*, they hoped it would offer an independent alternative to the formally mandated Red Cross, engaging directly with populations in distress rather than filtering its activities through national governments. In addition to directly caring for suffering people, this new group soon came to reserve the right to speak out on their behalf, practicing a form of advocacy under the name of *témoignage* (witnessing).[3] After a number of small

---

3   As I discuss and reference more extensively in other work (Redfield 2006), témoignage has been an expanding rather than static emphasis for MSF; while the spirit may have been present for some at its inception, the group's original charter was relatively modest on this score and, as Anne Vallaeys (2004) details, the question of whether not the group should take

emergency interventions and an eventual schism at the end of the decade, MSF grew through the 1980s, becoming both fully international in organizational terms and more technically proficient on the ground. The end of the cold war only increased MSF's scope and profile, as it and other non-governmental organizations played an increasingly central role in response to disasters and political turmoil. By the time the group won the Nobel Peace Prize in 1999, the acronym "MSF" designated a consortium of 18 loosely aligned national sections, with a collective annual budget over 300 million euros (the bulk derived from private, not institutional sources) and operations in over 80 countries. In human terms it included some 1500 expatriated volunteers and modestly salaried office workers, as well as some 10,000 national staff resident in mission sites. From a marginal and oppositional French group, the "doctors without borders" clearly had grown into an established transnational presence, no longer simply French nor simply centered around physicians.[4]

MSF was also a movement in partial transition. While maintaining (and periodically reaffirming) a core commitment to emergency operations in impoverished countries, different MSF sections had also experimented with a variety of other missions addressing an expanded conception of crisis, including efforts to address the health needs of marginal populations in Europe and elsewhere and longer-term efforts to address specific diseases in contexts where they were endemic. By the late 1990s MSF had dropped its earlier resistance to HIV/AIDS work and increasingly involved itself in campaigns to combat that spreading epidemic. And within some quarters of the organization, particularly the French section, momentum had been building for a new initiative to address the perennial problem of unequal access to medicines on the part of afflicted populations, together with an increasing lack of pharmaceutical products to combat unprofitable conditions.[5] On the eve of the Nobel

---

public positions constituted its first internal struggle. For additional descriptions of MSF in English see Bortolotti (2004) and Fox (1995). Brauman (2000) provides a broader background overview history of humanitarianism and Barnett (2005) outlines its current tensions.

4   By 1999–2000 only about a quarter of the volunteers were doctors, and fully 45 percent of field postings non-medical. For this and all other figures see MSF (2000), 82–85. The number of national staff that year was 9,570; however it would rise above 12,000 by 2001. The percentage of private funds within the budget came to 74 percent in 1999–2000; it too would rise to over 80 percent in the following years before dipping again. In 2004–5, total international income was up over 450 million euro (MSF 2005). While different national sections vary in their fund-raising abilities (not to mention sensibilities, the combination of which has at times produced as much conflict as cooperation), overall MSF has achieved remarkable success in deriving most of its income from private citizens rather than institutional donors, an economic strategy it sees as essential to maintaining operational independence.

5   In the early 1990s, MSF largely saw HIV-AIDS as falling outside its particular expertise and best left to others. The small projects by MSF Switzerland in Uganda constitute an exception (field notes 2003). The spreading impact of HIV-AIDS into other health concerns, along with the advent of antiretroviral therapy precipitated a reappraisal by the end of the decade. Another step towards MSF's eventual pharmaceutical epiphany occured in 1995, when the manufacturer of a meningitis treatment known as oily chloramphenicol abruptly decided to cease production just after the organization had successfully lobbied the WHO to recognize the treatment. The scramble to fashion an alternative supply source put drug issues on the group's agenda (Rankin 2005, 93–96).

award, MSF launched a "Campaign for Access to Essential Medicines," denouncing global inequities in biomedical supplies, and demanding new measures to address the problem. The subsequent award of the prize, together with the publicity and funds it generated, would fuel the rapid growth of MSF's advocacy work over subsequent years. As a number of those involved with the campaign have noted to me, the timing of the Nobel produced a fortuitous conjuncture for the new initiative.

Thus far the Access Campaign appears a relative "success" within the orbit of MSF's projects, although an ever incomplete and potentially troubling one to some within the organization. Over the short span of its existence it has played a role in the larger advocacy struggle to reduce drug prices in contexts of poverty. During this time issues of pharmaceutical production and pricing achieved a measure of media prominence with political effects; a WTO conference held at Doha, Qatar, in 2001 produced a grudging declaration about the right of states to consider Trade-Related Aspects of Property Rights (TRIPS) relative to public health concerns, and a few specific struggles showed signs of partial resolution. Most notably prices for antiretroviral drugs (ARVs) used to treat AIDS patients fell precipitously, due to a combination of generic production in Brazil and India, a legal struggle in South Africa, and concerted pressure on the part of activists and non-profit organizations (Hoen 2002). Yet the overall imbalance has remained little changed; corporations found ways to circumvent the Doha declaration in negotiating with weak states, and despite a remarkable shift towards the provision of ARVs by states and international organizations, the majority of people with HIV/AIDS remain without access to the drugs, and are unlikely to receive them in the near future (MSF 2003, 2006). At the same time the Access Campaign has expanded MSF's commitment to advocacy into extensive lobbying activities, frequently conducted in concert with other nonprofit and advocacy organizations, and aimed at an audience of state and institutional actors. Such activities sit uneasily with some in the organization, as they conflict with its historic focus on field operations, as well as its independent and generally rebellious, anti-bureaucratic ethos. MSF continues to depend on its global array of medical missions as a source of legitimacy for its testimony about pharmaceutical issues, even as the Access campaign stretches it into more rarified, and potentially complicitous ground.

From its inception the Access campaign included an even more daring departure for the MSF movement: a collaborative effort to directly fund and coordinate the research and development of drugs for "neglected" diseases. Surveying the greater terrain of human afflictions, MSF distinguished four categories of conditions relative to the pharmaceutical market (MSF 2001a). The first is that of "global diseases," maladies such as cancer or cardiovascular disorders that affect all populations, including wealthy ones where profits can be made. Unsurprisingly, the focus of pharmaceutical corporations rests here. The second category is that of "neglected diseases," maladies such as malaria and tuberculosis that occasionally strike people who live in wealthy countries, but largely affect poorer ones. Such conditions are generally marginal to pharmaceutical profits and hence to research. The third category is that of "most neglected diseases," maladies such as sleeping sickness and leishmaniasis that exclusively affect populations in economically marginal environments. Because they offer no real opportunity for profit at all, these conditions fall almost completely outside the market and corporations pay virtually no attention to them. The fourth and final category is that of conditions "other than purely medical," defects such as wrinkles, cellulite or baldness that obsess wealthy populations and constitute a significant and growing area of pharmaceutical research (MSF 2001a, 11).

Facing this constellation of diseases only partially addressed by commercial drug development, MSF first assembled a working group to study the problem, and then decided to join with several partner organizations and launch an effort known as the Drugs for Neglected Diseases Initiative (DNDi).[6] Incorporated as legal entity in Geneva in July, 2003, DNDi began the task of identifying both shorter and longer-term projects that would modify or enlarge the arsenal of medications available to combat neglected diseases, especially the most neglected. Early examples of potential products suggested by DNDi included an oral dose of eflornithine (used to treat sleeping sickness), and fixed dose artemisinin-based combinations for chloriquine resistant malaria. Rather than plunging directly into comprehensive research and development itself, the initiative was designed to operate as a virtual drug development organization, eliciting, supporting and coordinating a portfolio of projects within existing infrastructures. The goal was to circumvent the marketplace by focusing on medical need, and treating drugs as "public goods" (DNDi 2004).

The eventual relative success of DNDi, along with parallel ventures such as One World Health (a nonprofit organization in San Francisco funded by the Gates Foundation), remains to be seen. But like the related drug campaign, DNDi has already proved internally controversial for MSF, generating much debate within sections about the plan to devote five percent of their respective budgets to its funding. The Dutch section of the organization in particular opposed participation in the venture, arguing that it strayed too far from MSF's traditional focus on crisis intervention, and its operational expertise on frontline medicine. Certainly drug development involved a far different timeline than most humanitarian projects, with projects estimated in terms of years, even decades at the outset. And like the related advocacy initiative, involvement in pharmaceutical research and development required new forms of knowledge, considering medical compounds in terms of policy documents and international treaties regarding intellectual property.

Taken together, the Access Campaign and DNDi represent MSF's most explicit venture into the economics of suffering. Whereas the group classically denounces political failure and frequently calls for political responsibility in the form of state action, here MSF is seeking to shift market economics into a moral equation, one where life is never fungible. In the words of the head of the Access Campaign: "This inequality is incompatible with the concept of humanity. Fighting the fact that millions of lives are considered of less value than a fistful of dollars, is about preserving the basic morals of human civilization for the future" (quoted in MSF 2003). The effect

---

6   In addition to MSF, founding partners in DNDi included the Oswaldo Cruz Foundation in Brazil, The Indian Council of Medical Research, the Institut Pasteur in France, the Malaysian Ministry of Health and the Kenyan Medical Research Institute. The new organization also worked in association with the UN-World Bank-WHO program known as TDR (Research and Training in Tropical Diseases). For further details see MSF (2003) and the DNDi website (www.dndi.org).

of this reorientation of MSF's already global frame from populations to drugs, I suggest, is to extend humanitarian defense of life into the moral economy of suffering at a deeper technical level, repositioning neglect beyond particular bodies and into the apparatus of treatment itself. It also suggests something analogous to a right to healthcare, understood less as an abstract principle than as a material practice.

Small Happenings in Local Communities

Imagine the outcry in North America or Europe if a drug for, say, congestive heart disease didn't work in one-third of patients, and killed up to 10% of those who took it. Yet those are the shocking statistics for a 50-year old drug called melarsoprol, used to treat sleeping sickness – MSF website, 2003.[7]

Here I will return to a specific landscape of neglect, in this case northern Uganda, and small happenings in local communities. MSF first sent a mission to Uganda in 1980, just after the fall of Amin, and continued with various emergency interventions through the long years of ensuing chaos. After Yoweri Museveni came to power in 1986 and the country grew relatively stable, MSF had to decide whether to leave or develop a different sort of mission. As it happened, the field director for MSF-France of the time had written a thesis about sleeping sickness, then reaching epidemic levels in some areas of the country. Following his initiative and the efforts of many successors, a sleeping sickness program emerged, one that would continue in successive sites in the north until 2002. This program would not only become MSF-France's first long-term, disease-specific mission, but also play a background role in its later development of the Access Campaign and the DNDi. Slowly, over the years, MSF developed a degree of expertise in the treatment of sleeping sickness, conducting epidemiological studies of its programs and experimenting with different courses of treatment its clinics.

Sleeping sickness (African trypansomiasis, in this case *trypansomiasis brucei gambiense*) easily provides a paradigmatic example of MSF's "most neglected disease." A neurological disorder, it is transmitted by an insect vector – the tsetse fly – that infests marginal areas near vegetation and water across a central swath of Africa, and consequently mostly bites poor people.[8] Fatal if untreated, the condition has nonetheless enjoyed little in the way of pharmaceutical research, and the

---

7   Declan Butler, "Raiding the Medicine Cabinet," MSF website, information July 7, 2003 (http://www.msf.org/countries/page.cfm?articleid=F64F06F1-E7A7-44CF-87B9DAE4057D981F).

8   "Poor" here designates poorer people within already poor contexts. In complaining about lack of state funding for the sleeping sickness program members of the team joked that the only way to get attention for the disease would be to release tsetse flies outside the houses of the elite. Lyons (1992) underscores the role of the sleeping sickness in regional colonial history, covering an epidemic that struck Uganda in 1899–1905 amid a study of northern Congo/Zaire and suggesting that ecological effects of colonial policies themselves contributed greatly to outbreaks of the disease. This suggests a larger pattern of interventions and counter-interventions interacting under the divergent desires for wealth and health: in effect a greater colonial pharmakon. For further discussion of colonial medicine in Africa see Vaughn (1991).

dominant first line treatment for the second stage of the disease remains melarsoprol, a compound derived from arsenic first developed in 1949 that is notorious for its painful application and sometimes-fatal side effects. The mixed results of this quintessential pharmakon led MSF to favor treatments with eflornithine (DFMO), first licensed in 1990. However, in 1995 the manufacturer, Aventis, announced it would no longer produce eflornithine, which was proving unprofitable despite its high cost. An extensive lobbying campaign by MSF and others, coupled with the appearance of Vaniqa™, an eflornithine-based product marketed by Bristol Myers Squibb as the solution to wealthy women's unwanted facial hair caused Aventis to shift course, and agree to restart production in 2001. Moreover, Aventis and other manufacturers committed to direct some resources to humanitarian ends.[9] For a moment, at least, MSF's moral claim had helped sway the market. And yet the triumph was limited, given that the $40 million estimated to launch a truly comprehensive sleeping sickness program at a global scale remained nowhere to be found.

On the ground in Uganda, MSF itself decided to close its own program in Omugo in 2002. Local prevalence of the disease had shrunk to an unremarkable 0.3 percent, and after more than 15 years of operation in a series of sites the group felt it was time to hand over responsibility to the government. MSF's new mission in nearby Arua focused on HIV-AIDS, and that program was expanding to offer ARV drugs to several hundred patients, part of a new global initiative begun in 2000. For all of the organization's impressive resources, it could not do everything, everywhere, all the time. By the time of my visit to the area, only a small Ugandan team working for MSF's research affiliate Epicentre remained devoted to sleeping sickness, finishing off the last epidemiological studies. The program was clearly dying: no government funding had appeared for salaries, equipment or fuel, the only regularly operating vehicle was the last MSF land cruiser and the now expiring drugs on clinic shelves still all bore that organization's logo. While hoping that someone would arrive to pick up the pieces, the local staff and other medical personnel also recognized this collapse as indicative of a norm rather than an aberration. "Our limitations are national limitations," the director of one hospital told me, standing in front of a largely barren supply room. Waves of international aid come and go; the training of the sleeping sickness assistants might now go to waste, but at least they still had their donated bicycles.

Here we find the familiar shadow of poverty behind MSF's drive to address suffering infrastructural inequities in access to medicines, as well as the limitations of its ever-impermanent field missions. By moving beyond the immediacy of suffering bodies to focus on the commodification of medical materials, the Access campaign produces a different humanitarian configuration. At the same time, however, it also leaves some individuals and populations behind. Places like northwestern Uganda

---

9   See MSF (2001). As an article in 2002 noted, eflornithine is effective only against the gambiense varient of trypanosomaisis and remains expensive at $400–800 for a 14 dose treatment. Resistance to melarsoprol also appears to be rising. While the pentamadine prescribed for stage one of the disease is relatively safe, most patients only seek treatment when in the more debilitating stage two of the disease, which requires a treatment compound that can cross the blood/brain barrier (Ssemakula 2002).

run a regular surplus of neglected suffering, and one can die there from many things beyond either AIDS or sleeping sickness.

The Ugandan projects devoted to sleeping sickness and AIDS mark different points on MSF's trajectory into pharmaceutical activism, as well as some of the essential tensions of its sweeping endeavor. Whereas HIV-AIDS is a global pandemic threatening people in many walks of life, sleeping sickness is a regional disease limited to the marginal poor. Whereas many seek fame (and some also fortune) in searching for new treatments for AIDS, few researchers give much thought to sleeping sickness. With its drug campaign, MSF tries to address both the needs of the neglected and those of the "most" neglected. AIDS, however, often ends up at the rhetorical spear point of the effort. Given its greater media visibility, the vast advocacy coalitions constructed around it, and the sheer weight of medical need this is hardly surprising. DNDi, by contrast, concentrates more strictly on the "most" neglected" diseases. Rather than changing pharmaceutical availability through policy, it focuses on extending pharmaceutical reach by creating more "public goods" beyond the market.

Taken together, MSF's drug efforts and the two Ugandan projects also echo an observation made by Veena Das about the different resonance of expert knowledge and democratic desires in poor countries:

> The issue in this context is rarely that of our stake in "humanity" or "the human condition" as many have supposed, but rather how we can make institutions concerned with large issues of "human dignity" or "human rights" responsive to the small happenings in local communities far away from the eyes of the media or of new technologies – happenings that could nevertheless have vast consequences for our experience of the body, nature and society (Das 1999, 126).

The ambition of MSF's drug advocacy presents a precise corollary to Das' observation in biomedical terms: to render large-scale institutions responsive to "small happenings in local communities." Following the campaign and the initiative thus promises to illuminate not only this latest phase of humanitarianism, but also the distribution of global neglect, mapped with material exactitude by pathogens and medicines. In an era where "drugs for life" may well reflect a new biomedical orientation (Dumit 2002), we should recall that such a slogan can echo differently in different medical settings, particularly those where life finds its measure in existence rather than fulfillment.[10]

Expanded ambitions notwithstanding, however, MSF's move to address structural inequities of global health at the level of pharmaceutical access encounters the same general limit of capacity as its emergency programs. Geographically mobile and staffed by a fluid and partly volunteer mix of amateurs and experts, the organization

---

10 Dumit deploys the phrase to address a remarkable reconfiguration of contemporary pharmaceutical understanding at the centers of biomedical productivity, such that conditions like depression can be understood as a chronic state of an inherently ill (or suboptimal) body. Viewed from the margins of biomedical consumption, however, the phrase "drugs for life" just as easily suggests current anti-retroviral therapies for AIDS, where the course of treatment is literary conceived to be life-long, and measured directly in miniscule and uncertain supplies.

is neither a state nor a corporation. The group has sufficient collective resources to run small programs and make some larger noise, nothing more and nothing less. The very values that produce MSF's moral authority also restrict its action: it will not yield its independence, nor sacrifice lives in the name of a greater good, nor settle on a single priority amid the vast sea of the neglected. In a humanitarian time frame, future and past can never eclipse the present, embodied as it is in the immediacy of suffering, and evoked in the urgency of crisis. News from the latest front holds clear social appeal inside as well as outside the organization, as reflected in the pages of both its newsletters and fundraising brochures. Even AIDS, the most prominently publicized and moralized of contemporary afflictions, produces only a partial sense of urgency when viewed from the routine of a specific program; more than one volunteer at the ARV program in Uganda referred wistfully to the drama of emergency interventions elsewhere. Less remarkable conditions that only affect marginal populations – such as sleeping sickness – are even harder to cast as happenings with "vast consequences," and remain beyond the focus of most local, let alone international media. They might, however, present the sort of limited problem that a nonprofit pharmaceutical venture can address, thereby positioning them on the horizon of new technology.

Human Rights, Humanitarianism and the Practice of Virtue

Contemporary anthropologists tend to approach human rights less as an abstract set of defined principles to be supported or contested, and more as a dynamic discourse embodied in practice, and deployed by particular human groups within specific struggles (e.g. Merry 2006; Riles 2006; Wilson 1997). In this sense human rights claims constitute a potential basis for social exchange, in which the gap between legal ideals and daily realities can itself serve as a representational resource, one calculated in terms of suffering. From such a perspective, any "crisis' in human rights can only indicate a state in which the meaning of terms like "human rights violation" have become altered through their frequent deployment, and the strategies developed to respond to them. Similarly, from an anthropological perspective, humanitarianism designates not only a moral adherence to the alleviation of suffering, but also what people do while pursuing that good.

The fact that MSF has ventured into addressing pharmaceutical topics during a period of perceived crisis in humanitarianism suggests that this development marks a potential reorientation or redistribution within humanitarian sensibility, whereby economic factors contributing to suffering become newly tangible in the absence of medical materials. The forms of response that MSF has generated to further its goal of greater pharmaceutical equity – the Access campaign and DNDi – involve operations on a different time scale than those of its field operations: policy analysis, public advocacy and scientific research. These activities in turn involve MSF in alliances and coalitions with other groups and institutions pursuing similar ends, testing its historic value of independence even while the organization seeks to reassert autonomy in the face of military cooptation of humanitarian rhetoric.

Thus the actual practice of virtue grows complex and contradictory when examined at the level of ethnographic and historical detail. Within a regime of value focused on human life, an individual death can constitute a personal tragedy, a symbolic reference or an organizational opportunity. In certain cases it becomes all three. Although humanitarian organizations have long focused on the suffering of ordinary individuals, they have usually mobilized in response to extraordinary conditions, such as famine and displacement. By concentrating on global inequities in pharmaceutical availability and research orientation, the drug initiatives widen the scope of what counts as a humanitarian crisis. Deaths from unprofitable diseases have acquired additional moral weight in this sense, and are no longer "ordinary." In these practical terms one edge of humanitarianism now overlaps with international efforts to promote social and economic rights. For all of MSF's continued avoidance of human rights rhetoric, its efforts to address the problem of neglected diseases, along with HIV-AIDS, have effectively positioned the group to assert something analogous to a universal right to healthcare. The focus remains restricted to specific and quite tangible problems related to pharmaceutical access. At the same time, however, that goal is implicitly expansive; in identifying structural deficits in the global supply of drugs, MSF has recognized poverty, a condition for which it offers no cure.

Pharmaceutical issues emerged as a significant topic of international treaties amid the dramatic spread of the AIDS pandemic. As well as altering local conditions, debates and advocacy surrounding AIDS produced new configurations within the broader politics of international health and the moral framing of disease. At a moment when antiretroviral therapy promises survival, access to drugs defines an important attribute of public welfare. Thus scholars can speak of "biological" or "therapeutic" citizenship, as well as "pharmaceutical" governance (Petryna et al. 2006; Biehl 2006; Nguyen 2005). Such matters are hardly contained within individual nation states, but rather intimately connected to transnational networks and international organizations. When MSF altered course and launched into the provision of AIDS treatment, it hoped to spur state action. By the end of 2005 it was supporting well over 50,000 patients with its own ARVs, and faced problems of governance of its own (Calmy 2005). AIDS care ultimately involves social dimensions well beyond the physical treatment of individual bodies (Heald 2003; Kleinman et al. 1997; Whyte et al 2006).[11] Nonetheless, it continued to agitate for increased attention to less-publicized conditions, particularly those restricted to marginal settings. Issuing briefings on topics such as "What to Watch for in Free Trade Agreements with the United States" (MSF 2004), and launching efforts at nonprofit, need-driven drug research, the organization countered claims to intellectual property rights with an alternative conception of pharmaceutical products as a public good.

---

11 HIV-AIDS represents a particularly clear instance for the general anthropological emphasis on social aspects of suffering (Kleinman et al. 1997). Delivery of quality care requires quality health infrastructure, and antiretroviral therapy is a continuing, indefinite form of treatment. Moreover, it only restores bodies, not social relations, which MSF generally perceives to lie beyond its purview. For further anthropological work addressing the global life of pharmaceuticals see Lakoff (2006); Laplante (2003); Petryna (2005);Van der Geest et al. (1996); and Whyte et al. (2002).

What I wish to suggest is that something like a rights claim can emerge in practice as well as from principle. In the case of MSF's ventures into pharmaceutical advocacy and research, it does so in between legal treaties, laboratories and suffering bodies. Such human rights would necessarily address the material state of populations as well as states and legal persons, and they would redefine the circulation of goods in moral terms. Human dignity would now involve molecular reactions (Rabinow 1999). Whether or not these developments prove "successful" in the sense of achieving their initial aims, they mark a shift in humanitarian sensibility. Faced with the tension of states appropriating aspects of their moral discourse for their own ends, a humanitarian organization expands its focus to address market failure. Along the way it strives to highlight the suffering of victims of unprofitable diseases, and exposes the structural inequities of global health. Once ordinary forms of death can thus be recast as potentially extraordinary.

I will close this chapter with the image of a second body, this one fitfully inhabited by a departing mind. Idi Amin, after all, was not the only Ugandan to die in the summer of 2003. On my last day visiting the sleeping sickness program, I met a patient in the latest stages of the disease in a dilapidated regional hospital not far from the Sudanese border. Wearing a green T-shirt with the name "Versace" printed across the front, she exhibited signs of dementia when awake, dancing slightly and chanting phrases only she fully understood. She had recently given birth, and her own mother now attended both her and her child, since she herself was beyond any such maternal duty. The nurse accompanying me explained loudly (presumably for the benefit of others in the ward as well as me) that no drug could reverse the neural damage now, and so this patient was beyond the reach of cure. On seeing me the woman in the Versace T-shirt shouted two remaining words with foreign significance – "America!" and "Entebbe!" – before returning to her song. Along with Amin she lingered at the edge of existence, although the close of her life would inspire far less moral commentary. Both the staff and other patients around her seemed to recognize this woman as already departed; it was only a matter of time before her body followed behind. Her madness and impending demise lent her a degree of fleeting visibility within the ward, quickly erased by the continuing flow of human misery. Unlike the former dictator, this woman cast no long shadow of notorious excess and several hundred thousand bodies, only the slight shadow of a tragic, but unprofitable disease. Even in this corner of Uganda, sleeping sickness was far from the only health problem, and neither a national nor international priority. The very unremarkable nature of her fate, however, reveals both another horizon of humanitarian ambition, as well as the recognition of its continuing frustration.

Works Cited

Biehl, João (2006), "Pharmaceutical Governance," in Adriana Petryna, Andrew Lakoff, and Arthur Kleinman, eds, *Global Pharmaceuticals: Ethics, Markets, Practices*, Durham, NC: Duke University Press, 206–239.

Barnett, Michael (2005), "Humanitarianism Transformed," *Perspectives on Politics*. 3: 4: 723–740.

Bortolotti, Dan (2004), Hope in Hell: Inside the World of Doctors Without Borders, Buffalo: Firefly Books.

Bradol, Jean-Hervé (2004), "Introduction: The Sacrificial International Order and Humanitarian Action." in Frabrice Weissman, ed., *In the Shadow of Just Wars: Violence, Politics and Humanitarian Action*, Ithaca, NY: Médecins Sans Frontières and Cornell University Press, pp. 1–22.

Brauman, Rony (2000), *L'Action humanitaire*, Paris: Flammarion.

Calmy, Alexandra (2005), "Alive at Five: Lessons Learned from AIDS Treatment in Resource-poor Settings," *Access News* 12 (November): 1.

Das, Veena (1999), "Public Good, Ethics and Everyday Life: Beyond the Boundaries of Bioethics," *Daedalus*, 128: 4: 99–133.

Daston, Lorraine (1995), "The Moral Economy of Science," *Osiris*, 2nd Series, 10, *Constructing Knowledge in the History of Science*, 2–24.

DNDi (2004), "An Innovative Solution," Informational brochure, April 2004.

Dumit, Joseph (2002), "Drugs for Life," *Molecular Interventions* 2: 3 (July): 124–127.

Farmer, Paul (2003), *Pathologies of Power: Health, Human Rights, and the New War on the Poor*, Berkeley: University of California Press.

Fox, Renée (1995), "Medical Humanitarianism and Human Rights: Reflections on Doctors without Borders and Doctors of the World," *Social Science and Medicine*, 41(12): 1607–1616.

Heald, Suzette (2003), "An Absence of Anthropology: Critical Reflections on Anthropology and AIDS policy and practice in Africa," in George Ellison, Melissa Parker and Catherine Campbell, eds, *Learning from HIV and AIDS*, Cambridge: Cambridge University Press, 210–237.

Hoen, Ellen 't. (2002), "TRIPS, Pharmaceutical Patents, and Access to Essential Medicines: A Long Way from Seattle to Doha," *Chicago Journal of International Law*. 3: 1: 27–46.

Kleinman, Arthur, Veena Das, and Margaret Lock, eds (1997), *Social Suffering*, Berkeley: University of California Press.

Lakoff, Andrew (2006), *Pharmaceutical Reason: Knowledge and Value in Global Psychiatry*, Cambridge: Cambridge University Press.

Laplante, Julie (2003), "Le Médicament aux frontières des saviors humanitaires et autochtones," *Anthropologie et Sociétés*, 27: 2: 59–75.

Leopold, Mark (2005), *Inside West Nile: Violence, History and Representation on an African Frontier*, Santa Fe, NM: School of American Research Press.

Lyons, Maryinez (1992), *The Colonial Disease: A Social History of Sleeping Sickness in Northern Zaire, 1900–1940*, Cambridge: Cambridge University Press.

Médecins Sans Frontières (MSF) (2000), *Activity Report, 1999–2000*, MSF International.

Médecins Sans Frontières (MSF) (2001a), "Fatal Imbalance: The Crisis in Research and Development for Drugs for Neglected Diseases," MSF Campaign for Access to Essential Medicines/Drugs for Neglected Diseases Working Group Report.

Médecins Sans Frontières (MSF) (2001b), "Supply of Sleeping Sickness Drugs Secured," Press Release, New York/Geneva, May 3, 2001.

Médecins Sans Frontières (MSF) (2002), "AIDS: The Urgency to Treat," Supplement to Messages, 123. December.

Médecins Sans Frontières (MSF) (2003), "Access: Three Years On," *Access News*, 8 (February).

Médecins Sans Frontières (MSF) (2004), "Access to Medicines at Risk Across the Globe: What to Watch out for in Free Trade Agreements with the United States," MSF Campaign for Access to Essential medicines Briefing Note (May).

Médecins Sans Frontières (MSF) (2005), *Activity Report, 2004–5*, MSF International.

Médecins Sans Frontières (MSF) (2006), "Too Little for Too Few: Challenges for Effective and Accessible Antiretroviral Treatment," Briefing document, XVI International AIDS Conference, Toronto, 2006.

Merry, Sally Engle (2006), *Human Rights & Gender Violence*, Chicago: University of Chicago Press.

Nguyen, Vinh-Kim (2005), "Anti-retroviral Globalism, Biopolitics and Therapeutic Citizenship," in Aihwa Ong and Stephen Collier, eds, *Global Assemblages*, Malden, MA: Blackwell, 124–144.

Petryna, Adriana (2005), "Ethical variability: Drug development and globalizing clinical trials," *American Ethnologist*, 32: 2: 183–197.

Petryna, Adriana, Andrew Lakoff, and Arthur Kleinman, eds (2006), *Global Pharmaceuticals: Ethics, Markets, Practices*, Durham, NC: Duke University Press.

Rabinow, Paul (1999), *French DNA: Trouble in Purgatory*, Chicago: University of Chicago Press.

Rankin, Johanna (2005), A New Frontier for Humanitarianism? Médecins Sans Frontiers Responds to Neglected Diseases, unpublished Honors Thesis, International Studies, UNC-Chapel Hill.

Redfield, Peter (2006), "A Less Modest Witness: Collective Advocacy and Motivated Truth of a Medical Humanitarian Movement," *American Ethnologist*, 33: 1: 3–26.

Rieff, David (2002), *A Bed for the Night: Humanitarianism in Crisis*, NY: Simon & Schuster.

Riles, Annelise (2006), "Anthropology, Human Rights, and Legal Knowledge: Culture in the Iron Cage," *American Anthropologist*, 108: 1: 52–65.

Ssemakula , John Kiwanuka (2002), "No Longer Asleep: African Sleeping Sickness is Back," *Medilinks* 31 May, 2002, http://medilinks.org.

Thompson, E.P. (2001 [1991]), "The Moral Economy of the English Crowd in the Eighteenth Century," in Dorothy Thompson, ed., *The Essential E.P. Thompson*, New York: New Press, 316–377.

Vallaeys, Anne (2004), *Médecins Sans Frontières: La biographie*, Paris: Fayard.

Van der Geest, Sjaak, Susan Reynolds Whyte, and Anita Hardon (1996), "The Anthropology of Pharmaceuticals: A Biographical Approach," *Annual Review of Anthropology*, 25: 153–178.

Vaughn, Megan (1991), *Curing Their Ills: Colonial Power and African Illness*, Stanford: Stanford University Press.

Weissman, Fabrice, ed. (2004), *In the Shadow of "Just Wars": Violence, Politics and Humanitarian Action*, Ithaca, NY: Médecins Sans Frontières/Cornell University Press.

Whyte, Susan R., Sjaak Van der Geest, and Anita Hardon (2002), *Social Lives of Medicines*, Cambridge: Cambridge University Press.

Whyte, Susan R., Michael Whyte, Lotte Meinert, and Betty Kyaddondo (2006), in Adriana Petryna, Andrew Lakoff, and Arthur Kleinman, eds, *Global Pharmaceuticals: Ethics, Markets, Practices*, Durham, NC: Duke University Press, 240–262.

Wilson, Richard, ed. (1997), *Human Rights: Culture and Context* (London: Pluto Press).

Notes

The author wishes to acknowledge past and present members of MSF for their time and engagement. Alice Bullard and Diane Nelson provided initial prompts for this chapter, Joe Dumit, Rachel King, Jaco Homsy, Andy Lakoff, and Adriana Petryna essential orientation, and Silvia Tomášková the usual patient assistance. The National Endowment for the Humanities and the University of North Carolina both supported ongoing research, and audiences offered early commentary at the 2003 annual meeting of the Society for the Social Study of Science in Atlanta and the 2005 conference on "Human Rights in Crisis" held at the Georgia Institute of Technology.

Conclusion

Alice Bullard

The historian's perspective on human rights is perhaps best conveyed in *Human Rights and Revolutions*, a book that documents the fitful pursuit of human rights via violent upheavals as much, if not more than, via the rule of law (Hunt, Young, and Wasserstrom 2000). Such a broad historical perspective might induce us to view the present crisis with equanimity. If enemy combatants are detained without right to trial or adequate protection, nonetheless their number is much lower than the Japanese Americans interred in camps during World War II. If dissent is currently stifled, nonetheless the courts are asserting their power more robustly than they dared in previous war situations (Stone 2004; Lessig 2004). If human rights law is partially eclipsed today, a future era will undoubtedly usher in a climate more favorable to such claims.

Such arguments suggest a long term evolution of rights culture. Nonetheless, an evolution, with inevitable setbacks and partial eclipses, cannot remove the haunting fear produced by US government agents engaged in torture. Nor can it redeem the suffering, the lives lost and destroyed, by reckless actions. Advocates of international human rights law such as Mary Robinson, moreover, are less than sanguine about the current situation. Speaking at the International Rule of Law symposium in Chicago in 2006, Robinson lamented the "balance that was lost in the aftermath of 9/11," as she described the deterioration of guarantees and freedoms and the targeting of human rights advocates as terrorists (Robinson 2007). Writing with a characteristic restraint, Robinson remarked how the Eminent Jurists' panel to which she belongs, "was taken aback by the testimony" in their hearings in Washington D.C., noting with dismay and deep concern "the extent to which fundamental rights and freedoms [have] been undermined over the past five years" (Robinson 2007, p. 8; for a wide-ranging discussion of US infractions, see UNHCR 2007).

Robinson's words echo the message of Barr's contribution to this volume; the Eminent Jurists' panel's on-going examination of human rights during the Global War on Terror has found much cause for worry in societies around the globe (Eminent Jurists' Panel 2007). Writing about the United States, this panel reported that the moral leadership of the United States had been seriously undermined by treatment of unlawful combatants and prisoners from the Iraq war and in Afghanistan. Perhaps not surprisingly, the panel decried the post 9/11 erosion of the rule of law both in the United States and overseas (Eminent Jurists' Panel 2006).

In this collection the culture of crisis is bound up with the culture of human rights. "Human rights in crisis" can mean both human rights threatened and human rights defended. Indeed, the culture of human rights is bound intimately to the culture of crisis. In the first and most prominent instance, the crisis centers on a challenge or threat to state sovereignty. Such crisis has multiple impacts on human rights culture – the state in crisis can retreat from protecting the rights of individuals in order to bolster the power of the state; the state in crisis is often a weakened state, one fearful of strong, activist citizenry regardless of their political orientation; in the extreme, the state in crisis offers no viable framework for a peaceful social existence prompting flight to more stable and accommodating societies. The state in crisis, as we have seen, can violate the human rights of those attacking it, as well as those of its own citizens. Those in flight enter a no man's land from which only with great difficulty can they emerge with rights intact. Detainees are denied full recourse to the law, human rights defenders are harassed and stand accused of terrorism, migrants seeking better lives are jailed or denied legal immigration on suspicion of prostitution or other crimes.

Asserting successful claims to human rights, as these chapters demonstrate, demands not just the existence of laws and treaties, but also individual and political will to enforce these laws. The culture of human rights rests above all on the willingness to defend the dignity of human life fueled by a compassion for human suffering. Human rights activists, including the contributors to this volume, are products of robust human rights culture just as surely as they are builders of such a culture. The Center for Justice & Accountability (CJA), like Doctors Without Borders (MSF), or the many women's groups discussed by Freeman, have developed in human rights culture and give it further life and definition. Their success stories are hopeful beacons to others. In the case of the CJA, the victims of torture who succeed in prosecuting their claims in US courts stand as a rebuke (if not as a directly useful legal precedent) to tactics employed in Guantanomo and Abu Ghraib.

Torture, Law, Power

Hajjar places the United States on a map of types of torturing regimes: literal denial, interpretive denial, and implicatory denial each appear as established methods—used by states such as Great Britain in its fight against the Irish Republican Army and Israel against the Palestinians – of escaping public disavowal of a bedrock guarantee of human dignity. The 1984 UN Convention against Torture is explicit that no exceptional circumstances ever provide legitimate grounds for torture. The United States is a party to this convention; the US Torture Victim Protection Act of 1992 provided explicit recourse for those who have suffered torture (see Eisenbrandt's discussion in this volume).

Hajjar reminds us of the fundamental truth that the constitutional ban on cruel and unusual punishment, along with *habeas corpus* and the separation of powers, "served as a foundation of the modern rule of law, because it was understood as essential for conditions of human dignity, liberty, security and due process to thrive." Detentions, rendering, and rough interrogations during the War on Terror have broken with this guarantee in the US Constitution against cruel treatment as well as with international law.

The legal prohibitions on torture and the deep philosophical underpinnings of this prohibition are not universally respected around the globe; as Hajjar informs us, the United States joins about two thirds of the world's governments in its new, albeit disavowed, use of torture. In the case of torture, as with other human rights, legislation and ideals bear little direct relation to practice. The specter of agents of the US government engaged in torture, however, is new and apparently results from high level decisions to abandon the rule of law, to assert that terrorists have no legal rights, and consequently to make any methods of interrogation and detention allowable. Asserting that terrorists have no rights is a *de facto* disavowal of the very idea of human rights. According to Hajjar, Vice President Dick Cheney, his staff member David Addington and legal advisor John Yoo, developed a policy framework that placed the president above the law, allowing any executive action he desired in the name of combating terrorism. Subsequently, in 2002 US interrogators began using extreme and violent interrogation tactics in Guantanomo and from there the practice spread in 2003 to the Iraqi prison, Abu Ghraib.

Court challenges to the lawless culture of the War on Terror culminated in the June 2006, US Supreme Court decision in *Hamdan v. Rumsfeld*. The court ruled that prisoners captured in the "war on terror" have rights under the Geneva Conventions, including protection from torture and degrading treatment. The *Hamdan* ruling also declared the statute for the military commissions in Guantanamo unconstitutional, and raised the possibility that those responsible for violation of the Geneva Conventions could be prosecuted. In response to the *Hamdan* decision, the Administration successfully organized a campaign to pass the Military Commissions Act (MCA) of October 2006. As Hajjar details, this act essentially gave President Bush everything he desired, even provoking the capitulation of Republican dissenters. The new (as of 2007) Democratic majority in Congress could alter or repeal the MCA, but preoccupation with the Iraq War, investigations of the Administration and the presidential election cycle make it unlikely. Lawyers defending the detainees are prepared to challenge this new legislation in the nation's courts.

The landscape portrayed by Hajjar lies in uneasy juxtaposition with the achievements of the Center for Justice & Accountability (CJA) as detailed in Eisenbrandt's chapter. The CJA has, since its founding in 1998, used the Alien Tort Claims Act and subsequently the Torture Victims Protection Act of 1992, to bring civil suits in the United States against perpetrators of crimes against humanity. The working principle of CJA is derived from the Nuremberg Trials of 1946, which proclaimed that crimes against international law are committed by men, not by abstract entities. CJA employs multiple strategies to enforce legal accountability for human rights abuses, including pursuing civil suits in the United States, pursuing the deportation of human rights abusers, aiding in the extradition of human rights abusers from the US for prosecution, and participating in suits brought in other nations. The role of civil suits in the United States is not simply to obtain judgments, but also to produce new facts and establish responsibility via the discovery process, witness testimony, and the testimony of the accused. CJA also uses trials to generate public awareness of the possibility of punishing human rights abusers. This heightened awareness, for example, has led to El Salvadoran calls for a repeal of their amnesty law.

The CJA has successfully used the principle of "command responsibility" – that high government officials are responsible via a chain of command for abuses carried out by those lower in the government hierarchy – in winning cases in US courts. Eisenbrandt reminds us that the post-World War II war crimes tribunals used command responsibility to convict Nazi officials as well as the Japanese General Yamashita. Command responsibility, as Hajjar points out, has thus far been denied by the Bush administration; while low ranking personnel have been tried and imprisoned for specific acts in Iraq, no higher level official has been held accountable. As Hajjar phrases it, despite the dots that clearly carry up the chain of command, all the investigators have resolutely refused to connect them. Most recently, on 27 March 2007, Chief Judge Thomas A. Hogan of the Federal District Court for the District of Columbia dismissed a case against Donald Rumsfeld filed by the American Civil Liberties Union and Human Rights First, on the grounds that as a government official Rumsfeld was immune to suit. Moreover, the judge held that the plaintiffs – who alleged Rumsfeld was responsible for torture they suffered while in US custody – could neither invoke rights under the US Constitution nor under international law. Nonetheless, Judge Hogan noted that "'the facts alleged in the complaint stand as an indictment of the humanity with which the United States treats its detainees'" (ACLU 2007).

The 2006 Military Commission Act amends the War Crimes Act that makes violations of the Geneva Conventions criminal; this change moreover was made retroactive back to September 11, 2001, essentially immunizing officials in the United States from any prosecutions for war crimes under US law. Working with the principle of universal jurisdiction, various human rights groups, many of them co-ordinated into unified work by the Center for Constitutional Rights, have essentially moved their operations abroad. They have turned to Germany to provoke the prosecution of Rumsfeld, General Sanchez, former White House counsel (and from 2006–2007 the Attorney General) Alberto Gonzales, the former head of the CIA George Tenet and others (Zagorin 2006).

Thus the arena of the conflict between the sovereign executive, sometimes considered unfettered by law, and the legal culture of human rights, is broadened and displaced. If the executive reigns supreme within his or her state, international human rights law may give courts in other states the authority to prosecute such sovereigns. The 1999 arrest and subsequent prosecution of the former Chilean dictator, General Pinochet, has been seconded by the CJA case against the former president of Guatemala, Efrain Rios Montt, a proceeding that has not yet been settled (Eisenbrandt). Nonetheless, despite the doctrines of command responsibility and universal jurisdiction, the primacy of politics has not yet been displaced in favor of the rule of law.

Is it imaginable that high level US officials actually stand trial and face conviction for crimes against humanity? The US Pentagon protested in 2004 when German courts considered indicting Rumsfeld. Suits filed in Belgium against Americans who led the Iraq War were dropped when Rumsfeld threatened to cut off funding for a new NATO center in Brussels (Deusche-Welle 2004). The political pressure in 2007 to halt renewed German legal processes against Rumsfeld and other officials is strong and explicit, and demonstrates the distinct limit of court-based power over and against political power (Spiegel Online 2007). The political influence of the strongest states remains a reality in today's world. Whether or to what extent this can be compatible with human rights culture remains to be seen.

Crisis and the Promise of Law

According to Burchill, crisis is rooted in the system of human rights law, in the form of a permanent contradiction between International Human Rights Law (IHRL) and sovereignty. Burchill portrays a historical pendulum in which the 1990s euphoria over an international system that integrated human rights into international law gave way to a post-9/11 crash, in which human rights have been cast in opposition to state security. Yet this crash, in Burchill's interpretation, only revealed an ever-present paradox within the attempt to legislate human rights. Given the ultimate power of sovereign states, Burchill argues that the true power of human rights resides in its rhetoric, through which a sense of norms and expectations are created. It is the rhetoric of human rights, rather than legal constraints, that create grounds for expectation that high ideals can be delivered as quotidian reality. The rhetoric of rights, according to him, creates a culture of human rights that will eventually hold sway over sovereignty.

If rhetoric is to rule, it is imperative that we retain our capacity to be shocked and outraged by violations of human dignity – and yet the power of rhetoric callous with regard to human rights is not to be underestimated. Burchill implies that if we cannot count on the power of international human rights law, nonetheless we can take comfort in the pervasive rhetoric that generated such laws and is deployed by NGOs. But, if sovereignty threatens the rule of law in the international arena, the rhetoric of sovereignty, of national defense, of counter-terrorism, and of "illegal aliens" – to name just the most prominent rhetorics of sovereignty – challenge and threaten to override the rhetoric of human rights.

Indeed, the recommendation to put our faith in rhetoric instead of law, offers those dedicated to human rights culture uneasy comfort. Barr's depiction of the plight of human rights workers during the post-9/11 era emphasizes the power of the rhetoric of sovereignty. Barr points out, for example, the President of Colombia who refuted the principle of distinguishing between combatants and noncombatants. She cites the words of the former Indian Deputy Prime Minister used to condemn human rights defenders, "If the opposition opposes the ordinance they will be wittingly or unwittingly helping the terrorists." Such language is all too familiar to American ears, used by now to hearing opposition to Presidential policies condemned as aid and comfort to terrorists. The rhetoric of fear and hatred, good versus evil, loyal fighters and treasonous opposition, can effectively short-circuit claims to rights and the defense of the right of everyone to dignity.

Human Bodies, Meaning, and Media

Looking at human rights from the point of view of the body, rather than law, we encounter the materiality of existence, the inherently gendered aspect of human life, the warmth of flesh and blood over and against the letter of the law. Bodies live in and through culture. The media broadcast, magnify, and sometimes distort, cultural patterns. Fostering a robust human rights culture requires grappling with the materiality, the sex and disease of bodies; it requires influencing cultural assumptions, defusing stereotypes, and skillfully engaging mass media.

The culture of counting bodies of those fallen in warfare or victimized by more haphazard violence reminds us that the rhetoric of universal human dignity is far from the reality. The 654,965 excess civilian mortality in Iraq – counted only recently by independent scientists and as yet hotly contested by American officials – are bodies still awaiting symbolic vestiture. The pierced or mangled body recorded only as collateral damage or perhaps not even recorded at all is a brute reminder of the flesh, the blood, the materiality of life. Bodies speak in many ways, reminding us of the indignities suffered in life and death. Only in counting each individual body – in creating an account of the individual life and death – are we assured that the body symbolizes human dignity. The anonymous flesh of the uncounted dead figures rather as a wound, an open sore, and a well spring of indignity in our world.

That the human species comes always in two sexes, female and male, only became a vibrant part of human rights discourse in the 1970s and 80s. Freeman's celebratory history of the enshrinement of women's human rights in international law, is nonetheless clear eyed and unsentimental about the ultimate impact of such achievements. Freeman recognizes that activist women must continue to press for women's human rights, continue to secure funding and to attract media attention as viable human rights projects. Mainstreaming of women's issues declared the 'revolution' over rather too quickly, threatening to submerge women's distinctive position in society in the onslaught of the presumed masculine standard. The crisis for women's human rights is a crisis of funding and of competence: bringing rights from a promise in an international treaty to a reality in the actual lives of real women around the globe is an epic challenge.

The complicated vulnerability of female bodies, even in the United States protected against domestic violence only beginning in the 1970s, is evident in Haynes' chapter on trafficking. Women are the majority of the estimated 600,000 to 800,000 individuals trafficked across international borders each year. Engaged in domestic employment, sweat shops, or sex work, these women pursue precarious lives. Despite the Palmero protocol and the Trafficking Victim Protection Act of 2000 (TVPA 2000), attaining legal immigration status remains an enormous challenge for these women. Their bodies and lives remain imperiled, illegal in the society, and dominated by traffickers. The traffickers, as criminals, are pursued; those trafficked, as victims, are often overlooked and left to languish in dire situations.

Haynes notes with sad irony, that it is those who can claim most convincingly to be victims – those who can successfully tell the victim story in the courtroom and in the media – who can benefit from programs such as the TVPA 2000. Forced sex and sexual abuse figure prominently in media portraits of trafficked women. The more broadly applicable, but more subtle stories about economic exploitation, inequality, and grinding poverty, are not sexy, do not sell, and hence are less frequently told. Attempting to prove one's status as a victim involves a difficult negotiation between the public image of a sexualized victim and the reality of a complicated life. The real victims rarely correspond to the images of victims presented in the media, and hence have difficulty eliciting sympathy and justice.

Meanwhile, the United States has structured its immigration laws to allow only "real victims" legal status and to preclude economic refugees, as though victims cannot also be people seeking economic opportunities. In the United States, Haynes argues, "the legal fiction is that one can either be a victim or a capable person of free will, but not both" (Haynes, p. 112). In this respect, the crisis for the individual must be complete, no remnant of dignity or self-direction is allowed to co-exist in the victim of trafficking. In Haynes' chapter, the law reinforces the media in its emphasis on lurid, sexualized crisis; trafficking policies admit only thoroughly broken victims.

Haynes proposes that successful trafficking programs need to move away from the culture of complete crisis and sexual victimization, and to adopt instead a focus on how primarily young women from around the world are so easily enticed into exploitation. She normalizes the quest for human rights, suggesting that the desire for a life with opportunity and dignity leads to sometimes desperate gambles and illegal means. Criminalizing trafficking, in her analysis, has the perverse effect of disallowing a focus on the broad array of human rights of those trafficked. Haynes proposes a restructuring of this outlook, so that the particular vulnerabilities of victimized migrants are understood, and solutions are offered that recognize the individual dignity of the victimized migrants.

For the volunteers at MSF the focus on the body is essential to efforts to enrich and sustain the dignity of life. Redfield is particularly interested in MSF tackling massive deaths from unprofitable diseases. Working from an ethnographic perspective on human rights, he focuses tightly on an outpost in Uganda that fights river blindness. Redfield describes how MSF strives to use a vision of dignified human life to drive the defense of human rights past the culture of crisis and toward an enrichment of healthcare opportunities. In this MSF performs work akin to that envisioned by Haynes *vis-à-vis* individuals caught up in trafficking. Both seek a restructuring of the moral economy, a renewed vision of the right and the good, and hence a more truly empowering human rights culture. This transformation in both cases would move toward an emphasis on and appreciation for dignity in daily life and away from the prevalent coupling of human rights to crisis situations.

The media love of crisis sustains a culture in which bodies in extreme peril seem somehow more valuable than those sustaining banal, constant degradation. Sexualized bodies in peril, as Haynes notes, are a media favorite. Aided by mass media, crisis is nearly omnipresent in our world; crisis is the emergency of the present, the on-going, ever-present emergency (Redfield, p. 139). Dramatizing immediate suffering and intervention, crisis calls forth humanitarian actions, including medical aid and also the defense of human rights of those in peril. Crisis as well calls forth the executive power of the sovereign to defend an imperiled people or state or privilege, and possibly to inflict damage on individuals and their rights.

Disdaining the role of the media in human rights culture, however, is a double-edged sword. As much as some defenders of human rights seek to move beyond sensationalistic stories of victimization, others are dependent on the media to bring stories of abuse into public discourse. The success of international defenders of human rights, such as the CJA, just as the plight of the 'unlawful combatants' detained at Guantanomo, are in part dependent on media scrutiny. The media plays a significant role as well in fostering interest in various types of human rights; as Freeman's chapter points out, women's efforts to secure human rights have suffered as donors have moved on to other, somehow more current, preoccupations. Restructuring the moral economy, to borrow Redfield's phrase, requires not the abandonment of media, but the adroit participation in it. Indeed, as Haynes notes in passing, the mushrooming interest in human rights over the past twenty years can in part be attributed to the fact that, "'human rights and suffering have become a mass media commodity that serve a function in the growth of capitalistic mass media throughout the world'" (Haynes, footnote 4).

Enriching and refining human rights culture by moving beyond the culture of crisis so beloved by the media appears a difficult prospect indeed.

Final Thoughts

Opposed to the conviction that national and international law will eventually succeed in establishing actually attainable universal human rights is the conviction that human rights are utopian ideals, that humanitarians are saints, and that dedicated human rights advocates are tilting forever at windmills. The chapters in this volume largely inspire a more resilient dedication to the on-going pursuit of human rights. As we have seen in this volume crisis impels the defense of human rights even as it provides occasion for the violation of those rights. Dwelling on the violation of rights and the threat to the culture of human rights may motivate others to take on further issues and projects. The possibilities for engagement are vast. Crisis provides exceptional moments when activists attempt to make concrete the utopian ideals of human rights. Human rights work takes place in multiple arenas; dedicated activists sustain a vibrant human rights culture; human rights work continues to renew, broaden, and enhance our understanding of human rights. Enforcing laws and enhancing human rights culture by refashioning our moral vision are central to these projects.

Works Cited

American Civil Liberties Union (ACLU), Press Release: ACLU and Human Rights First Express Disappointment at Dismissal of Rumsfeld Torture Case (published online 27 March 2007) http://www.aclu.org/safefree/detention/29209prs20070327.html, accessed 29 March 2007.

Deutsche-Welle Lawsuit Against Rumsfeld Threatens US-German Relations, http://www.dw-world.de/dw/article/0,1564,1427743,00.html published 14 December 2004, accessed 29 March 2007.

Eminent Jurists Panel, Press Releases (updated March 2007) http://ejp.icj.org/, accessed 23 March 2007.

Eminent Jurists Panel, USA: Emiment Jurists Panel concludes US hearings, Press Release, (published online 14 September 2006) http://ejp.icj.org/, accessed 23 March 2007.

Hunt, Lynn, Young, Marilyn, and Wasserstrom, Jeffry (eds) (2000), *Human Rights, Citizenship, and Revolutionary Traditions*, New York: Rowman Littlefield.

Lessig blog (Lawrence Lessig), "World War One" (published December 16, 2004 03:53 PM) http://www.lessig.org/cgi-bin/mt/mt-search.cgi, accessed March 23, 2007.

Robinson, Mary (2007), "The Rule of Law; Striking a Balance in an Era of Terrorism," *International Law News* 36:1 (winter) 1 and 6–8.

Spiegel Online, WANTED FOR WAR CRIMES, Rumsfeld Lawsuit Embarrasses German Authorities (published online 26 March 2007) http://www.spiegel.de/international/world/0,1518,473987,00.html, accessed 29 March 2007.

Stone, Geoffrey R. (2004), *Perilous Times: Free Speech in Wartime from the Sedition Act of 1798 to the War on Terrorism*, New York: W.W. Norton.

United Nations High Commission for Human Rights (2007), "Preliminary Findings on Visit to United States by UN Special Rapporteur on the Promotion and Protection of Human Rights and Fundamental Freedoms while countering Terrorism" (published online 25 May 2007) http://www.unhchr.ch/huricane/huricane.nsf/view01/15B4F3535CE9EB5FC12572E600569287?opendocument.

Zagorin, A. (2006), "Exclusive: Charges Sought Against Rumsfeld Over Prison Abuse," *Time* (published online 10 November 2006) http://www.time.com/time/nation/article/0,8599,1557842,00.html, accessed 29 March 2007.

Index